BEYOND RISK

Conversations with Climbers

BEYOND RISK

Conversations with Climbers

NICHOLAS O'CONNELL

FOREWORD BY
GREG CHILD

THE MOUNTAINEERS

In memory of Wolfgang Güllich, 1960–1992

5 4 3
5 4 3 2 1

Published by The Mountaineers
1011 SW Klickitat Way, Seattle, Washington 98134

Published simultaneously in Canada by Douglas & McIntyre, Ltd., 1615 Venables Street, Vancouver, B.C. V5L 2H1

Published simultaneously in Great Britain by Diadem Books, London. All trade enquiries U.K., Europe and Commonwealth (except Canada) to Hodder and Stoughton, Mill Road, Dunton Green, Sevenoaks, Kent TN13 2YA

Manufactured in the United States of America

Edited by Linda Gunnarson
Cover design by Watson Graphics
Book design and layout by Barbara Bash
Typesetting by The Mountaineers Books

Cover photo: Lynn Hill (Photo by Philippe Fragnol). Insets: *top:* Jeff Lowe (Photo by John Roskelley); *center:* Reinhold Messner (Photo courtesy Diadem archives); *bottom:* Wolfgang Güllich (Photo courtesy Wolfgang Güllich). Back cover photo insets: *top:* Sir Edmund Hillary (Photo by Nicholas O'Connell); *center:* Catherine Destivelle (Photo © George Lowe); *bottom:* Warren Harding (Photo © Galen Rowell). Frontispiece: TomoČesen. (Photo © Januz Skok).

Library of Congress Cataloging in Publication Data
O'Connell, Nicholas.
    Beyond risk : conversations with climbers / Nicholas O'Connell.
      p.   cm.
    ISBN 0-89886-296-5
    1. Mountaineers--Interviews. 2. Mountaineering--History--20th century. I. Title
GV199.9.O36   1993
796.522'092'2--dc20
    [B]   93-22723

CONTENTS

FOREWORD

Climbing has evolved rapidly over the last hundred years. A climber of the 1930s, or earlier, would be startled to see the shape of climbing in the 1990s. The severity of a 5.14 sport climb, the crowds of people clambering over cliffs, and contests on artificial climbing walls would bear little resemblance to the climbing scene of the 1930s veteran. Arguments over ethics, bolts, and the right to climb, and $50,000 Everest permits would baffle the vintage climber. The notion of ascending the highest mountains without bottled oxygen, and modern inventions like spring-loaded camming devices for slotting into cracks, synthetic mountaineering boots that protect the feet from subzero cold, and ropes strong enough to restrain a charging rhino would seem, to our 1930s climber, like science fiction visions by H. G. Wells.

These steps in the progress of climbing, whether in pushing free-climbing grades to higher levels or making an alpine-style ascent of an 8000-meter peak, come about through inspired acts of vision by individual climbers. Their minds and bodies are completely attuned to what they are doing, and their achievements are not made by accident. Occasionally, a dedicated climber comes along whose career is filled with milestones that set the standard of the day and of the future. The shape of a particular branch of climbing is sculpted by his or her achievements. Sometimes, a name alone defines a style of climbing.

When we think of alpinism, we recall Walter Bonatti pushing the limits in the European Alps. Reinhold Messner comes to mind in discussions of Himalayan mountaineering. Any mention of soloing big mountains includes talk of Tomo Česen. Lynn Hill is synonymous with sport climbing. Wolfgang Güllich defines the power of free climbing. And a climber like Royal Robbins, whose signature is found on the big walls of Yosemite, represents traditional American rock climbing.

If we wish to understand where climbing came from and where it is headed, a good first step then is to learn something about the people who have set the pace in this sport. Nicholas O'Connell's interviews with seventeen of the many climbers who have shaped climbing as we know it today bring together voices from different disciplines of the multifaceted sport of climbing. He has conversed with pivotal climbers from many countries. They come from a variety of eras. Their life histories are vastly different. The sum of their contribution to the sport is immense.

Traveling far and wide to interview his subjects, the author has let them speak their minds without indulging in his own personal interpretations. The result is a collection of casual, honest self-portraits of the world's most accomplished climbers. With Nicholas's gentle prodding, the climbers in this book reveal their personalities and the important moments in their careers with greater frankness than might have resulted from a formal magazine profile.

The climbers interviewed here did not set out with a conscious plan to shape the course of climbing. They did not become climbers in order to achieve something great—climb at a new level of difficulty, experience an ordeal that could be transformed into a widely read book. Before any of that could happen, they had to commit themselves to their sport totally. Climbing shaped them just as they shaped climbing.

Nicholas's constant curiosity about what forces drive these climbers is apparent, and he doesn't shy away from asking the question climbers hate most: Why do you climb? *Why* is the single parameter of the climbing game that no one has really worked out. An answer to that question has long appeared to be an astounding deficit in a pursuit in which the participants have mastered an unusual skill set, that of coping with literal fears of height and life and death.

There will probably never be a concise, intelligible answer as to why climbers accept the generally arduous, often uncomfortable, even downright dangerous side of climbing, but, after reading this book, I was left with the impression that it is in the voices of climbers—in their informal, off-the-cuff remarks, and in their unadorned recollections of their lives—that the greatest truths about climbing are revealed.

—Greg Child, 1993

ACKNOWLEDGMENTS

Writing a book is a lot like climbing expedition-style in the Himalaya, with many people contributing toward the total effort. Some of these people carry much of the burden without receiving an appropriate share of the credit for the final achievement. For this reason, I would like acknowledge the following people for the crucial roles they played in completing this project:

Donna DeShazo, Margaret Foster, and the staff of Mountaineers Books demonstrated early interest and patient support throughout the long process of putting this book together.

Ken Wilson of Diadem Press, England, proved invaluable in developing the book. His encyclopedic knowledge and unabashed love for climbing added immeasurably to the quality of the finished product.

Linda Gunnarson represented the Platonic ideal of an editor, responding enthusiastically to my efforts, while encouraging me to do still better.

Mirella Tenderini arranged and translated the interviews with Cassin and Bonatti, and she and her husband, Luciano, put me up at their wonderful home overlooking Lake Como in the foothills of the Grigna.

George Bracksieck published several of the interviews in *Rock + Ice* and generously provided advice, phone numbers, addresses, and vital back issues when needed.

The editors at *Climbing* magazine also helped out with phone numbers, addresses, and detailed background information on the climbers.

Dan Levant of Levant & Wales offered valuable counsel throughout the writing and publication of the book.

Virginia Baker and Katrina Reed allowed me special borrowing privileges at the Mountaineers' outstanding alpine library, a resource that proved indispensable in preparing the book.

Climbers Jim Wickwire, Steve Swenson, Greg Child, Steve Roper, Greg Murphy, and others contributed expert advice and criticism at various stages of the manuscript.

Climbing partners Mike Barton, Brad Taylor, Ken Johnson, Lee Gibbon, Steve MacAulay, Ed Kim, Jan Kalinsky, and others lured me away from the word processor to actually go climbing, proving that there was more to the sport than writing about it.

My parents, family, and friends supported me through the seemingly endless task of putting the book together. I would especially like to thank Clara Menhuin-Hauser for comic relief, Lisa Sowder for political incorrectness, and my brother Richard and Dennis Shaw for helping solve a potentially disastrous computer software problem.

And finally, I would like to express my deepest gratitude to the climbers themselves, who gave so generously of their time and attention during the interviews and throughout the process of writing and editing *Beyond Risk*.

INTRODUCTION

WHILE WRITING THIS BOOK I was sometimes asked whether climbers indeed have a death wish. The assumption seemed to be that anybody who attempts such hazardous and improbable objectives must be mentally unbalanced in some way, that consciously or subconsciously climbs must be suicide missions, species of Russian roulette, where losing means death and winning means—what does it mean?

After interviewing some of the world's leading climbers and thinking about the significance of their chosen activity, I can honestly say that nothing could be farther from the truth. What animates climbers is not a death wish, but a *life wish*, a desire to live—fully, intensely, completely. I have never met a group of people more truly alive—physically, emotionally, intellectually, spiritually. Rather than courting danger for its own sake, they do so as a means of deepening and enriching their experience of life.

As a group, then, they should be seen not so much as thrill seekers but as truth seekers. They climb not just for the adrenaline or exercise, but for the opportunities to gain insight into themselves and the world around them. Long, exhausting, nervy routes serve as the purgatories through which they must pass to test and perfect their character.

For climbing is about more than the completion of a difficult route; it is also about the completion of oneself. Rather than just another sport or pastime, it can be seen as a path to self-knowledge, a means of growth and renewal in contact with nature, a way of experiencing in a short, concentrated time the extremes of human emotion, the extraordinary joy in being fully alive, and the naked fear in facing up to great risk, thus providing a glimpse into the essential nature of human life.

Because climbing contains such a remarkable concentration of human experience, it can be seen as a microcosm for the rest of life. It requires courage in adversity, grace under pressure, and generosity and patience in exasperating circumstances—all of the qualities necessary to succeed and remain reasonably sane in everyday life. Because climbing represents the human drama in all its myriad aspects, it makes a fitting metaphor for other aspects of life.

Perhaps it is this metaphorical dimension of mountaineering that explains its appeal not just to climbers, but to the general public as well. Many people who have trouble ascending a flight of stairs take great interest in the stories coming out of the climbing world: Reinhold Messner's desperate search for his brother amidst the avalanche debris on Nanga Parbat, Doug Scott's epic crawl off the

Ogre, Voytek Kurtyka's and Robert Schauer's mental telepathy during their harrowing ascent of Gasherbrum IV, Kurt Diemberger's despairing descent from K2 after Julie Tullis died, Tomo Česen's dramatic accounts of his ascents on Jannu and the south face of Lhotse. These are just a few of the many moving stories related in this book, stories that are meaningful not just to climbers, but to anyone interested in the larger drama of human life. These stories concern more than grades, ratings, and route descriptions; they also chart the mysterious topography of the human spirit, demonstrating that climbing can serve as a powerful symbol for human aspiration in all its various forms.

It was this sense of the larger significance of mountaineering that led me to begin interviewing climbers. As a climber myself, I was keen to meet these people in person and question them in depth about their approach to the sport. I wanted especially to talk with those who had played a significant role in shaping the history of climbing. I hoped that if I selected carefully, choosing those figures who were not only historically important but also representative of a particular period or style of climbing, the book as a whole could suggest the overall scope of climbing in this century.

To give context to the interviews and make clear how they sketch out the range of modern climbing, I've included a brief history of mountaineering. Following this history are the interviews themselves, in which some of the world's top climbers relate in their own words incredible stories of triumph and tragedy, of peaks climbed and partners lost, of personalities tested and transformed by the extremes of human emotion.

Mountains have always captivated the human imagination. Rising steeply out of their surrounding valleys and foothills, they have long stood as symbols of purity, idealism, and spiritual aspiration. To the Greeks, they were the dwelling places of the gods. To the Hebrews, the site where Yahweh revealed himself and communicated with his people. For many ancient peoples they served as the point of intersection between the human and divine spheres, where the gods could descend from their thrones in the heavens and where humans could ascend to query them about the mysterious workings of the world. Not surprisingly, anything having to do with mountains carried with it a strong element of mysticism, a condition that persists to this day.

But if people found mountains fascinating, they also were frightened of them. They approached mountains tentatively and respectfully and seemed in no great hurry to climb them. Moses' free-solo, oxygenless ascent of Mount Sinai to retrieve the Ten Commandments may have set an early standard for climbing style, but no matter how influential theologically, it did little to spur further mountaineering development. It wasn't until the eighteenth century in Europe that people began scaling summits systematically.

At 15,771 feet, Mont Blanc is the highest point in Western Europe. When

Michel-Gabriel Paccard and his guide, Jacques Balmat, succeeded in climbing it in 1786, the ascent proved an immense psychological breakthrough for climbers and marked the beginning of the sport of mountaineering. Climbers then turned their attention to lower, though not necessarily less challenging objectives such as the Jungfrau, Monte Rosa, Matterhorn, and the Grépon. A Golden Age of peak-bagging ensued, during which the majority of Alpine peaks saw first ascents, usually by their easiest routes.

Mountaineers then focused on finding more technical ways to the top. As these routes tackled steep faces, they often proved difficult to negotiate without resorting to some form of artificial aid, and so around the turn of the century in the eastern Alps, climbers such as the Italian Tita Piaz and Austrians Otto Herzog and Hans Fiechtl began to employ pitons and other hardware, first to protect themselves from falling and later to pull themselves up hard sections.

Not all climbers agreed with the use of such techniques, however. The Austrian Paul Preuss denounced artificial aid as a retrograde step in Alpinism. He put his words into action by free-soloing a number of difficult technical routes, including the first ascent of the east face of the Campanile Basso in 1911. Though Preuss was killed while attempting the north face of the Manndkogel in 1913, he was an inspiration to many subsequent free climbers, including Reinhold Messner.

Despite the objections of Preuss and others, the reliance on artificial aid and protection continued, especially in the eastern Alps. There, climbers used pegs, stirrups, and double ropes to surmount increasingly steep and even overhanging sections of rock. The principal exponent of these new aid-climbing techniques was Emilio Comici, an Italian climber who put up hundreds of new routes, including such classics as the north face of Cima Grande in 1933. On this and many of his other routes, Comici demonstrated his preference for the diretissima, or route that followed as closely as possible the path of a vertical line from ground to summit.

If Comici had realized the full implications of this ideal, he may not have embraced it so enthusiastically. For as German climber Anderl Heckmair pointed out, such a philosophy taken to its logical extreme would result in excessive bolting without regard to the natural features or weaknesses of the rock. Subsequent ascents have borne out Heckmair's critique, with routes such as the 1963 Kauschke, Seigert, Uhner Super Direct on the north face of Cima Grande more closely resembling engineering feats than climbs.

Nevertheless, Comici's example attracted numerous followers, including such outstanding figures as the young Riccardo Cassin. After learning the fundamentals of aid climbing from Comici, Cassin quickly put these techniques into practice, first repeating many of Comici's hardest climbs and then putting up difficult new routes of his own, including the north face of Cima Ovest in 1935. Not content with his successes on the Dolomite limestone of the eastern

Alps, Cassin took aim at challenging objectives in the western Alps as well, especially the great north faces.

In the pre–World War II era, these north faces represented the next frontier in climbing. The first to fall was the north face of the Matterhorn, climbed in 1931 by Germans Franz and Toni Schmid. The Eiger north face proved a more formidable objective, however, claiming numerous lives before Germans Anderl Heckmair and Ludwig Vörg and Austrians Fritz Kasparek and Heinrich Harrer found a way to the top in 1938. The Walker Spur of the Grandes Jorasses beat back numerous attempts before Italians Cassin, Gino Esposito, and Ugo Tizzoni reached the summit in 1938.

After World War II, development continued in the Alps. With the great north faces having been ascended, climbers sought still harder challenges. The outstanding figure of the postwar period was unquestionably the Italian Walter Bonatti. His route on the east face of the Grand Capucin in 1951 set a new standard for continuous alpine aid climbing, while his solo of the southwest pillar of the Petit Dru in 1955 ranks among the greatest climbing achievements ever. This audacious alpinist demonstrated his flair for the dramatic by soloing a new route on the north face of the Matterhorn in the winter of 1965 before retiring from mountaineering to pursue other adventures.

Bonatti's example inspired many other alpinists. The English climbers Chris Bonington, Don Whillans, and Ian Clough and Polish climber Jan Djuclosz succeeded on Mont Blanc's central pillar of Frêney in 1961. South Tyrolean wunderkind Reinhold Messner, to whom Bonatti dedicated his book *The Great Days,* followed in the master's footsteps by doing such hard solo routes as the northeast face of Les Droites in 1969. French alpinist René Desmaison repeated many of the hardest Alpine routes in winter and pioneered a new line on the north face of the Grandes Jorasses in the winter of 1973. These and many other outstanding ascents brought Alpine exploration to a resounding finale as the range's major problems were steadily mastered. After the 1970s, climbers concentrated on speed ascents, filling in routes, and sport climbing on the higher peaks and faces.

American climbers began to make their mark in the early 1960s, with major technical advances on the great rock walls of Yosemite National Park and elsewhere. With big-wall aid-climbing techniques developed by Royal Robbins on Half Dome in 1957 and Warren Harding on El Capitan in 1958, American climbers were able to grab major first ascents in the Alps, including the west face of the Petit Dru, climbed by Robbins and Gary Hemming in 1962, and the south face of the Aiguille du Fou, claimed by John Harlin, Tom Frost, Hemming, and Stuart Fulton in 1963.

In addition to developing big-wall techniques, Americans advocated a return to the principles of free climbing, with aid used only where free climbing proved impossible. Inspired by the superclean ethic of British rock climbers such as Frank Smythe, Joe Brown, and Don Whillans, Americans adapted the principles of free climbing to the steep granite walls of Yosemite and other climbing areas around the United States. Royal Robbins, Chuck Pratt, Yvon Chouinard, John Gill, Layton Kor, and others pushed the grade to 5.11 and paved the way for the next generation of free climbers, including Jim Bridwell and Ray Jardine, who raised the standards to 5.12 and 5.13, as well as soloists Henry Barber, John Bachar, and Peter Croft, who extended the boundaries of boldness, speed, and technical difficulty. Word got around that Yosemite had become the world center for rock climbing and soon European climbers began making pilgrimages to this new mecca.

The Yosemite influences were quickly transposed back to Europe, where they re-energized a scene dominated by Alpinism. Jean-Claude Droyer eliminated aid on Alpine routes, such as that of Comici's on the north face of Cima Grande in 1978, as well as putting up hard new free routes on non-Alpine cliffs such as the Verdon Gorge. German free climbers Reinhard Karl, Kurt Albert, and Wolfgang Güllich drew their inspiration from Yosemite as well as the Saxony region of Germany, where Bernd Arnold had established routes in the 5.13 range. Rather than ascending peaks, these climbers concentrated on short, extreme "sport" routes, and the result was a free-climbing explosion in the mid-1980s and early 1990s, with Güllich, Jean-Baptiste Tribout, and Ben Moon leading the way.

Whereas free climbers in Yosemite had focused mostly on cracks, these European sport climbers turned their attention to face climbing, choosing overhanging limestone as their favorite medium. Since this rock seldom featured a continuous crack line in which to place protection, these climbers bolted extensively, and frequently while on rappel, as there were few stances from which to place bolts on lead. This rap-bolting technique caused a furor in American climbing circles, representing as it did a radical departure from traditional ground-up style, and resulted in the hard feelings, fist fights, and deep divisions that have rocked the climbing community ever since. In Great Britain feelings also ran high as climbers sought reconciliation between the old styles and the new.

Despite the controversy, sport climbing continued to win new adherents, particularly among those first coming into climbing. With its emphasis on numerical grade, sport climbing soon lent itself to organized competitions, with climbers battling it out on artificial walls in front of judges and spectators, a far cry from traditional climbing and a development that threatened to further divide the climbing community. But as these events proved popular with the public and provided climbers a way to make a living, their scope and number increased.

The first of these competitions was held in Bardoneccia, Italy, in 1985, and many others soon followed. The French in particular excelled at this aspect of the sport, with figures such as Patrick Edlinger, Didier Raboutou, Jean-Baptiste Tribout, and François Legrand dominating men's climbing from the mid-1980s to the present, with an occasional challenge by Jerry Moffatt, Simon Nadin, and others. In the women's division, Catherine Destivelle and Lynn Hill battled it out for a couple of years before Destivelle quit to pursue alpine climbing in 1989, leaving Hill to begin her reign as the queen of competition climbing, a reign that has been challenged in recent years by Isabelle Patissier and Robyn Erbesfield.

Destivelle jumped back into the spotlight with a winter solo of the Eiger north face in 1992, a feat that earned her the reputation of being perhaps the finest all-around female climber in history. The advancement in free-climbing standards brought about by sport climbing and the growing numbers of women in what had been an aggressively male activity promised to change the face of climbing not only in the Alps, but elsewhere around the world.

Meanwhile, in the Himalaya and other high mountain ranges, development continued, but at a much slower pace than in the Alps. Whereas in the Alps at the turn of the century climbers were taking aim at technical routes, in the Himalaya they were just beginning to probe the foothills of these great peaks.

In 1895, Albert Mummery made an important early attempt on Nanga Parbat but disappeared without a trace. In 1907, Tom Longstaff, Henri Brocherel, and C. G. Bruce ascended Trisul, which at 23,360 feet was the highest peak yet climbed. A 1909 Italian expedition sponsored by the Duke of Abruzzi unsuccessfully attempted the southeast spur of K2, now called the Abruzzi Ridge. British climbers, including George Mallory and E. F. Norton, attempted Everest in 1922, when their expedition reached 27,300 feet, and then again in 1924, when Mallory and Andrew Irvine disappeared while trying to climb the northeast ridge.

German climbers concentrated first on Kangchenjunga, with Paul Bauer leading strong but unsuccessful attempts in 1929 and 1931, and then on Nanga Parbat, with Willi Merkl organizing expeditions in 1932 and 1934. The second ended in disaster, with Merkl and eight others perishing in a blizzard while trying to descend from the peak's Silver Saddle (24,560 feet).

British climbers Frank Smythe and Eric Shipton proved more fortunate on Kamet (25,447 feet) when they reached the summit in 1931. Shipton later joined forces with H. W. Tilman to map out many of the interior valleys of the Himalaya, while in 1936 Tilman and N. E. Odell managed to climb the difficult Nanda Devi (25,645 feet). But the most astonishing achievement of the pre–World War II period was undoubtedly the 1939 American attempt on K2, where Fritz Wiessner came within a few hundred feet of the 28,250-foot summit, a feat unfortunately clouded by the disastrous loss of four men.

After World War II, climbers resumed their efforts in the Himalaya, concentrating especially on peaks in excess of 8000 meters. A French team led by Maurice Herzog was the first to succeed on an 8000er, climbing the 8091-meter Annapurna in 1950. With the 8000-meter barrier broken, climbers then redoubled their efforts on Everest, the world's tallest peak, and as such the greatest prize in mountaineering history. So much energy and attention was devoted to Everest that when a doughty New Zealander named Ed Hillary and Sherpa

Tenzing Norgay succeeded in climbing it as part of a British expedition in 1953, the whole world stood up and took notice.

After the ascent of Everest, high-altitude climbing progressed rapidly. As was the case in the Alps, the ascent of the highest peak paved the way for ascents of lower, often more difficult summits. Shortly after Everest fell, 8000-meter peaks such as K2, Kangchenjunga, and Gasherbrum II saw first ascents, usually by big parties forcing their way up the easiest routes. The majority of these teams employed expedition-style tactics, whereby climbers used supplemental oxygen and fixed ropes to work their way up a mountain in a series of steps. Such tactics required a huge team and complicated logistical organization, but they proved a necessary phase in high-altitude mountaineering, permitting climbers to ascend extremely hazardous peaks in relative safety.

However, not all mountaineers chose to employ such tactics. Austrian Hermann Buhl's solo, oxygenless ascent of Nanga Parbat in 1953 demonstrated that alpine-style tactics could succeed at altitude. His expedition to Broad Peak in 1957 took high-altitude alpine-style climbing still further, with the entire team—Buhl, Kurt Diemberger, Markus Schmuck, and Fritz Wintersteller— reaching the top without supplemental oxygen or fixed camps. Alpine-style ascents such as these established a foundation upon which the next generation of Himalayan climbers would build.

After Everest and all the other 8000-meter peaks had been climbed by their easiest routes, the next step became finding more demanding ways to the top. Reinhold Messner and his brother, Günther, made a major advance in 1970 with an ascent of the Rupal Face on Nanga Parbat as part of a German-Austrian expedition. Later that year a British expedition led by Chris Bonington climbed the formidable south face of Annapurna. Bonington followed that up with a successful British expedition to the southwest face of Everest in 1975. A Yugoslavian expedition organized by Ales Künaver overcame the daunting south face of Makalu in 1975, with several members reaching the top without supplemental oxygen. Polish climber Andrzej Zawanda took things a step further by pioneering winter climbing in the Himalaya, leading successful winter expeditions to Everest in 1980 and the southeast face of Cho Oyu in 1985.

While most teams attempted such routes in expeditionary style, still others opted for a pared-down, alpine-style approach. Messner proved the great innovator within this tradition, practicing a style of high-altitude alpinism that allowed him and Peter Habeler to establish a new route on Hidden Peak in 1975 without porters, fixed camps, or bottled oxygen. They followed that up with the even more impressive feat of climbing Everest without oxygen in 1978. Later that year Messner pushed the limits still further with his solo, oxygenless ascent of Nanga Parbat. Just as he had in the Alps, Messner took climbing in the Himalaya to an astonishing new level, thereby establishing his reputation as the greatest climber of the modern era.

Others soon followed in his footsteps. Spanish climbers Nil Bohigas and

Enric Lucas completed an extraordinary alpine-style ascent of a new route on the south face of Annapurna in 1984. Polish mountaineers Jerzy Kukuczka and Voytek Kurtyka undertook remarkably committing traverses of Hidden Peak and Gasherbrum II in 1983 and Broad Peak in 1984. Shortly thereafter, they split up to pursue separate interests. Kukuczka entered the race to climb all the 8000ers and was killed on Lhotse in 1989, while Kurtyka continued to seek out aesthetic new lines on lesser-known peaks. Kurtyka's 1985 route on Gasherbrum IV with Austrian Robert Schauer set a new standard for boldness and severity of line. In recent years, he has teamed up with Swiss climbers Erhard Loretan and Jean Troillet to make one-day ascents of such routes as the west face of Cho Oyu and the south face of Shisha Pangma in 1990.

Alpine-style tactics proved attractive to many other climbers as well, often on some extremely technical routes. American Jeff Lowe specialized in high-grade ice routes such as the 5000-foot north face of Kwande, which he climbed in 1982 with David Brashears, and technical rock routes such as Taweche, which he ascended with American John Roskelley in 1989. Englishman Doug Scott developed a multipeak style of acclimatization whereby he scaled lower peaks in preparation for lightning-quick ascents of peaks such as Shisha Pangma, which he completed in 1982 with Alex MacIntyre and Roger Baxter-Jones.

But the figure who took high-altitude climbing to a whole new level was the Slovene Tomo Česen. His free solo of the south face of Lhotse in 1990 represented not just a quantum leap forward in terms of high-altitude climbing, but a new synthesis of all the various specialties within the sport. The route demonstrated that comprehensive mastery is the key to keeping adventure and commitment in mountaineering. This visionary ascent brought all of the sport's divergent branches back together and pointed out a clear path for the future in climbing.

In light of Česen's route on the south face of Lhotse and other important recent ascents, where is climbing likely to be heading in the future? What are the new "great problems" that remain to be solved? How can climbers push the limits and still keep excitement, adventure, and commitment in climbing?

For answers to these questions, read on: seventeen of the world's most outstanding climbers offer their perspectives on these and many other issues, illustrating in graphic and compelling detail where climbing has gone in the past and where it is likely to be headed in the future.

⛰ REINHOLD MESSNER

*The true art of climbing is survival, and the point at which
that becomes most difficult is when, having mastered what till
then has been considered the epitome of achievement, you try to
go one stage further. To venture where no one has been before,
and where hardly anyone wants to follow—or even understands
what it is you are trying to do. It is there, in that unknown
region, where sensations and experiences are found that are of far
greater intensity than any from "well-grazed" lands.*

—Reinhold Messner, *All 14 8,000ers*

AS THE MOST INFLUENTIAL high-altitude climber of the modern age, Reinhold
Messner has brought to fruition all the advances made in climbing over
the previous half-century, purging the sport of excessive technological
aids while relentlessly pushing the limits of the possible. During the height of his
career in the 1970s and 1980s, Messner consistently upped the ante in climbing,
not only tackling increasingly difficult routes but also completing them in a
progressively stripped-down style. In paring equipment and supplies to the
minimum and eschewing artificial aids such as bottled oxygen and expansion
bolts, Messner ushered in an era of fast, free ascents in the Alps and alpine-style
and solo ascents at altitude. His climbs became the standard by which all others
were judged.

This single-minded—some might say obsessive—search for new and harder
challenges has won Messner not only praise but also misunderstanding and
criticism. He has been called crazy more than once in his career, but upon close
inspection his climbs reveal not foolhardiness, but precise calculation, immense
self-confidence, and bold execution. The proof of this lies in his survival. He has
been one of the few high-altitude climbers who not only continued to push the
limits, but who returned to tell people about what lay beyond them. He credits
his talent for survival to the experience gained over a lifetime of living in the
mountains and climbing them.

Messner was born in 1944 in Brixen, a town in the South Tyrol region of
Italy. He grew up not far from there in Villnöss, a mountain village surrounded

19

Reinhold Messner. (Photo by Alison Chadwick Onyszkiewicz; Diadem Archives)

by impressive spires and peaks. Several years after he learned to walk, he began climbing, first on Sass Rigais, a nearby peak, which he ascended with his parents, and later on more technical routes such as the east face of the Kleine Fermeda, which he climbed with his father. He eventually teamed up with his younger brother, Günther, and others to tackle the most difficult climbs in the Alps: in 1965 he and Günther repeated the North Face Direct of Les Courtes and the North Face Direct on the Triolet in the western Alps; in 1966 he and Heini Holzer climbed the notorious Philipp-Flamm Route on the Civetta in the Dolomites as well as several other difficult test pieces; in 1969 he soloed the north face of Les Droites, the Philipp-Flamm Route on the Civetta, and a new route on the south face of the Marmolata. Also in 1969, he made a one-day ascent of Mont Blanc's central pillar of Frêney with Erich Lackner, a feat that paved the way for other speed ascents, such as his and Peter Habeler's record ten-hour climb of the Eiger north face in 1974. By the time Messner was twenty-five, he had done most of the hardest routes in the Alps, many of them solo, and was ready to move to high-altitude objectives.

He got his first taste of high-altitude climbing in 1969 when he climbed Yerupajá Grande (21,759 feet) as part of a Tyrolean expedition. The following year he went to Nanga Parbat with an expedition led by Dr. Karl Herrligkoffer. There, he and Günther succeeded in climbing the Rupal Face, but triumph turned into tragedy on the descent when his brother was killed by an avalanche. Driven near to madness with grief, Messner descended, eventually returning home to tell the story to his heartbroken family.

After taking time to recover emotionally and physically from the tragedy (he lost six toes to frostbite), Messner returned to the Himalaya in 1972 to climb the south face of Manaslu with a Tyrolean expedition. He was the sole team member to reach the summit. On the descent, climbers Franz Jäger and Andi Schlick failed to find their tent and perished in a blizzard. Inexplicably, some members of the European press blamed Messner for not doing more to prevent their deaths, and although Messner didn't take the accusations seriously, he was still hurt by them.

Smarting from the criticism and fed up with big teams, he decided to forgo large expeditions in favor of small, experienced, cohesive teams. His first experiment in this direction took place in 1974 on his solo of the south face of Aconcagua in Argentina. He returned to expedition climbing briefly in 1975 when he accompanied Riccardo Cassin's Italian expedition to the south face of Lhotse. Avalanches forced the expedition to retreat, but later that year Messner teamed up with Peter Habeler to do the north face of Hidden Peak in one long push, without fixed camps, bottled oxygen, or the support and safety net provided by a large expedition. The two followed up this coup with an even bolder stroke in 1978 when they climbed Everest without oxygen via the south col. Not content to stop there, Messner summited on K2 without oxygen in 1979 and the following year achieved one of his ultimate objectives with a solo, oxygenless ascent of the north face of Everest.

Other amazing feats followed. He traversed Gasherbrum I and II in 1982 with Hans Kammerlander and in 1986 achieved yet another tour de force when he and Kammerlander ascended the west face of Lhotse, thus completing Messner's quest to climb all fourteen of the 8000-meter peaks in the world. Having achieved that goal, Messner shifted his focus from high-altitude climbing to other projects, such as polar exploration. In 1989 he and Arved Fuchs crossed Antarctica on skis, pulling their supplies behind them on sleds. Messner continues to climb, mostly choosing new routes on remote peaks as his objectives.

Messner has been married once, to Uschi Demeter in 1972. They were divorced in 1977 because, as Messner admitted, "In the end my single-minded obsession with the mountains was too much for our marriage." In 1981 his girlfriend, Nena Holguin, bore him a daughter. He now lives in a castle in the South Tyrol with Sabine Stehle, with whom he has two children.

Since 1979, Messner has made his living by lecturing, writing scores of books, guiding, teaching, and endorsing products. In the process he has achieved a near film star status in Germany, Austria, Italy, and other European countries. While on a lecture tour of the United States he took time out for an interview in the lobby of a resort hotel in Snowbird, Utah. Messner is a tall, robust figure with unruly brown hair, a bushy beard, and a wild gleam in his eye. In addition to being an exceptional athlete, he is a man positively bursting with ideas, opinions, and pronouncements on everything from climbing to wilderness preservation and from philosophy to filmmaking.

Is danger a necessary part of climbing?

Yes. Without danger of death, climbing is no longer climbing. I'm not seeking death on the climb—exactly the opposite—I'm trying to survive. But it's very easy to survive if there's no danger of death. Climbing is the art of surviving in very difficult situations that involve the danger of death. And the best climber is not the one who does a crazy thing once or twice and dies the second time; the best climber is one who does many things on the highest level and survives.

How were you able to survive your many climbs?

You need a lot of experience. You need a lot of preparation. You need a lot of energy. You need good instincts for the mountains. And you get these things only after years of climbing.

And also you need a lot of luck. Nobody should overstretch his luck. For this reason, I don't do ten expeditions a year. I do two or three. And if I feel I have enough luck in my rucksack, I do another one. But I'm not able to go immediately from one to the next. I would make mistakes. I would fall. I have made many mistakes in my life and I have been lucky a few times. But if you are always risking your life, you will surely die.

You should know, "This I can do, and this I cannot do." This is one of the basic parts of climbing, to know in every second, "This is my limit. I cannot go above it. I should stay a little bit below." And if you go above too many times, you will surely die climbing. And the art of climbing is surviving and not dying.

So you know your limit very well.

But I have to learn it again every time. You don't know exactly what is your limit. And you forget it very quickly. After a few years of not climbing you lose not only your power and your strength, you also lose the knowledge of your limits. And to know that you can do something, you have to try, like a jumper who tries first two meters twenty, then two meters twenty-one. You have to try it and you have to feel it.

I am a very cautious man. If I have the feeling, "Maybe I cannot do this," I wait for a long time until I'm sure I can do it. I'm not going to risk it.

How did you get started climbing?

I got into climbing by going with my father. He brought the whole family to the mountains. I've been climbing since I was five years old.

Did you like climbing right from the start?

Yes, I liked it very much. When I was a small boy I liked to go to boulders fifty or sixty feet high rather than to the mountains. But when I was about fourteen I loved to climb mountains. At fifteen or sixteen, I did some moderate solo climbing. I would go from the village into the mountains and back in one day.

> *". . . THE BEST CLIMBER IS*
> *NOT THE ONE*
> *WHO DOES A CRAZY THING*
> *ONCE OR TWICE*
> *AND DIES*
> *THE SECOND TIME;*
> *THE BEST CLIMBER IS ONE*
> *WHO DOES MANY THINGS*
> *ON THE HIGHEST LEVEL*
> *AND SURVIVES."*

Who taught you to climb?

The simplest things I got from my father. And I met some very good climbers—Sepp Mayerl, Heini Holzer—and I learned a lot from them. By twenty or twenty-one, I knew how to handle things technically.

So you took to it quickly.

Yes, I came in at a very high level. At eighteen and nineteen I became interested in doing the most difficult climbs in the Alps and in being one of the best. First on rock and later on ice too. And by the time I was twenty I did maybe 80 or 90 percent of all the difficult Alpine climbs. And so I understood that there was nothing left in the Alps, and I went to the Himalaya.

What accounted for your success on these difficult Alpine routes?

I trained for climbs like the Eiger north face and the classical big climbs in the Alps, and I had a lot of experience because I'd been climbing for fifteen years. This experience helped me to find a good route by myself, to understand the weather quickly, to know that this rock is good and this rock is bad, to learn the structure of the mountain, of the rocks. If you have a lot of experience, you know if this gully will go to the left or the right; you'll see it instinctively from the rock, from the geology. And this I got when I was a child, without even thinking. And this is my power today, especially these things.

So it was this early experience that allowed you to do more difficult climbs quickly and safely?

Yes. When I came to the Himalaya I was the youngest on the team, but I felt quite quickly that I had more experience than the older ones, because I had been climbing for so many years before. Most of them had five to ten years maximum, and when I came to the Himalaya, I had twenty years of experience.

When did you begin doing high-altitude climbing?

In 1969 I was invited to South America, and there I first put my nose into high-altitude climbing. We did a very good climb there [east face of Yerupajá Grande], and when I came home I did a lot of Alpine climbs. In 1969 I did the most difficult routes of the Alps solo—the most difficult rock climbs, the most difficult ice climbs. And I was invited again by an expedition leader to Nanga Parbat, and we climbed the Rupal Face of Nanga Parbat.

Why did that particular face appeal to you?

The Rupal Face was very important for me because since 1963 many climbers had tried it. Everybody failed. The most important European climbers were there, especially from the German-speaking countries. This was really a difficult face on a high mountain, one that is much bigger than the Eiger face—three times the Eiger face, four times the Matterhorn north face—and I was interested to know what was going on there.

When you got back from Nanga Parbat, was it difficult to explain your brother's death to your parents?

It was very difficult for me to help my parents and brothers understand what really happened, because they didn't know what high-altitude climbing was all about, and we were a very close family, and still are.

My brother and I climbed every weekend in the summer. We climbed like invulnerable people. We heard that somebody was killed here, and somebody was killed there, and we had to help rescue people sometimes, but we had the feeling that we would never die climbing. We felt that we could do the craziest things and that it would have been impossible for us to fall.

We started for Nanga Parbat in the same mood. After the decision to climb down the west face, it was difficult for the first hours because we did not know if we could handle it, but we were not thinking, "We will die down

*Rupal Flank of Nanga Parbat, climbed by Reinhold and Günther Messner in 1970.
(Diadem Archives)*

there." We were just going, and the tragedy came in seconds, and I had to understand in seconds that there's also death involved in life and in climbing.

For a while, I did not really accept the fact that my brother had died. I was living like he was still alive. And in the last ten years of going on climbs, or living in the mountains, or in dreams and so on, I have the feeling that he's still alive.

And clearly it was much more difficult to express it to my mother than to myself, because I had the experience, I was there, I lived it. But my mother could never have this experience. She could never understand what Nanga Parbat was. She could see it on the map, but nothing more.

"I WENT BACK TO SEARCH FOR MY BROTHER, TO SEE THE AREA AGAIN, TO UNDERSTAND WHAT HAPPENED.

Is it fair for climbers to put their loved ones through things like that?

I think we have the right to do it. I think it's fair. I think there is no difference if you die at twenty or at sixty. It's more difficult for a wife or a child or a mother to understand it than for a climber himself; it's never a tragedy for the one who dies, because the one who dies is not living the tragedy. The tragedy is only with those who survive. But a climber who is married or who is growing up in a family is evolving like this, so the family sees this and lives with it.

Why did you go back to Nanga Parbat the following year?

I went back to search for my brother, to see the area again, to understand what happened. In 1973 I went back to try a solo ascent of Nanga Parbat, but I was not mature enough then. Maybe the whole thing was not mature— nobody else was thinking about climbing an 8000-meter peak solo. And later on [1978] I did the first solo ascent of an 8000-meter peak on Nanga Parbat. I did it there because it was my first 8000-meter peak, because my brother was killed there, because it was an important mountain for me. It's still the most important 8000-meter peak for me.

Why did you keep pushing the limits in high-altitude mountaineering?

I always wanted to do something more difficult. In 1970 it was the Rupal Face that attracted me. After the bad experience of the death of my brother, and a year to recover from that, I knew that I could do more.

And again in 1972 I did a classic, fixed-rope expedition when I went with a team to Manaslu. After Manaslu the critics said, "He is responsible [for the deaths of climbers Andi Schlick and Franz Jäger]. This climbing is too dangerous." They didn't die because I was there; they died because they were not prepared for such difficult things. And partly because of that I began to think, "Okay, in the future, I do them alone so that I am responsible for nobody."

And because of this pressure, and also because in the meantime I understood it should be possible to climb a peak without fixed ropes and so on, I tried to solo Nanga Parbat in 1973. But I was not able to live in such difficult situations alone. I was able to climb in 1973 maybe better than in 1978—I was very strong in 1973—but I was not able to be up there alone, having nobody to speak with, no other faces. It was very difficult. It took me a long time to learn. I was especially weak in this area.

Did your alpine-style ascent of Hidden Peak help pave the way for a solo ascent of Nanga Parbat?

Yes. After the Hidden Peak climb [1975], I knew that I could do difficult climbs exactly like in the Alps and that the next thing would be a solo ascent. The Hidden Peak climb was a new thing, but we [Messner and Peter Habeler] went with the feeling, "If it's impossible, we will go down, we will stop." But we were quite lucky and we had good weather and we were able to do it.

And when we succeeded on Hidden Peak, I knew immediately that this would change the whole of Himalayan climbing. Because if you go up with two climbers, you can do a climb with only $5000. Many people can get $5000.

Was it difficult to break through the psychological barrier of climbing Everest without oxygen?

It was difficult because, before we started, people told us, "It is not possible. You're risking your life. You will lose your brain up there." We were only part of this big Austrian expedition, and when the first team came down, they said, "Don't even try. It's impossible." It was a difficult decision because we didn't know if we would have a chance to go back to Everest another time, and Everest is Everest. And I was very determined then, and I was thinking, "Even if we don't succeed, let's go as high as possible. Let's try it."

We had medium-good weather; we didn't have really good weather. We went from the south col to the summit in a little more than eight hours. That's a quick ascent. It demonstrates that it's not so difficult. Since then, many people have done it—some twenty without oxygen. And you will see, in twenty years most people will climb without oxygen.

Do you think it should be climbed without oxygen?

I would not make a rule of it. Everyone is free to do it with oxygen or without oxygen, but if somebody's doing it with oxygen, he should be responsible to bring the bottles down to base camp.

I would never say that everyone has to do the same thing. For a long time, especially in the sixties, I was always preaching, "Everybody has to climb without bolts. I'm climbing without bolts. Bolts are ruining the faces."

Today I would say, "I am climbing without bolts. I have my own rules. But if you like to climb with bolts, do it." And so I say with oxygen.

Why did you end your partnership with Peter Habeler?

In 1978 it was finished and it will be finished forever. He's a very good climber, but he's a man in whom I lost confidence. He signed a contract for a book, which was written by a journalist. And this book was so much bullshit that I could not accept it. If you sign a contract, you're responsible for what's in it.

And at least a thousand times I had to answer questions about the book. I had it up to here. And then people understood that our partnership was over. Because if I've lost confidence in someone, if there is something not right between us, then I make a break. I cut the rope forever.

Does this apply to the rest of your life?

Also normal life. I'm very strict in my views. And if I have a good friend, I have a good friend. A good friend would never do things like this. Peter Habeler and I were good climbing partners, but we were not good friends. We met once or twice a year. We did good climbs. On all my climbs with him, I organized and financed things. And it was not nice to read in this book that he organized and financed the Hidden Peak expedition. He did not pay one schilling. I had to work for a year to organize and finance it. [Habeler denies this, maintaining that he helped organize and finance their expeditions. He argues that Messner simply resented the attention that he (Habeler) got from the book.]

You've done a lot of your recent ascents with Hans Kammerlander. Is he a good partner?

Yes. I met him in 1970. He worked in my climbing school. He was a very strong climber. He went into climbing as a small boy, like me. I invited him on Cho Oyu in 1983, and I thought, "Maybe he's exactly the man I need for the next trips."

When did you get the idea to traverse Gasherbrum I and II?

In the early eighties, after the Nanga Parbat solo, I was just beginning to study other adventures. I still had the dream of soloing Everest, but I was sure I would not be able to do the first traverse of two 8000-meter peaks, because somebody else would do it. It was the logical next step. But still by 1984 nobody had done it, and I had the time, and I went there [with Kammerlander] and I tried it and I succeeded. And it may be the most difficult thing I ever did. And it's not been repeated. Nobody has been able to do two 8000-meter peaks without any support, without fixed ropes, without depots, without anybody on the mountain. Now it would be difficult because you would not be able to find two 8000-meter climbs without anybody on them. And if you have a lot of teams, it's not possible to do a traverse by clear and fair means.

And now I'm sure it's possible to traverse Lhotse and Everest, to go up on the south or eastern side of Lhotse, climb down to the south col, up to Everest, and down the other side. It's much more difficult than the Hidden Peak traverse and ten times more difficult than the Hidden Peak north face in 1975; but it's possible, and in the next ten years somebody will do it.

Did your attempt to climb all fourteen 8000ers become a race?

For me, it was never a race. It was a race for somebody else. Not for me.

Do you think it was a race for Jerzy Kukuczka?

He said sometimes it was a race for him, sometimes not. Maybe at the end he was racing because the press was pushing, but in a playing way, not in a competitive way.

We met many times. We were very good friends. We had no problems. But the press likes to make up a race. It's much better to write, "He did thirteen, and now who will win?"

What challenges remain in the Himalaya?

Quite a number of faces, such as Makalu's west face, Dhaulagiri's direct south face, and many others. There are many 6000- and 7000-meter peaks with difficult, difficult routes, and there are still many traverses to do, especially combinations.

Did you study climbing history when you were growing up?

Ever since I was sixteen or seventeen and I love it still. I have a huge library of maybe 2000 climbing books, especially from the older times. I've begun a new library of polar books, but I'm still following alpine history, and maybe when I'm sixty or seventy I will write a climbing history. I would like to do it. But I would need at least ten years.

You seem very conscious of climbing history.

Yes, I like it. For maybe ten or fifteen years, I was ahead in Himalayan climbing because I knew exactly the history. If someone wants to go ahead of others in climbing, he should first look back at the whole history, and then he will know where to go.

So that would guide a climber.

Yes, even now. Free climbing is now over 100 years old. The first free climb in history was done in 1890. The evolution of free climbing is a very interesting story. It originated in the Dolomites. [And also in Great Britain, where climbers eschewed the use of bolts, pitons, and sometimes even nuts, considering them "unnatural" techniques.] In 1911 the rules of free climbing were written in a book by Viennese climber Paul Preuss. Free climbing is not an invention of the 1950s or 1960s, it's an invention of the last century. Today they climb much more difficult faces than in the 1890s, but the view and the approach are still the same. Preuss says that we should not change the rock to our needs, but we should train ourselves so that we are able to adapt to the rock. It's logical. If you really know what climbing is, this is the only answer.

> "*AND IF WE DESTROY THE IMPOSSIBLE WITH BOLTS OR TECHNICAL TRICKS, WE DESTROY CLIMBING.*"

After the Second World War, people came slowly again to climbing, and they went exactly the opposite way in the Dolomites and in the western Alps. They used more and more technical aids to do the walls in a direct line. They were not looking to do them free; they were looking to do them any way. Not by fair means, but by any means.

Only after the Yosemite revolution with Yvon Chouinard and Royal Robbins, and later on Ron Kauk, did this idea come back to Europe. [Chouinard and Robbins reduced artificial aid to a minimum and relied as much as possible on free-climbing techniques, thus paving the way for a revolution in free-climbing standards. In the mid-1960s they led the way in using leader-placed nut protection in lieu of pitons, an idea they had picked up from British climbers. Kauk followed in their footsteps until he began rap-bolting routes, a radical departure from the ground-up ethic of his predecessors.] Americans had become leaders in these views, and the Europeans in the meanwhile had forgotten them, so they had to get them back over a long circle. And now in the last ten years, rock climbing again has become a sport trying to put the limit higher and higher, and this is possible only when technical aids are there only to prevent falling [and not for pulling up on]. They are really climbing free today, like a hundred years ago.

Why are rules important to climbing?

Rules are not important. From the beginning, climbing was an anarchical way of living with nature. And climbers should make rules on their own. But if each one of us is saying, "I can put bolts over there. I can leave fixed ropes over there," we slowly destroy our playground. So there is at least one rule: we should leave the mountains as we found them.

And that's what you were fighting for in your early climbs?

Yes. I was always for pure free climbing in the classic way. I was never a free climber able to climb 5.13. Maybe I climbed 5.10 in my best years, in 1968 and 1969. That was the limit then. Nobody did more. Nobody was even thinking that maybe someone would climb 5.13, and now they are doing 5.14.

Did people think you were crazy for advocating free climbing?

Yes, especially in Europe. In 1965, I wrote my first article, "The Murder of the Impossible," in which I put down the idea that if we use more technical equipment, we will destroy the impossible, and without the impossible, climbing will lose the most important motivation. Nobody can do the impossible, but we can go near the impossible. And if we destroy the impossible with bolts or technical tricks, we destroy climbing.

What about the use of bolts?

I never used a bolt in my life, like I never used an oxygen bottle in my life. This is still part of my philosophy. If I cannot climb a mountain without an oxygen bottle, I don't go up. If I can't climb a wall without a bolt, I don't do it. I would not like to rape a wall or rape a high mountain. But today they need bolts for high-level sport climbing. But I would prefer that they do it on artificial walls.

But on a natural wall, we should leave it like it is. Just the normal piton put in a crack, or the nut, is a compromise. The nut is a better thing, because you put it in and you take it out, and if you don't put it in with the hammer, you don't destroy the rock. But just putting in a piton again and again slowly destroys the rock.

I put in a lot of pitons for belaying [and protection from falling], but 99 percent of the time I didn't use them for getting up. And in the mid-sixties, when I became quite a good rock climber, I always said the pitons should be there for belaying [and protection] but not for putting in a ladder. I should find a way to do a climb free or I should leave it undone. This was more or less the idea of "The Murder of the Impossible."

When you do a climb, is the struggle between you and the mountain rather than you and some other climber?

Not even between me and the mountain. I'm trying to live with the mountain. I'm not fighting with the mountain. But it's a relationship between the mountain and me and not between me and someone else. If I have a partner or a group, I try to live with them and I try to have no fighting between the members if I am leading. I try to give them the mountain as a motivation or the face or the line. I never had the feeling that there was a competition going on with other climbers.

Is climbing ever a religious experience for you?

In a large way, yes. There are many ways to pray. And praying is a meditation. For Buddhists, praying is nothing but to forget everything, to be empty, and to be open for new experiences.

> *"FOR ME THERE'S NO DIFFERENCE BETWEEN CLIMBING AND LIVING."*

But meditation is not our Western way. We are not able to do it. We have an active approach to life. But I think through climbing I reach the same goal. And in this way climbing is for me praying, because if I climb, I am so concentrated that I become empty and open for new experiences.

So this is one of the reasons you climb?

This is one of the motivations that remains. After the competition years, I see it with a loving eye.

Do you still need to climb?

Yes. I'm still interested in going on climbs, but I no longer climb very high peaks like Everest, K2, or other 8000-meter peaks. But I still dream about climbs in Tibet and South America.

Why is it that you climb?

There is no answer. If I asked you, "Why are you living?" what would you say? For me there's no difference between climbing and living. Climbing is one of the center points of my life. So I should answer, "Why am I living?" I feel life is a positive possibility to express myself, to know myself, to know the world, to be with people. But I would not make a distinction between why I am living and why I am climbing. For me it's the same thing. I'm not dividing it. For me, climbing is part of my life.

And for me it also would be difficult to answer why I am writing, or why I am farming, or why I am trying to make films. Again, I try a new possibility to express what I know, what I feel, what I can do. I like to be creative.

What effect has climbing had on your body?

I lost some of my toes. This was the worst thing. For a long time I had problems with my knee, so I decided maybe ten or fifteen years ago to have a pause every year for three or four months, to do nothing. And it helped. So I don't have any problems with the knee.

Did oxygen deprivation have any effect on you?

No. I don't have any problems from that. I'm doing research with a Swiss university because they're studying bodies after high altitude, studying the brain especially. And they're doing it every year, so I know about everything that happens in my brain. At the moment I'm quite sane.

Do you think that climbing is a decadent activity?

Yes. Decadent in that it's not a basic need. Only when people have a house and enough to eat and drink—what they need basically to live—are they thinking of climbing or going to the theater or creating works of art. I don't see it in a negative way. I see it in a positive way.

So you see climbing as creative?

Yes, I put climbing on the creative side, not on the sportive side. I like to express my capabilities and also my fears in my climbs. My climbs are really artistic works. The lines remain there, and somebody can go there and have the same experience.

If you sit below Taweche [a peak in the Solu Khumbu region of Nepal], and if you know that John Roskelley and Jeff Lowe climbed the northeast face in winter [1989], you can feel something of what they experienced. Looking at their climb gives you an experience that is like the experience of looking at a painting.

A good line on a good face is a work of art. It's like life. We live it and afterward it's gone, but there remains something, there remains a line.

▲ RICCARDO CASSIN

The preparations for a bivouac are lengthy, often a race against darkness; but when, having arranged everything, you look for the most comfortable place to sleep—and heaven knows it's nearly always uncomfortable—then in a sense the whole mountain is present in you: you get the feeling of being part of it, and that is poetry too. Each one feels it in his own way, according to diverse habits, desires and personality; but each one of that ill-matched bunch who are real climbers, even though he may not find the means to express what he finds in language, at the bottom of his heart is still a poet even if—especially when young—he finds it shameful to confess.

—Riccardo Cassin, *Fifty Years of Alpinism*

RICCARDO CASSIN may be reluctant to speak of the poetry that underlies his climbing, but others who have observed the severe, classic lines of his routes haven't hesitated to compare them with poems. As one observer remarked of Cassin's ascent of the southeast ridge of Torre Trieste, "On those 700 metres of rock you wrote a poem."

Cassin has been penning this kind of impressive poetry for a long time. The patriarch of Italian climbing, he has achieved legendary status not only for his extraordinary athletic achievements but for his remarkable longevity as well. A potent force in extreme alpinism for more than fifty years, he continued to push the limits on rock, snow, and ice long after most climbers his age had settled comfortably into their rocking chairs. In addition, he served as a model and mentor to a number of younger climbers, including Reinhold Messner, his most famous protégé.

The career of this grand old man of climbing comprises several phases. Born in 1908 in Savorgagno, in lower Friuli, Italy, he began climbing in 1926 on the limestone towers of the Grigna, a rock-climbing center near Lecco in northern Italy. Teaming up with such partners as Mario Dell'Oro (Boga) and Mary Varale, Cassin reeled off a dizzying list of first ascents and developed the skills, courage,

Riccardo Cassin. (Courtesy Cassin collection)

and tenacity that would later prove of critical importance on some of the most difficult peaks in the world.

Italian climber Emilio Comici's visit to the Grigna in 1933 served as Cassin's introduction to aid climbing and other techniques developed in the Dolomites.

Fired with enthusiasm by this visit, Cassin became determined to put these techniques into practice not just in the Grigna, but on big Dolomite walls as well. His perseverance paid off in 1934, when he, Boga, and Gigi Vitali made the second ascent of Comici's route up the north face of Cima Grande.

His apprenticeship completed, he went on to pioneer many new aid routes in the Dolomites, including a first ascent with Vittorio Ratti of the north face of the Cima Ovest in 1935. On this and other Dolomite climbs, Cassin demonstrated a mixture of skill, determination, and audacity that allowed him to succeed on the steepest and severest of routes. His unwillingness to retreat unless forced into it resulted in many breakthroughs under the worst weather conditions. In 1937, he, Ratti, and Gino Esposito made the first ascent of the northeast face of Piz Badile despite a storm during which two other climbers (Mario Molteni and Giuseppe Valsecchi) died of exposure.

Though he specialized in rock climbing, Cassin also developed his skills on snow and ice, permitting him to extend his horizons to mixed routes in the Alps. Like many climbers of his generation, he had hoped to make the first ascent of the north face of the Eiger. But when Anderl Heckmair, Ludwig Vörg, Fritz Kasparek, and Heinrich Harrer got there first in 1938, Cassin turned his attention to the Walker Spur of the Grandes Jorasses, one of the last great problems in the Alps at that time. Despite less than ideal weather, he, Gino Esposito, and Ugo Tizzoni tackled the route. The wall had beaten back all previous attempts, but Cassin's skill in making delicate traverses allowed them to cross the crux pitch and claim their first ascent.

After this and other successes in the Alps, Cassin was ready to move to more extended climbs, but personality conflicts sometimes got in the way. Cassin was excluded from the 1953 Italian K2 expedition purportedly for health reasons, but more likely because of his strong personality. Despite the snub, Cassin proved that he wasn't quite ready for retirement by leading an Italian expedition to Gasherbrum IV in 1957. The expedition put Walter Bonatti and Carlo Mauri on the summit.

That climb would have capped many a career, but Cassin wasn't finished yet. In 1961 he led a team of young Italian climbers to the Cassin Ridge on Mount McKinley, one of today's classic alpine test pieces. Storms buffeted them all the way up the mountain, but Cassin's indomitable will won out when they summited in mid-July. Weather conditions worsened, however, and they endured an epic descent. Several members of the team suffered frostbite, but all of them managed to get off the mountain.

Still not content to retire, Cassin looked to South America in 1969 for a new extreme route. Relishing his role as expedition leader, he brought another group of young climbers with him to attempt the west face of Jirishanca in the Peruvian Andes. Their ascent of this nervy ice climb temporarily sated Cassin's need for adventure.

In 1975 Cassin set out for perhaps the most ambitious objective of his career, the immense south face of Lhotse. He assembled a formidable team for the task, including a young climber named Reinhold Messner. At first the expedition made good progress, but then two devastating avalanches swept through base camp, injuring several porters and climbers and wreaking havoc on the tents and supplies. Cassin had no choice but to abandon the expedition. For the first time in his life, a peak had forced him to back down.

After that expedition, he retired from extreme alpinism. He didn't give up climbing, but he pursued it less avidly. He devoted more time to his family and to overseeing the small factory where he manufactures pitons, crampons, ice axes, and other equipment.

Cassin and his wife, Irma, were married in 1940. They have three sons and several grandchildren. Today the Cassins live in the hills above Lecco in a chalet beneath the imposing limestone pillars of the Grigna. The interview took place there on a balmy evening in midsummer, with Mirella Tenderini, a friend and neighbor, doing the translating. Cassin is not a tall man, but he is an imposing presence: his long arms are knotted with muscles, his clear blue eyes glitter with a shrewd and practical intelligence, and his big, square jaw moves with force and resolution as he makes his points. Even at eighty-five, Cassin possesses the energy and dynamism of a natural phenomenon.

Do you like to take risks?

Yes, I like to do things that are considered dangerous, but I overcome the risk by being skilled and prepared. I only take calculated risks. And if you take this approach, even the most difficult climb is no more dangerous than a walk.

Is risk one of the reasons that you climb?

No. It's not just the risk. It's because climbing is a sport and I've always loved sports, all kinds of sports—running, basketball, skiing, boxing. I think that what I really like is sports and competition. And of course there is competition in climbing, even though people maintain that there is not. If there is not a direct competition with other climbers, there is always a very strong competition with oneself.

What distinguishes climbing from these other sports?

There is more adventure in climbing than in other sports, and the competition with oneself in climbing is more exciting than the competition that you have with other athletes.

But why did you choose to pursue climbing rather than another sport, such as boxing?

I chose climbing because it appealed to me much more than boxing. As far as boxing is concerned, I fought fifty matches and was close to going to the Italian national championships, but at that point my boxing trainer said, "You have to choose," because to box and to climb are two different things, which require different kinds of training. Mountaineering is something that asks for steady, prolonged effort, whereas boxing asks for velocity, and the kinds of training needed for those things were incompatible. I chose to give up boxing because I liked mountaineering so much.

I've always enjoyed climbing. I had a preference for limestone because there is more elegance and technique in climbing on Dolomite limestone, and it's safer than other rock and ice climbs. But in principle I enjoy all kinds of climbing. And I don't just like climbing. I like very much to go on long walks in the mountains with my dog. I love the mountains in all their aspects.

How did your fascination with climbing get started?

I was born in Friuli, a region in northeast Italy, and from there, I used to see the mountains far above. In 1926 I came to Lecco to work. When I arrived, the friend who had gotten me the job took me to Lake Como. I'd never seen such a big lake. I thought it was the sea. And I said, "How beautiful it is. This is paradise." I fell in love with the lake and decided to stay there.

So I was working in Lecco as an apprentice in masonry, and the very first weekend in Lecco, I went with friends to Monte Resegone. Two weeks later I went to the Grigna for the first time, and after that, every weekend I went to the mountains. At first, I went around just as a tourist, walking, not climbing.

Then when I was eighteen I started to rock climb. I climbed the Segantini Ridge, which is very easy but very exposed. And I felt a bit dizzy, and I told myself, "Oh, Cassin, this is not the sport for you."

But the next weekend I went to the Angelina Spires, with walls of fifty meters. At these Angelina Spires, we had only fifty-meter ropes. There were eight of us, so we had to rope and unrope because the ropes were not sufficient for all of us. And on the second pitch my comrade Boga [Mario Dell'Oro] was off-route, and he said, "I don't know how to go now." I said, "Wait, wait. I'm coming." So I unroped myself and went up the right route. When we came upon another difficult passage, I climbed on Boga's shoulders to get to the top. When I got to the top, I unlaced my belt and helped him up. That's the way we climbed in those early days.

Luckily, Boga could climb down from that difficult passage we had overcome. Everybody got to the top. But then there were two pitches to descend to get down off the Angelina. And there is a very small ledge for one person between the first and second pitch. We managed to stay in aid on that ledge and I was the last one to descend, but we did not abseil. We didn't know the abseiling technique at that time. Later, when Comici came to the Grigna, we perfected the abseiling technique. At that time we just descended on the ropes. And I managed to make the descent safe for everybody.

But we understood that it was not sensible to climb that way. So we decided to make several teams of two, and since we had only two ropes, we arranged shifts to use the ropes. I went with Boga, and in a short time we had climbed all the spires in the Grigna.

In 1932 I went with a friend to climb the Corna di Medale [south southeast face]. When we were making a difficult and delicate traverse, a stone fell on my head, and I fell and hurt my knee slightly. Three weeks later, I recovered and went back to the Medale with Boga and succeeded.

From that time on, everything I did was a first ascent, with no previous attempts. My rule was to attack and succeed in one attempt. When I went on a new climb, a new route, I or someone on my expedition always got to the top. The only time I didn't succeed was in 1975 on Lhotse, the only time in my life.

What kind of line did you look for on your first ascents?

With the help of binoculars, I usually chose the most logical and correct route to climb. I seldom made a mistake. It's natural to travel the most logical line.

When I went to repeat a route, I wanted to follow the instructions, but I always made some mistake; so the only way was to put the guidebook in my rucksack and to climb by instinct. In that case I always found the right route.

We were not interested in establishing more than one route on a wall. Once a wall had been climbed, it no longer had any interest to me and to people in general. It was only later that I went to walls where there was already a route and looked for a more difficult one.

Did people criticize your use of artificial aid?

Yes. I was much criticized. They treated me very badly. But, in fact, on routes where I had used fifty pitons, other people used seventy pitons. So I climbed with less aid than other climbers.

Did you agree with the ideas of Paul Preuss, the great advocate of free climbing?

Oh, yes. I admired him as a great climber, but I must say his ideas were not supported by life because he died [on a climb]. I've always maintained that it's better to use one piton more than to lose your life.

When I went to climb the Comici Route on Cima Grande, I met Raffaele

Carlesso and Hans Vinatzer, who was a great climber of the time. Since they were two and we were three, I told them to go ahead because they were faster. But they were slower than us and I led right behind them. I often had to wait for them, so I spent the time taking pitons out, because I thought there were too many.

Was the northeast face of Piz Badile one of your most difficult climbs?

No. It wasn't one of the most difficult, but it was one of the most dramatic because we had the misfortune to meet two climbers [Mario Molteni and Giuseppe Valsecchi] who were on the route before we started, and they were already exhausted. Afterward I thought I should not have agreed to let them join us. If I had not accepted, they perhaps would have descended, and they might still be alive. [The two climbers died of exposure.] So the beautiful ascent was transformed into tragedy. But that was the only time that someone with me has died, and these were people we met accidentally on the route. I have never come back from an ascent having lost a climbing partner.

Did their deaths make you question the value of climbing?

This thought occurred to me, but it must be said that they died because they were not in a position to do such a difficult climb. They were not prepared.

Were a lot of people vying for the Walker Spur before you climbed it?

Everybody was, but most of the people attempting the Walker Spur were from the western areas of the Alps, and the pitch that nobody was able to overcome, and that I overcame, was something for someone who specialized in Dolomite climbing. The crux pitch was a traverse with no protection at all for twenty meters. When I first arrived there I found some matches and cigarette butts at the base of the crack. I thought, "My goodness, someone has already succeeded." I discovered later that no one had been able to get past it, because being on the crack without protection was very frightening.

So I succeeded in reaching the end of the crack and climbing the overhanging ice pitch. Sometime after that, the ice collapsed and the pitch was easier. The second ascent, made ten years after the first ascent, was not along the crack, but straight up, which was not possible until the collapse of the overhanging ice. And that crack has never been climbed again, as far as I know.

Was there a strong nationalistic impulse behind your Walker Spur ascent?

I had a strong anti-German feeling, so much that even in climbing I was always in competition with the Germans. You must understand that I'm from Friuli, and it is a region that for a long time was under Austrian domination. We grew up with pro-Italian and anti-German feeling because, to us, German-speaking people were considered one people, and it was a tradition for us to be suspicious of the Germans.

This also played a great part in my decision to fight against the Germans during World War II. At the beginning of the war I was a member of the Fascist Party like most everyone else in Italy. I was not interested in politics and didn't realize much about what was going on. But in 1939, when Italy entered the war beside the Germans, I strongly objected, and so I tore up my party card and joined the partisans, who were starting to organize against the Germans.

That must have been a very dangerous thing to do.

Yes. It was a risk not only for myself but also for my family and for the people who lived near me. I had arms and ammunition hidden in my house, and if the Germans had discovered them, it would have been dangerous for everybody. But during the war life was very risky anyway. Shortly after I joined

Riccardo Cassin on the Corno del Nibbio below the Grigna Range, Italy, 1938. (Diadem Archives)

the partisans I became a leader and had to take all kinds of risks. The Americans made nine air drops of ammunition, food, and clothes into the Grigna. My group received the materials and then hid them.

Did this make a difference in the war effort?

Yes. While the Germans and Italian Fascists fought us they were distracted from fighting the Allies, who were coming up from the south of Italy.

Have you always been a natural leader?

Yes. Whether I wanted it or not, people would come to me for advice and to make decisions. During the war, I, who had not done military service, found myself the commander of a group of partisans.

Did you enjoy leading climbing expeditions?

I would have preferred to be one of the group, but I was often asked to be the leader and so I acted as the leader. I did my duty.

Did you lead by example?

Yes, I believe in leading by example. If you want to get results, you have to do things, not just say them. On Gasherbrum IV, I made many trips a day for eight days with a load heavier than the ones the porters carried. Since I did that, the other climbers had to do the same. I set a good example for the porters and for everyone else.

How did you choose the climbers for the Gasherbrum IV expedition?

They were people whom I knew, and they were the best climbers at the time. My team on Gasherbrum IV was simply wonderful. People like Walter Bonatti, Carlo Mauri, and especially Bepi De Francesch, were very generous and carried material beyond the point where the porters had stopped.

After making several trips up and down the mountain, I reached Camp IV and felt ill. The doctor of the team told me, "You cannot continue. You must go down and you're not to come up anymore." I went back down and I felt better. So I started up again, alone, working, working, working, and reached 7500 meters. I found myself only 450 meters from the top, but there was an overhanging pitch above me. I left pitons and my hammer at the point where I could use them the next day and then descended. But unfortunately the monsoon came and I never got another chance to climb it. [Bonatti and Mauri made the first ascent.]

Was it difficult to move from climbing in the Alps to climbing in the Himalaya?

It's exactly the same except for the altitude, which requires more time for adaptation. Above 6500 meters it's important to go very fast because you cannot benefit from staying and getting used to it. If you stay, you don't get used to it; you get sick. The only thing to do is to go very fast. Experienced climbers know that and try to move quickly when they are above that altitude, unless they use oxygen, which is an artificial adaptation.

What climb are you most proud of?

I'm proud of all of my climbs, but the one that I enjoyed most was McKinley because I had such a wonderful group of young people. I was the father and mother of all of them. It was wonderful.

Why did you climb the ridge rather than the south face of McKinley?

The spur was the most logical route. I studied McKinley very carefully and flew over it and discovered that the ridge was the most beautiful route to the top.

> "... *I BELIEVE IN LEADING BY EXAMPLE. IF YOU WANT TO GET RESULTS, YOU HAVE TO DO THINGS, NOT JUST SAY THEM.* "

So you chose the route for its beauty?

Yes. It's difficult because of altitude and conditions, but it's still considered the most beautiful route on McKinley. It's a route that everyone would like to do.

Were you tempted to do an alpine-style ascent of the ridge rather than an expedition-style ascent?

No. At that time no one was thinking of doing routes like that one alpine style.

What are the advantages of expedition-style climbing?

It's safer. It's easier to evaluate the difficulties. It's possible to prepare the route. On McKinley, we had too large a party to climb it alpine style. To climb alpine style, it's necessary to have no more than three or four people.

Is expedition climbing a thing of the past?

Progress has been so great in so many senses that expeditions like the ones I did in the past make no sense now. When I was on the Baltoro for Gasherbrum IV, I had 500 porters because we had to leave from Skardu, whereas now you can go higher with roads. And the gear and food were heavier then. Once you had to carry two kilos of food per day; now you can bring food that weighs a lot less. And today the climbers are better prepared; they can climb alpine style. A small group of climbers can organize their own small expeditions; it's not necessary to have big expeditions with lots of people.

What were the challenges of that type of climbing?

The main problem with big expeditions is having people together who are different in character and convictions. In my experience that is the hardest thing. On Gasherbrum IV, there were nine of us, but on Lhotse there were thirteen, and luckily I had the experience of being the manager of a factory and was used to dealing with workmen, so I knew that with some people I had to shout and with others I had to be kind. The personality conflicts are really the most difficult things with big expeditions.

Was your 1975 attempt on the south face of Lhotse ahead of its time?

Evidently it was, if you consider that the 1981 Yugoslavian team with twenty-two people was not able to do it, and even Messner, who was with me at that time, went back in 1989 and didn't get higher than we did at that time. It was only in 1990 that Tomo Cesen was able to climb it.

Was it hard to accept defeat on Lhotse?

Yes. It was difficult, but we had to turn back because there was nothing else we could do. The weather was very hard on us. Two avalanches swept through base camp. It was better to give up than to risk anyone's life.

In my climbing career I was very lucky because I or a member of my team always succeeded in reaching the top of the mountains that we wanted to climb. The only unsuccessful attempt was on Lhotse and of course it was a disappointment.

Was this a psychological blow?

Defeat is always hard to accept, but I had to accept it and so I did.

Are you a fatalist?

No, I'm not a fatalist, but I believe that there is a destiny, which, however, is in our own mind.

Do we have control over it then?

Yes, there is a destiny that you can maneuver. It's like good luck. There is such a thing as good luck, and when good luck is within your reach, you have to grab it. In life and in mountaineering you need good luck and you need to be swift enough to grab it.

Is a strong will necessary as well?

A strong will is the motor of success, but it's something that some people have and some people don't. A strong will can endure sacrifice. A strong will can take pleasure in work, in difficult tasks. There is a pleasure in work and sacrifice because it allows you to accomplish what you're striving for.

Has that been the case with you?

Yes. I have a strong will and I attach to it so great a value that if I had to start my life all over again, I'd be very happy to start as I did, very poor, son of an immigrant who died in Vancouver, B.C., in a mine, provided that the only gift I were given would be a strong will.

Are you a stubborn man?

Yes, I have great force of will. That I know I have. I am certainly competitive. When I'm not in competition with someone else, I'm in competition with myself. In my opinion, life is partly competition. For the rest, I don't think I have anything special. I consider myself a normal person like anybody else.

Did your stubbornness make you want to go back to Lhotse?

Yes. But it was very difficult to get permits, very difficult to raise money. Those difficulties made it impossible to return. And I was sixty-six, and I decided not to go on any more expeditions.

> *"IN LIFE AND IN MOUNTAINEERING YOU NEED GOOD LUCK AND YOU NEED TO BE SWIFT ENOUGH TO GRAB IT."*

What did you think of Tomo Česen's ascent of the south face of Lhotse?

Extraordinary. Such an ascent is something that can be accomplished only by someone who devotes himself completely to mountaineering. Tomo is also a very high-level free climber and ice climber. He is very well prepared and he climbs at a very high level.

Jerzy Kukuczka was an extraordinary mountaineer, but he couldn't have done what Tomo Česen did because he was not a free climber of Tomo's caliber. He was very strong, determined, and had great qualities as a mountaineer, but he wasn't a great free climber, whereas Tomo is.

What impressed you most about his ascent of Lhotse's south face?

The clever idea of climbing it at night, because that face is very dangerous. I called it the walking mountain because when it snows you can actually see the mountain moving. So it's unlikely that if you climbed it by day that you could avoid all the ice- and stonefall.

Tomo is very intelligent, and he studied the route that was attempted by the Yugoslav party in 1981. He got the diary of the expedition and studied it in detail so that he was prepared technically, athletically, psychologically, and historically. He knew every move for the ascent and he knew every move for the descent. On top of that, he did the real south face. Other attempts were made by climbing Lhotse Shar and then traversing.

Are climbs like his the way of the future?

As far as I know, there are no other walls of that difficulty, perhaps the west face of Makalu, which is still to be climbed. But the west face of Makalu is safe, whereas the south face of Lhotse is very dangerous.

Have climbing techniques and equipment changed much over the years?

Yes, they've changed enormously, and it's easy to understand—man used to travel by bicycle and now he goes to the moon. And it's the same in mountaineering. Techniques and technology have allowed climbers to make enormous progress. There is better equipment, which makes climbing safer and easier. In the old days the equipment was bulky and heavy—a piton could weigh half a kilo, and if there was a small crack, it wouldn't fit. Now the pitons are of every shape and dimension and it makes the climbing much, much easier.

When I started, I found it natural to climb, but now it seems even easier because climbing has evolved so much. Because of better shoes, better gear, better knowledge, I find it easier in my eighties to do some sections that were very hard sixty years ago.

Are climbers today more skilled than their predecessors?

Their technique now is much more sophisticated and they perform more difficult climbs, but that's because of technique and technology, which cannot be compared with the techniques and technology of yesterday.

Are there some principles of climbing that haven't changed despite the changes in gear and technique?

I think that basically it's the same as it's always been. What attracts climbers to the mountains is adventure, and since adventure is proportional to a person's expectations, there are different kinds of adventure. So for one person, adventure is a difficult climb in the Himalaya, and for someone else adventure is climbing to the top of the Grigna. And so each person finds his own adventure, and his motivation is always the search for new adventure. In the end it's always a search for excitement, a search for adventure.

How have climbing competitions changed climbing?

Climbing competitions are just an aspect of climbing. Competition climbing is not the whole of climbing; it's just an athletic sport. Of course competition climbing has brought the level of climbing up, and people who practice competition climbing are more prepared to do actual climbing and mountaineering. So it's natural and expected that climbers today perform at a higher level because they practice so much.

When we were young, we also practiced. We went to the [Corno del] Nibbio, which is a part of the Grigna, and practiced climbing on that crag. So there is continuity; things haven't changed that much. If I were twenty, I would be doing competition climbing.

Has your attitude toward the mountains changed over the years?

It has become softer, because thanks to technique and experience, I've found it's now easier and less painful to climb than when I was young. Now I climb as a second, and to me it's less strenuous than when I was young. My great problem is my knees—they don't work as well as they used to. But fortunately I still have a lot of strength in my arms, so I succeed that way.

The difference between climbing and many other sports is that in other sports, when the physical capacities weaken at a certain point, people usually give up the sport and their lives become deprived of something that was important. In climbing there is always the possibility to go on, maybe lowering the performances, but still enjoying it so much that one can go climbing at fifty, sixty, eighty.

Why do you continue to climb?

[Laughs] Because I like it. I'm older. I cannot do what I did before. I must climb at lower levels, but I'm content with that. I like it and I do it. And when one can no longer climb in a satisfactory way, one can still do other things in the mountains.

I think that hard work keeps men healthy. When I get up in the morning, I like to think of something I'll do that day. And it's always something that is strenuous and hard so that I can exercise. I enjoy working. I enjoy strenuous exercise. Then I come home tired and happy.

What was your last big climb?

Piz Badile in 1987. The year after, I was prepared to go to the Walker Spur, and I was fit to do it; but I became ill when I got there, so I had to give it up. After that I did other climbs, but not at that level because of my knees.

To what do you owe your remarkable health and longevity?

Work much and drink little. Eat without excess and keep fit.

What are your plans for the future?

At eighty-five I have no specific plans, but I still plan to go climbing.

⛰ SIR EDMUND HILLARY

*The heroes I admired in my youth seemed to possess abilities
and virtues beyond the grasp of ordinary men. My desire to
emulate them was very great but I never succeeded in approaching their high standards. Fearful at heart in moments of danger,
I found it difficult to produce the calm courage of the heroic
mould.... In a sense fear became a friend—I hated it at the time
but it added spice to the challenge and satisfaction to the
conquest. I envied those who in success clung to a measure of
peace and tranquility—I was always too restless and life was a
constant battle against boredom. But the compensations have
been great—certainly more than I deserve. I have had the world
lie beneath my clumsy boots and have seen the red sun slip over
the horizon after the dark Antarctic winter. I have been given
more than my share of excitement, beauty, laughter and
friendship.*

—Sir Edmund Hillary, *Nothing Venture, Nothing Win*

WITH THE FIRST ASCENT of Everest in 1953, Sir Edmund Hillary solved
the greatest problem in mountaineering history and became the
world's most celebrated climber. This socially awkward beekeeper
from rural New Zealand who had taken up mountaineering as a hobby suddenly
found himself transformed into an overnight sensation. Rather than wilting
under the scrutiny of the world's gaze, Hillary grew in the spotlight, using his new-
found publicity to help finance further adventures as well as fund the construction
of schools, hospitals, and other development projects in the Solu-Khumbu region
of Nepal. This modest, unassuming young man soon developed into the leading
adventurer of the twentieth century and eventually apotheosized into a near-
mythic figure.

As a youngster, Hillary loved to read and dream of great adventures. A
turning point in his life came at age sixteen when he spent the winter holidays at

Sir Edmund Hillary with his wife, Louise, and a Tibetan lama. (Photo by Mike Gill; Diadem Archives)

New Zealand's Mount Ruapehu. There, he learned to ski, clambered around the snow-clad slopes, and generally reveled in the cold, crisp mountain air. The trip awakened an appetite for mountain adventure that has never left him.

After serving as a navigator on Catalina flying boats during World War II, Hillary returned to his father's bee-keeping business in New Zealand but spent every spare moment climbing in the local hills. Then in 1947 he met Harry Ayres, a prominent New Zealand climber, and they teamed up to do a number of climbs in the southern Alps of New Zealand, including the first ascent of the south ridge of Mount Cook in 1948.

Having completed his apprenticeship in New Zealand snow and ice climbing, Hillary branched out in other directions. In 1950 he traveled to Europe and climbed the Jungfrau, Monte Rosa, and several other moderately difficult peaks. In 1951 he and George Lowe, Earle Riddiford, and Ed Cotter broke new ground by doing first ascents of mountains such as Mukut Parbat (23,760 feet) in the Garhwal Himalaya. When the renowned British explorer Eric Shipton heard about the success of their trip, he invited Hillary and Earle Riddiford to join him on the 1951 Everest reconnaissance.

The Everest reconnaissance proved pivotal for Hillary in many ways. During this trip he came into his own as a climber, demonstrating superb fitness and stamina as well as an ability to acclimatize quickly. As a result of these qualities, he became Shipton's climbing partner, accompanying him up the side of Pumori to get a better view of the southeast ridge of Everest. From there they spotted a line through the treacherous Khumbu Icefall, up the western cwm to the south col and along the southeast ridge to the summit. They came away convinced that the route would go.

Two years later Hillary returned to attempt the route as a member of the 1953 British Everest Expedition. John Hunt, a British army colonel, led the expedition, the Everest Committee having summarily sacked Shipton for alleged lack of progress in planning. Despite some ill will toward the Everest Committee for mandating this change in leadership, the expedition rallied around Hunt, who proved an outstanding leader in his own right. He ran the expedition smoothly and efficiently, getting men and materials in position to make a bid for the summit. After Charles Evans and Tom Bourdillon made the first attempt, reaching 28,700 feet before turning back, Hillary and Sherpa Tenzing Norgay were chosen to make the second attempt. After a long and arduous climb up the southeast ridge, they reached the summit (29,028 feet) on May 29, 1953, becoming the first men to stand on the top of the world.

After the hubbub surrounding the ascent had subsided (among other things, the queen of England knighted both Hillary and Hunt for the accomplishment), Hillary continued to climb and pursue other adventures. In 1958 he led an expedition across the Antarctic to the South Pole. In 1959 he organized a search for the Abominable Snowman but found little in the way of physical evidence to support the existence of this creature. In 1960 he led an oxygenless attempt on Makalu that succeeded in getting Peter Mulgrew within 800 feet of the top. In 1963 he headed a team that climbed Kangtega (22,300 feet). The following year another group under his leadership ascended Tamserku (21,730 feet). In 1977 he journeyed by jet-boat up the Ganges, the longest and holiest river in India.

Although he continues to participate in expeditions and other adventures, in recent years Hillary has devoted much of his time to improving the lot of the Sherpas and other hill people of the Himalaya. In 1961 he raised money to build a school at Khumjung in the Solu-Khumbu region. Soon after, many other Sherpa communities requested similar assistance for schools, hospitals, roads, bridges, and other improvements. Hillary helped finance these projects by touring and lecturing in New Zealand, the United States, Canada, and other countries. He founded the Himalayan Trust in 1962 to distribute the money he had raised and oversee the construction of these projects.

Over the years the trust's mission has grown and changed. In recent years it has tackled such problems as deforestation brought on by the increasing numbers of climbers and hikers visiting the Himalaya. As more and more trees have been chopped down for firewood, erosion has devastated many of the hillsides. To counteract this, the trust helped establish Sagarmatha National Park, which comprises much of the Solu-Khumbu. Within the park, the cutting of trees for firewood is restricted; trekkers and climbers are requested to use kerosene and other fuels for cooking. The park has also undertaken an aggressive tree-replanting program. Though the park was initially resisted by some of the Sherpas, support for it has taken hold, especially since it was Hillary who helped establish it, a man whom many Sherpas regard as their king.

Hillary was born in Auckland, New Zealand, on July 20, 1919. He grew up in Tuakau, a small country town forty miles south of Auckland. He graduated from the local school at age eleven, two years earlier than normal, and went on to attend Auckland Grammar, one of the most highly regarded schools in New Zealand. After graduating, Hillary spent a few years at the local university before becoming bored with academic life and entering the military. After World War II, he helped his father with the bee-keeping business until he became known as a climber and adventurer. Thereafter, he made his living from lecturing, writing, designing outdoor equipment, and conducting business ventures.

In 1953, he married Louise Rose. They had three children—Peter, Sarah, and Belinda. In 1975 Louise and Belinda were killed in a plane crash outside Kathmandu. In 1989 Hillary married June Mulgrew, the widow of Hillary's friend, Peter Mulgrew, who had died in a plane crash in Antarctica. The two now live in Auckland.

The interview took place in New Delhi, India, at the New Zealand High Commission, where Hillary was serving as ambassador to India. Dressed in a dark suit, white shirt, and red tie, he looked every inch the Western diplomat, but the garb couldn't disguise his powerful build and rugged toughness. With his big, capable hands, wild mane of graying hair, and immense, bushy eyebrows, he resembles nothing so much as a large, friendly lion.

Though Hillary immediately puts one at ease with his blunt, honest, down-to-earth manner, it's impossible not to be impressed with the multifacetedness of the man. Here's someone with the energy and ambition to make the first ascent of the world's highest peak, the presence and aplomb to succeed in diplomatic circles, and the enthusiasm and generosity to spend much of his own time raising millions of dollars for development projects in the Solu-Khumbu. In talking with Hillary, it quickly becomes obvious that he is not just another climber or political figure, but is instead that rarest of human beings—an authentic modern hero.

Was climbing Everest a lifelong ambition?

I can't say I had the ambition all my life to climb Everest. It was a developing thing. I started off as a beginner, became a competent climber, and then did first ascents. When the opportunity came for a crack at Everest, it seemed like a good idea. People's ambitions tend to grow as they become more competent at something. As they attain certain objectives, their objectives then become more difficult.

It's amazing how many people wanted to be the first person to climb Everest.

Well, they say they did. I run into people all the time who say they wanted to be the first person to do it, but most of them didn't do much about it. They were really just dreaming.

Were you afraid of the mountain as you were climbing it?

Yes. Being afraid was part of the whole deal. I have frequently been afraid of mountains. Fear can be stimulating; it can allow you to solve problems you might not otherwise solve. And when you're afraid and have to overcome it, it adds to the satisfaction. And without the satisfaction of overcoming these fears, some climbs wouldn't be worth the effort. Life is fairly miserable at high altitude, and you need something to give you satisfaction.

Were you confident from the start that you could climb it?

No. If at the start of a project you are confident of success, I can't see why you would go through with it. Maybe the objective is below your abilities. I planned to be fit, strong, and ready to give it a good shot, but never was I absolutely confident that I could climb it. If something is a big challenge and you don't know if you'll succeed, but you give it all you have and succeed, then that's the ultimate satisfaction.

How did you get started on the road to climbing Everest?

When I was sixteen, I went with a high-school party to Mount Ruapehu in the middle of the North Island of New Zealand, about 230 miles away from Auckland. This was during the winter and it was the first time I'd ever seen snow. I really enjoyed skiing and scrambling around in the mountains. I spent ten days there and it was the most exciting experience I'd ever had.

How did you learn to climb?

I did quite a lot of tramping and trekking in the hills with people who were more experienced than myself. And then I started getting interested in purely modest sorts of climbing. As I became more experienced I attempted more difficult things and so became more useful at it.

Later I became very friendly with Harry Ayres, who was the most outstanding guide in New Zealand. I based my abilities and techniques on his example.

Did you have other models?

George Mallory, definitely, the great man of Everest. He was an inspiration. He made the world aware that Everest existed. He was obsessed with Everest. His 1922 reconnaissance of Everest was as fine a piece of that kind of work as has been done.

". . . WHEN YOU'RE AFRAID AND HAVE TO OVERCOME IT, IT ADDS TO THE SATISFACTION. . . . LIFE IS FAIRLY MISERABLE AT HIGH ALTITUDE, AND YOU NEED SOMETHING TO GIVE YOU SATISFACTION."

Did you become a proficient technical climber fairly early?

In my early twenties I became fairly proficient at snow and ice climbing. I did the first ascent of the south ridge of Mount Cook and a number of other first ascents of snow and ice routes in the southern Alps of New Zealand. I was among the dozen or so who were at the forefront of New Zealand climbing.

Did your early climbs prepare you for the Himalaya?

Yes, there's no question. Doing a lot of mountain activity, particularly in New Zealand, I became a fairly competent all-around mountaineer, specializing in snow and ice climbing. So when I went to the Himalaya, I found it suited me really very well because the nature of the climbing was very similar. It involved crevasse techniques, icefalls, and avalanches.

When did you first go to the Himalaya?

I went to the Himalaya first in 1951 on a small, shoestring expedition from New Zealand. It was a very cheap trip; we used our own personal finances. We went to the Garhwal Himalaya, which is in the Indian Himalaya. We did first ascents of half a dozen peaks well over 20,000 feet. It was very exciting because in those days we were alone in the area. Nobody else was in there to climb anything.

What was your impression of the range?

Well, I totally enjoyed it. You could get out of your tent in the morning and look around at peaks in every direction, and you knew that none of them had been climbed. You could say, "Well, over the next few days we'll climb that one." And you'd know that no one had been there before. It was a great time to be climbing there.

When did you first visit the Solu-Khumbu?

In 1951, on the Everest reconnaissance. Eric Shipton and I climbed partway up Pumori to have a look up into the western cwm. It was the first time anyone realized the potential of the route. Mallory had dismissed it, as had Tilman, but when Eric Shipton and I went up Pumori Ridge, we saw the route was possible, even though the [Khumbu] icefall was a dangerous place.

Why were you invited on that 1951 reconnaissance?

Shipton had led an Everest reconnaissance during the 1930s and one of the members was a New Zealander named Dan Bryant. Shipton became very impressed with Bryant's ability as a snow and ice climber. In 1951 Shipton had selected a team of very good rock climbers from Britain, but he wasn't quite so confident about their ability on snow and ice. So when he heard about our Garhwal expedition, he invited two members of our party—Earle Riddiford and myself—to join him, largely because of the good opinion of New Zealanders he had developed from Dan Bryant.

What was Shipton like as an expedition leader?

I liked him very much and had great admiration for him. He was a great explorer, but he wasn't interested in organizing big expeditions. He disliked the complications of big expeditions and much preferred to head off with a small group into remote areas. So I wouldn't say he was enthusiastic or particularly good at being the leader of a very large expedition.

How did you perform on that expedition?

I performed well. I was fit and fast and acclimatized very well. Shipton invited me to be his climbing companion. I enjoyed that very much indeed. We had a very good time.

So the success of that reconnaissance set the stage for the 1953 expedition?

Yes. It's like in most sporting events. If a member does pretty well on an earlier trip, he tends to get invited back for the following one.

Why was Shipton replaced by John Hunt?

Well, the Everest Committee in London felt that the progress on planning the expedition was rather slow—which it may well have been because Eric really didn't enjoy planning and organizing large expeditions—so they rather arbitrarily replaced him, much to the annoyance of quite a few of us on the expedition.

Was Shipton disappointed?

Yes, he was very disappointed.

Did you feel that it was a poor decision?

Yes. Although his replacement, John Hunt, was certainly a much better organizer for a big expedition, I'm always inclined to think that if Eric had remained as expedition leader there was a very good chance that we would have been successful.

How did Hunt compare with Shipton as a leader?

He was a military man. He had been a senior army officer during the war. He had good organizing ability, but he was not a bossy chap. He didn't order you around. Obviously, members of a climbing expedition are fairly independent, and John Hunt was very good at handling a group of independent-minded people.

Was it more like a military operation than some expeditions?

No, I wouldn't say so, except that the organizing was efficiently handled and probably in more detail than most expeditions before then.

Did you have a strong team?

We had a strong team, a very united group, out to achieve the ultimate objective.

Why did the 1953 expedition employ expedition-style tactics?

Well, we really didn't know all that much different in those days. That was the way big expeditions were done. Alpine-style climbing was a much later development. Expedition style was the way people climbed on big mountains.

Was it a classic expedition-style climb?

Yes, but we were quite a small expedition. We had only ten climbing members, plus Tenzing Norgay, who made eleven. Tenzing was the *sirdar* [head Sherpa] on the expedition, but we regarded him as a member of the climbing team. And then we had about twenty-five Sherpas for carrying loads. But the actual size of the expedition was relatively small compared to many of the expeditions that came along much later. Some of the later Japanese and Italian expeditions were absolutely huge.

Did the Sherpas do a lot of the carries further up the mountain?

Yes, they did a lot of carrying. But we always escorted laden porters through the [Khumbu] icefall and higher on the mountain. We never sent a group of Sherpas by themselves. We felt a responsibility to travel with them and see that the correct and safe routes were used. Nowadays, of course, many expedition members don't move out of their tents until the Sherpas have carried all of the loads higher on the mountain.

How did you come to be paired with Tenzing?

I deliberately decided to team up with Tenzing because we seemed well balanced. The person I had most in common with was George Lowe, the other New Zealander on the expedition. I would have preferred to climb with George, who was also very fit, but John Hunt kept us separate because we were both particularly experienced on snow and ice. Since Tenzing was also fit, I joined up with him. We climbed together and fit in very well.

What was Tenzing like?

He was a very pleasant person with a charming smile. He had strong motivation to get to the top, which was really quite unusual for a Sherpa in those days, and he was a formidable climber. I don't think any of us on the expedition were hotshots in the sense that people are hotshots today—things have changed enormously—but he acclimatized well, he was determined, and he was very, very strong.

How did you and Tenzing come to be chosen to make a bid for the top?

Once we established the route up onto the south col and up the southeast ridge [Evans and Bourdillon reached 28,700 feet], we all withdrew off the mountain for a day or two. It was then that the final decision was made as to who was going to do what. And at that stage Tenzing and I were undoubtedly the fittest pair. So we were given the job of trying to get to the top.

Was there any grumbling because a New Zealander was chosen to be a lead climber on a British expedition?

No, not really. In those days New Zealand had quite a close relationship with Britain. We were New Zealand citizens but we were British subjects. Now a lot of that has changed. But in those days, although we were very much New Zealanders, we felt we were sufficiently British to be part of a British expedition.

Was it you or Tenzing who was the first on top?

It's completely unimportant as to who was first. It was a team effort; we reached the summit together.

How did you feel at the top?

I felt some satisfaction, but I didn't feel as ecstatic as people might think. We were tired. I was most excited when we were back down off the mountain and our problems were behind us. But it was a good mountain.

Did you enjoy climbing it?

I enjoyed it, but it's not much fun being above 25,000 feet. You just don't have the reserves of energy and vitality that you have lower. Alpine climbing at 12,000 to 14,000 feet is often a great deal more fun. In the European Alps, you can reach the summit, lie down on the rocks, and go to sleep. I've never heard of that happening on a big Himalayan peak. You head back down. You're very much aware that if you stay too long, you may not get off.

Did you realize what effect your climb would have on the rest of the world?

I had no idea whatsoever. In fact, I really thought that the world in general would be rather disinterested in the whole business. I was probably a bit naive about it. I had no conception that it would have the impact that it actually had.

How did climbing Everest change your life?

After climbing Everest, I had no sense of anticlimax—I was just as keen on climbing. Everest was not the end; it was just the beginning. And after I'd climbed it, it was easy to get support for other expeditions. There were advantages due to the publicity.

Did you begin to employ alpine-style tactics on these later climbing expeditions?

Yes. We certainly had fewer people in climbing peaks like Ama Dablam and Kangtega and Tamserku and things of that nature. We had only four members on Ama Dablam. We had six members on Tamserku. These were pretty much alpine-style ascents, but we never went as far as some of the modern climbers who climb solo or with just a couple of climbers.

Was the 1954 oxygenless attempt on Makalu your last serious mountaineering endeavor?

Yes, I suppose in many ways it was. I was the leader of a lot of expeditions after that, but I personally didn't go to the summit. But I did do some quite interesting climbing in New Zealand after that.

Was climbing Makalu without oxygen an ambitious objective at that point?

Yes. The whole program was quite extensive—studying high-altitude physiology as well as the mountaineering. And our approach to Makalu was a very energetic one. We crossed over from the Khumbu, carrying all our loads over two high passes and into the Barun Valley. Nobody really has used that approach since.

Why was that Makalu expedition a significant one?

It was significant in that we had a very extensive program of high-altitude physiology. And I think the program that we carried out set quite a standard for later research on the subject [adaptation to high altitude].

Did you come away thinking that somebody would eventually climb Everest without oxygen?

Yes, I had the feeling that ultimately Everest would be climbed without oxygen.

What was your reaction when Reinhold Messner and Peter Habeler accomplished that?

I was full of admiration. I was actually up at Khunde when both Reinhold Messner and Peter Habeler came down. They were a very fit and very tough couple. I think Messner has been the high-altitude man of the era. He's done amazing things. There may be other climbers who have greater competence in extreme technical climbing, but for operating at high altitude at a very high standard, I think Messner has been quite exceptional.

And it has always struck me that he has never been afraid to turn back. When the conditions were unsuitable when he was attempting Lhotse, for instance, he turned back and left it for the following year. For that reason he has survived.

Did your ascent of Everest help pave the way for Messner and other climbers?

Yes, I think it had a very stimulating effect on world mountaineering in general. It made quite a difference to the tempo with which mountaineering was developing. I think a lot of it was the publicity that we got. There's no doubt that interest in mountaineering took quite a leap forward and consequently mountaineering itself took quite a leap forward.

Has the number of climbers increased markedly since your day?

There's been a vast increase. I was up in the Khumbu recently and there were eight expeditions at base camp all trying to climb Everest at the same time. When I climbed it we were the only people there. I think we were the lucky ones in many ways. We were there in an early period when there were new things to do and when the place wasn't cluttered up with other expeditions.

What was the Solu-Khumbu region like back then?

It was fantastic. It was a beautiful area. The shrubs in the Khumbu were still very dense and the trees hadn't been destroyed. It was all very attractive, and the local people were much less sophisticated and very, very friendly. It was a wonderful time to be there.

They probably hadn't seen many Westerners.

Except that the Sherpas had always been great travelers and had gone off trading, particularly into Tibet and down into India. So many of them had seen foreigners, but outside their own area.

How did the local people treat you on that expedition?

The Sherpas treated us in an extremely friendly and generous fashion. We enjoyed them right from the start.

How has the Solu-Khumbu changed as a result of the climbers and trekkers visiting the area?

The standard of living has improved greatly for the local people. Homes in the Solu-Khumbu are more comfortable now. People have glass in their windows. There's so much more employment. But on the other hand, the environmental damage has been considerable. A lot of the forests have been cut down. We've done quite a lot of reforestation in the Khumbu area, but even so, the forest areas are certainly not what they were like when I first went there.

Are there more people living there now?

No, because the growth rate of the Sherpa population has not been particularly great. But there are more people employed from the hill areas. The Sherpas don't do much load-carrying nowadays. They look after the trekkers and climbers. Most of the low-altitude portering is done by hill people like the Tamangs and others who tend to be poorer than the Sherpas.

How did the building of schools and hospitals change the life of the Sherpas?

As far as the schools are concerned, a large portion of the kids now go to school. These kids are more able to meet the changes in society and to get better jobs. So instead of being peons around the place, they are very involved with trekking, hotels, and running the national park. So schools have helped that way. And if they get sick, they have hospitals where they can go.

Have the Sherpas adapted pretty well to these changes?

Yes. They've picked up a lot of habits from the Western expeditions that aren't terribly desirable, but they still retain very close ties to their customs and habits. Many of the more experienced Sherpas live down in Kathmandu, but during the monsoon season, when there's not a great deal of action, they all tend to go back to the Khumbu and take part in the major social and religious events there. So they still have strong ties to the old customs. They remain amazingly loyal to community and religion.

How did you become involved in the development of the Solu-Khumbu?

I became friends with many of the Sherpas. I lived in their houses and saw that they lacked many of the things that we just take for granted, such as schooling and health care. But while I was aware of this, I really didn't do anything about it until 1961. Around that time I was talking to some of the

Sherpas and asked if there was something we could do for them, and they all agreed that what they wanted more than anything was a school in Khumjung so that their children could get an education. That sounded like a pretty good idea, so I raised the necessary funds in the United States and we built the school. That was really the start of the whole thing.

Then other villages asked for help in building schools, hospitals, and all the rest. In the last twenty-five years, quite a portion of my time has gone into fundraising in New Zealand, the United States, Canada, and elsewhere for these projects. I've done vast numbers of fundraising lectures at Rotary Clubs and Lion's Clubs and schools and black-tie dinners. You name it and I've probably done it. It's been quite hard work, but I've found it quite worthwhile.

Have the schools and hospitals meshed well with the traditional Sherpa culture?

We've tried to ensure that they do. We've cooperated very closely with the local people and things have worked out well. I think we are fortunate that we are dealing with adaptable people. In the slums of Calcutta or somewhere like that, it can be really tough to do anything for people, whereas working with the Sherpas has been very satisfying and I've really enjoyed it.

Why did you form the Himalayan Trust?

The whole purpose of the trust is to support these various activities of helping the mountain people of the Himalaya. I formed it in 1962 with some people in New Zealand and then later added foundations in the United States and in Canada. We have one in Germany now. We have quite a number of people organizing fundraising activities.

What are the most pressing problems facing the Solu-Khumbu?

The environmental matters are as big a problem as anything. Too many trekkers, tourists, and mountaineers have come into the area too quickly. In 1992 there were some 11,000 trekkers and tourists who visited the Khumbu area. There are actually only 3000 Sherpas living in the region. So it's been a very heavy burden in many ways on the local people.

Why was Sagarmatha National Park created?

With the increase in tourism, more trees were cut down, and the effect of deforestation was devastating. The national park was designed to control this. The park was initially resisted by Sherpas, but now the majority have accepted the park as a good thing.

So the creation of the park has helped alleviate some of the problems?

Yes, I think it's helped substantially. In the park they are trying to restrict the cutting of firewood by expeditions. It's compulsory for people to use kerosene or gas, although by no means do people always observe these rules. It's been a long, slow business, but the creation of the park has been a step in the right direction.

Are they also replanting trees?

Our Himalayan Trust has been involved for a number of years in replanting trees. We plant 60,000 to 100,000 seedlings each year. We are making progress, but the trees grow very slowly.

Do you think that Everest should be shut down from climbing for a couple of years?

I actually suggested that a few years ago as a way of trying to stimulate people into being more careful about what they did to Everest. The most important thing is that expeditions on Everest should accept the responsibility of taking down off the mountain all the junk they take up there. There could be 500 to 600 empty oxygen bottles on the south col. I think expeditions to Everest or any big mountain have got to plan, organize, and finance the cleaning up of the mountain as well as the actual ascent of the peak.

> *". . . EXPEDITIONS TO EVEREST . . . HAVE GOT TO PLAN, ORGANIZE, AND FINANCE THE CLEANING UP OF THE MOUNTAIN. . . ."*

Can that be built into a climbing permit?

Well, it's pretty hard to do unless the people themselves are motivated to do it. You're not going to get a national park representative wandering up to the south col just to see whether it's tidy or not.

What appeals to you about the Solu-Khumbu and the other mountainous areas of the world?

The mountains have a beauty, a sense of challenge, and good, clean air to breathe, and often you have very good companions when you're in the mountains. The mountains have a great deal to offer energetic human beings.

Is this why you have continued to climb over the years?

Yes, and the danger has been an attraction. The fear has been a stimulating factor. It's been quite an important part of why I've done it. If you find something that's difficult and dangerous and perhaps a little frightening, but you persist and overcome it, that gives you a much greater sense of satisfaction.

Do you still climb?

Not so much. I still enjoy adventures, but they're more modest than they used to be. Several years ago I flew to the North Pole with Neil Armstrong [the former astronaut]. When I left Delhi, the temperature was 45 degrees Celsius, and at the North Pole it was -45 degrees Celsius. We landed on the snow. It was a great experience to step out onto that sea of ice. I felt a considerable sense of loneliness, but also a sense of adventure, seeing the ice spreading out in all directions. Space is one of the great challenges today, but there are still a lot of things to do here on Earth.

What are the challenges that remain for climbers?

Modern climbers find harder and harder things to do. They tackle steeper problems. They get a sense of challenge out of doing something more difficult than we did in the early days. But Everest is still no pushover. Even on our route [south col route], people still die.

What do you think of all the changes in mountaineering that have occurred in your lifetime?

The changes are absolutely unbelievable in many ways. The equipment has become so sophisticated and the climbers have become so expert at using it. So the development will go on. The ability of climbers to climb extremely difficult things will grow and grow.

Do you think there will still be adventure in it?

Yes. I think for quite a while yet there will be very difficult and often very dangerous routes left to be done. And the ability of modern climbers to move quickly will be very important in doing these routes. Modern climbers can cover a dangerous area much more quickly than we were able to. So they're taking more risks, but also reducing the danger by moving so much faster.

Are you disappointed that you can no longer climb the big peaks?

No. As you get physically less energetic, instead of being a physical bomb, you use experience and knowledge to plan and lead. It's just as satisfying to lead an expedition as to be the one who stands on the summit. And I also get tremendous satisfaction out of aiding the Sherpas. It's a big challenge. The hardest thing I do is raise money.

KURT DIEMBERGER

The darkness, the all-encompassing dreariness, lasted for a long time after the return from K2—as if the storm, like a bad spell, had not fully worked itself out. There were gaps in memory...full of fantasies; there were heroic poems...and clichés. There were invented "rescues"—when in fact nobody unable to climb down by himself could have survived. The most extreme opinions clashed together. But that time is over; it was a fight, but it was necessary—for the truth, for all those who will climb in the future.

—Kurt Diemberger, *The Endless Knot*

FOR YEARS THE IMMENSE, glistening pyramid of K2 had stood over Kurt Diemberger, remote and chill, more beautiful for him than any other mountain, a symbol of all that was unobtainable, a kind of eternal temptation. The winking facets of this huge, dark crystal beckoned him by day and bothered him by night, turning what started out as a whim to climb it into a kind of burning obsession. For a man made for the 8000ers, a pioneer of alpine-style tactics in the Himalaya, getting to the top of the 28,250-foot peak came to represent a long-cherished dream, the crowning achievement of a long and illustrious career. After several attempts, Diemberger finally realized his dream in the summer of 1986, but at a much higher price than he was prepared to pay. His partner, Julie Tullis, died on the descent, and Diemberger barely escaped with his own life. In all, thirteen climbers, many of them his friends, died on K2 that fateful summer. His ultimate dream had turned into the ultimate nightmare.

Diemberger traces his desire to climb K2 back to his childhood. As a boy he hunted for crystals in the Obersulzbachtal region of his native Austria. He journeyed far afield in search of quartz, epidotes, emeralds, and other stones, all the time exploring the mountains and getting to know their secrets. When he was sixteen he borrowed his grandfather's bicycle and traveled to the Hohe Tauern, a mountainous area south of Salzburg. While looking for crystals there, he happened to climb a nearby peak and felt for the first time the mountaineer's

63

exultation at standing on the summit. From that day forward it became his ambition to be a climber.

His grandfather's bicycle provided the means to pursue his new-found passion. He pedaled it back and forth across the Alps, exploring the countryside and climbing peaks such as the Marmolata and the Matterhorn. These ascents fueled his ambition for further adventures, and shortly thereafter he and his friends Erich Warta, Peter Heilmayer, and Wolfgang Stefan attempted the Dent du Géant on the Italian side of Mont Blanc. They never made it to the summit. Midway up the route, Erich slipped while traversing a snow slope and fell to his death. The incident burned itself into Diemberger's memory, making him even more careful and deliberate, but it didn't stop him from climbing. From that point on he teamed up with "Wolfi" to climb a number of the hardest north faces in the Alps.

One after another, these faces fell to the pair's crampons and ice hammers. In the early 1950s they concentrated on ice faces such as the Dent d'Hérens, Obergabelhorn, Breithorn, Lyskamm, Aiguille Blanche, and Grands Charmoz and the great Brenva Face of Mont Blanc. In the mid-1950s they moved to mixed routes and knocked off one of the great north face routes of the Alps when they ascended the north face of the Matterhorn. Not long afterward, Diemberger succeeded in climbing the Giant Meringue, a massive overhanging cornice on the Königsspitze that was thought to be unclimbable. The publicity surrounding this feat caught the attention of the renowned Austrian alpinist Hermann Buhl, who was looking for an ice climber to include on his 1957 expedition to Broad Peak. Because of this impressive accomplishment, Diemberger was invited to join the team.

Buhl's plan was to use *westalpenstil* (alpine-style) tactics on Broad Peak, thus becoming the first to attempt an 8000-meter peak in such a fashion. The four-man expedition consisting of Buhl, Diemberger, Markus Schmuck, and Fritz Wintersteller employed no high-altitude porters and used no bottled oxygen on the assault. They gradually made their way up the west spur, and on June 9, 1957, all four reached the summit of Broad Peak. Alpine-style climbing had come to the Himalaya.

From the top of Broad Peak, Diemberger got his first real glimpse of K2, its dark profile soaring above the surrounding peaks. Although it impressed him, he had no wish to climb it: it seemed too big and unapproachable to consider. Instead, he simply reveled at being in the midst of the amazing sea of peaks that make up the Karakoram. He felt so well and strong up in the rarified air that he vowed to return someday.

The following year found Diemberger back in Europe, climbing in the Alps and getting his start in filmmaking. He teamed up with Wolfgang Stefan again to ascend the Eiger and the Walker Spur of the Grandes Jorasses, thus completing their sweep of all three great north faces of the Alps. In addition, he and Franz

Lindner filmed their traverse of the integral Peuterey Ridge of Mont Blanc, perhaps the finest ridge traverse in the Alps. Diemberger gave up a whole summer of climbing to edit the film, but the effort paid off. His prowess as a filmmaker was to provide his ticket back to the Himalaya.

In 1960 Max Eiselin invited Diemberger on the Swiss expedition to Dhaulagiri, the "White Mountain" of Nepal. Diemberger served as both cameraman and climber on the trip, doing much high-altitude camera work and managing to climb the peak as well. His career as an expedition filmmaker was under way.

Thereafter, he continued to climb in the Alps but made numerous forays into the Himalaya. In 1965 he journeyed with his wife, Tona, and friends to do several climbs, including a first ascent of Dertona Peak in the Hindu Kush. Two years later he returned to the Hindu Kush to do alpine-style ascents of 6000- and 7000-meter peaks such as Tirich Mir. His love of adventure continued to lead him to remote corners of the Himalaya, to Greenland, or wherever there was new territory to explore or a new adventure to film.

Kurt Diemberger. (Photo by Ken Wilson; Diadem Archives)

While many of his mountaineering contemporaries had long since hung up their crampons and ice axes, Diemberger found that his climbing career picked up after age forty. In 1974, at forty-two, he summited on Shartse. In 1978 he climbed Makalu in the spring and Everest in the fall. In 1979 he ascended Gasherbrum II. In addition to climbing these peaks, Diemberger did much of the camera work for the various expedition films. His reputation as cameraman of the 8000ers had become secure.

Thereafter, he traveled back to the Himalaya every year to film and climb. In 1982 he attempted a route on the Diamir Face of Nanga Parbat with a French expedition led by Pierre Mazeaud. British climber Julie Tullis served as his assistant on the trip, and although neither one made it to the top, their film *Diamir—Bewitched by Nanga Parbat* won the 1983 Grand Prize at the San Sebastian Film Festival in Spain. They collaborated on subsequent films, including *Tashigang—Between the World of Men and the World of Gods* (1986), and eventually founded "the highest film team in the world."

Much of their film work took place within sight of the immense, dark pyramid of K2, and after seeing it from various angles, especially the north, they became determined to climb it. In 1983 they attempted it from the Chinese side, but bad weather forced them to turn back at 26,000 feet. In 1984 they approached it via the Abruzzi Ridge, but the weather again forced a retreat. In 1986 they succeeded in getting to the top, but a storm caught them on the descent. Holed up with five others in their high camp at 8000 meters, they tried to wait out the storm, but soon ran out of food and fuel for melting snow. Tullis died after a few days, and Diemberger barely escaped with his life. His heart-wrenching film of the experience, *K2—Dream and Fate,* won the 1989 Grand Prize at the Trento Film Festival. His book about it, *K2—The Endless Knot,* took top honors among books at the same festival and was runner-up for the prestigious Boardman-Tasker Award in England.

In recent years, Diemberger has continued to film and climb. He participated in the 1987 Italian expedition to measure the heights of Everest and K2, and in 1991 and 1992 he inspired and took part in an expedition to the east face of Broad Peak, where four other members summited.

Diemberger was born in Villach, Austria, in 1932. He grew up there and in Salzburg, and then moved to Vienna to attend the University of Commerce. He graduated with a degree in business and soon after took a job as a business teacher. He taught for five years before quitting to pursue a career as a freelance writer, filmmaker, lecturer, and climber. Diemberger has been married twice. He and his first wife, Tona, have two daughters, Hildegard and Karen. He and his second wife, Teresa, have a son, Ceci. Today they live in a house in the hills overlooking Bologna, Italy.

The interview took place there in August, when the weather was sweltering and Diemberger was lumbering around the yard like a big, amiable bear, tending his garden and watering his peach and apple trees. He is balding and powerfully built, with the missing fingers of his right hand serving as a grim testament to that terrible summer on K2. Though he remains a charming, amusing, sophisticated man—fluent in German, Italian, and English—he still can't prevent a hint of sadness from creeping into his voice when he talks about the highlights of his climbing and film careers, especially that decisive summer of 1986, when he realized his ultimate dream and began to be haunted by the nightmares that followed its fulfillment.

Why are the big Himalayan peaks so dangerous?

They are dangerous in part for the same reasons that other mountains are dangerous—avalanches, crevasses, storms, and all that. But these peaks are even more dangerous because the dimensions of these dangers are much bigger than in the Alps. In the Himalaya, for example, the avalanches go much further out; you have to climb much higher to get to the top and much further to get down to base camp; and you cannot be saved by a helicopter, which has a ceiling of 19,000 feet under the best of circumstances. So the higher you get, the more it becomes almost impossible to be rescued.

Also, the judgment of the people climbing these mountains may not be equivalent to the real dimensions of the dangers because they may judge them from their experience of lower mountains. Only after years of experience at high altitude can you have the right judgment about these dangers. You go on autopilot at high altitude, so if you have developed good judgment over years of being in the Himalaya, you will be more likely to make the right decision.

But even with a lot of experience, one thing that can almost never be avoided is that the human mind and body get restricted at high altitude. The human body's reserves are pretty limited and it's hard to tell beforehand exactly what they are. There are theories that one can be at 8000 meters for only thirty hours or so. For one person it may be true, but for another it may not be. And it will certainly depend on whether you have enough water and on your state of acclimatization. As a result, everyone's judgment at high altitude can become impaired, even if they are experienced.

So taken all together, I would say that these big mountains are so dangerous because they are at and sometimes beyond the limits of those who climb them. Many of the people who climb them don't have the proper experience or equipment or fitness or whatever. So climbing them then becomes a kind of Russian roulette.

Why did you fall under the spell of these peaks?

I don't know exactly why. It could be that they looked like giant crystals. It could be that I was simply curious and wanted to discover their secrets. It could be that I had a feeling I was born for living up high. Many years ago I was always very tired, sleeping all the time, except when I was in the mountains. So I went to a doctor, a blood specialist, in Italy. He checked my blood and said, "You should always live at least at 10,000 feet. That's the right place for you." And he was right; if I stay down too long, I close up like a marmot in hibernation. It's strange, but that's the way it is. I'm like a yak in this way. A yak can't live very long below 10,000 feet. It has to be up high. And it's the same with me.

How did you get started climbing?

Like many other boys, I liked to explore and discover things. And my father once took me up to a mountain where there were some crystals. The ones we found were not very beautiful, but I became interested in finding more. And when I was up in the mountains looking for crystals, I sometimes thought, "Why do these mountain climbers go up there? They don't find anything to carry down."

I was curious about this, and one day when I was looking for crystals in the Hohe Tauern, a mountain range outside Salzburg, I reached a high col. Larmkogel [9886 feet] was not far from there and I thought, "Why not try climbing to the top?" So I left the crystals behind and climbed the peak. I was up there all by myself with the clouds. Sometimes they were all around me and I could reach out and touch them before they drifted off. And I could look very far out and see down into the valley on the other side. This made me feel very good. I experienced that day what mountaineers feel on the summit. And I liked it so much that I knew I would do it again.

Since that time I've been a mountaineer. I was sixteen years old at the time, and when I came back down I told my parents I wanted to be a climber. They gave me all kinds of help. I remember the day my father gave me a rope and an ice axe. I was very happy then.

How did you learn to use the ice axe and rope?

When I was a student in Vienna, I met another student named Railli, and he told me about a climbing area near Vienna. We went out there to take a look and saw several other climbers already on the walls, which were 200 to 300 feet high and very sheer. Railli said, "Let's climb up here."

I followed him till we reached a point on the slab where there were just two tiny fingerholds. I looked down to where it fell away a hundred feet or so. I said to him, "I don't feel very comfortable."

He said, "Oh, that's nothing. Rely on the fingerholds and you will feel fine."

So I did, but I felt very nervous. And afterward I said to him, "I don't like going without a rope."

So the next day we climbed with a rope. He took me to a route that was a grade 5 [5.6] and told me, "You can lead that. There's a piton up there below the crux."

I climbed up and put a carabiner in the piton, but I couldn't see how I could manage to climb any further. He kept encouraging me, so I kept going. I got about six feet above that piton and I fell off. He had the rope around him, but it was loose; it was not a very good belay. So I fell quite a ways before he caught me. And the force of the fall was so great that it lifted him off the edge of the ditch where he had been sitting and threw him toward the bottom of the face. We were both shocked.

That was the end of my climbing for a while. Later I did it more properly and was really safe, but at the beginning it was quite harrowing.

Did you have heroes who were climbers?

Yes, I especially admired Hermann Buhl. I remember going to one of his lectures about Nanga Parbat. Afterward I went up to get his autograph, and on my alpine club membership card he wrote, "*Berg heil!*" which means, "Have a good mountain!" or "Be blessed for the mountains!" I kept it like a treasure.

Why did you team up with Wolfgang Stefan?

We started climbing together on the Dent du Géant. He was climbing ahead with my friend Erich Warta, and I was behind climbing with another friend, Peter Heilmayer, who was inexperienced and much slower. Erich was very experienced and had done a lot of rock climbing, as had Wolfi, but very often people fall when it's easy. And that's what happened. Erich fell to his death.

After that Wolfi and I teamed up and climbed together for many years. We would still climb together today if Wolfi didn't live so far away. And when I was in the hospital in Innsbruck after K2, Wolfi was one of the first to arrive to see me. He came all the way from Switzerland. I was quite touched.

What made you two such a good team?

We understood each other. We could rely on each other. We had the feeling that the other person wasn't gambling. And the longer you climb with someone, and have felt good with him, the more you get linked together.

When we were students, Wolfi and I gave all of our free time to the mountains. We had no money and lived on polenta and potatoes. We climbed like mad. We did many, many climbs in the Alps. We wanted to

Kurt Diemberger (left) and Albert Schelbert on the summit of Dhaulagiri, 1960.
(Diadem Archives)

climb everything. But after a while we realized that we could never climb it all, so we decided to concentrate on the big climbs.

About that time, Gaston Rébuffat's *Stars and Storms* appeared. The book earmarked the big north faces as the ones to climb. We looked at the book and said, "We can do those." And then we started doing big north faces like the Eiger, Grandes Jorasses, and Matterhorn. I can't remember all the faces that Rébuffat mentioned, but we did most of them.

Would you ever care to repeat the Eiger?

No. I don't usually repeat a climb unless I like it very much. But if I do like it, I can repeat it many times. The south ridge of Aiguille Noire is a fantastic climb, and I've done that three times. And I've done the Peuterey Ridge on Mont Blanc several times.

I've climbed Mont Blanc from many sides. It is an amazing mountain. It is the only peak in the Alps that can compare with the Himalaya. You must forget about the normal routes, which are crowded with people, but the Brenva Face and the Peuterey Ridge and the pillars on the Frêney side are fantastic. These are things like you find in the Himalaya.

Why did the classic north face routes in the Alps appeal to you?

I liked them because they were very wild and savage. We climbed them one after another, and eventually I became known as Austria's best ice climber. I then attacked the Giant Meringue on the Königsspitze. Wolfi wasn't with me that time because he was in love with a girl in the Dolomites. So it was his fault.

Why did you gravitate toward ice climbing?

I liked to climb ice because it's a crystalline element and I had started with crystals. I most liked those mountains that looked like big crystals. It's really a fascination to see a white mountain above the country, even if you're not a mountaineer.

Why did Hermann Buhl invite you on the Broad Peak expedition?

Because he heard that I had climbed the Giant Meringue.

What was he like as a man?

He was small-boned and delicate, serious and sensitive. He was very careful and precise in his plans and actions. You have to be like this if you are a solo climber. If you are not extremely precise and careful, you will not live very long.

What did you learn on the Broad Peak climb?

I found out that it was fantastic to be in the world of peaks in the Karakoram, a real ocean of steep and pointed mountains. And I found out about the loneliness and huge dimensions of the area. And I also found out that I felt well and strong. I found out that I was made for the Himalaya.

Why did you climb the peak twice?

It first looked as if Hermann Buhl wouldn't go on any further than 7900 meters. So I went on and got to the top. And on the way back down I met him. He had changed his mind and had decided to do it. I wanted to be with him up there, so I turned around and went back up with him. There was no danger of any breakdown in the weather, and the other two—Markus Schmuck and Fritz Wintersteller—had gone down.

Did it change you to have climbed an 8000-meter peak?

Yes, it changes you for a while. The effects of the altitude are a bit like a shock. It takes some time before you are normal again. But there are no rules about it; some people get over it fast, and others take a lot longer. Some people have been up there for a while and others for a short time. Some climbers acclimatize well, while others don't. It always has some effect, but it is not always the same, even for the same person.

How did Hermann Buhl's death on Chogolisa shortly thereafter affect you?

I thought about it a lot. It was always on my mind. But I didn't stop climbing.

Did you intend to return to the Himalaya?

We are in a different age now. At that time I didn't think I would ever get a chance to go to the Himalaya again. I got to go once and I thought that was a lot. Perhaps if I were very lucky I would get to go again. I didn't even imagine going the next year. In 1957 I climbed Broad Peak and in 1958 I climbed with Wolfi in the Alps. I was thinking back about climbing with Hermann in the Himalaya, but I was climbing the Eiger, Grandes Jorasses, and the Peuterey Ridge.

I didn't climb very much in 1959 as Max Eiselin from Switzerland invited me to go to Dhaulagiri for 1960. We worked for many, many months raising the money and organizing the expedition. It was a lot of work. It was much harder than it would have been today.

And Max had this idea of landing by airplane on the northeast saddle. At first I thought it was a crazy idea. Why should we do it, since we could have walked? But no, he was sticking to this idea. So I helped him find an airplane. It wasn't so easy, but we got it in the end. From the pure rules of mountaineering, it wasn't right to fly over all these valleys and then land up there at the saddle, but it was a great adventure. It was on the limits of the possible, because what we saved in miles of walking we made up in waiting up there with headaches because we hadn't acclimatized. It was a big thrill to be up there again.

What is the lure of 8000ers?

They are very, very big mountains. They are really something from another world. But this also applies to the high 7000-meter peaks. If you stand in front of Gasherbrum IV, or Masherbrum, they look very high and impressive—no different from an 8000-meter peak.

But the 8000-meter peaks have become a classification in people's minds. It isn't so much that way for the British or Americans; they measure the peaks in feet, and 26,000 feet is not as clear a figure as 8000 meters. I don't know who really created this category, but it has become a category and now people want to climb an 8000-meter peak.

From the climbing point of view, as far as thin air is concerned, there is no real difference between Gasherbrum II or Hidden Peak and Masherbrum; they are all fantastic mountains, and a few meters in height don't really make a great difference. It can be easier to organize and finance an expedition to a mountain that has the 8000 in front of it, and so for that reason this 8000 figure is an attraction; but in terms of size it's really a false category.

Instead, there should be a category for peaks between 7500 and 8200 meters and a category for peaks higher than that. To lump Everest, K2, Kangchenjunga, Lhotse, and Makalu with the other 8000ers is misleading because they are really a whole category higher than the others and cannot be tackled with the same approach. There should be another category for the five highest peaks, which really are a whole mountain above the other mountains. That would be a real category.

Do you find these mountains to be spiritual places?

Yes, they are spiritual places. And not only the mountains, but very often a spot near the mountains. There are certain such locations that are real power places. By accident I discovered one of them in 1978 when I was trying to climb Makalu. I hadn't been on an 8000-meter peak in eighteen years, and I developed a terrible cough while on the climb. I was coughing so much that I couldn't do anything. I took it as a very bad sign.

So I descended into the rhododendron forest below. I didn't know it, but this site of blossoming rhododendrons and huge Himalayan firs was a power place. I called it the Enchanted Forest. I stayed there for almost a week, meditating and thinking about what my life would be like without these big mountains, which was very difficult to contemplate. But by the time I had come to terms with the fact that I would never climb in the high mountains again, the cough began to go away and I started to feel so strong. There was such an energy within me.

I went back up to base camp, and the others were all surprised at how healthy I was. I said, "Tomorrow I'll try to climb Makalu." I felt so good all of a sudden. And so I did.

And this wonderful feeling went on. Only a few months later I climbed Everest, and the next year I climbed Gasherbrum II. And I could have easily climbed Lhotse the year after that, but my work as a filmmaker began to interfere with my mountaineering. I was feeling good and the weather was fine and our expedition had a permit for Lhotse, but my work was to film an Everest climb.

I asked the expedition leader, "Why can't I have just three days off and climb Lhotse?"

He said, "You can go for Lhotse, but first you must finish the film for Everest."

So I went up to the south col of Everest to do the filming, and while I was finishing it up, a heavy storm broke. It stormed for a week, and I was on the south col for many days. But if I had had the chance I would have climbed Lhotse. It's often a question of choosing the right day, and you cannot always choose the right day.

> *"I LOVED TO BRING THE ADVENTURE DOWN TO OTHERS, AND I LOVED TO FIX THIS EXPERIENCE THAT I HAVE LIVED."*

How did you start your filmmaking career?

In 1958 I made my first film with Franz Lindner. We climbed for five days over the whole Peuterey Ridge on Mont Blanc. That was a fantastic enterprise to go over that ridge and do that film. I still think it's one of the best things I've ever done.

I found out on that trip that I loved to create in photography. I loved to bring the adventure down to others, and I loved to fix this experience that I have lived. That's why I write and that's why I make films.

Then I filmed the Dhaulagiri expedition in 1960 together with Norman Dyhrenfurth. And by and by I became known as the cameraman of the 8000ers. Then I met Julie, got to know her, and in 1983 we founded the highest film team in the world. In 1986 we went to K2 and it ended there. But I'm still filming.

Did filmmaking often get in the way of your climbing?

Yes. Filmmaking slows you down. Quite often you're trying to both film and climb on the same trip, and it doesn't always work. So sometimes you will have to retreat from a climb. That's how I lost Lhotse. And that's how Julie and I lost K2 on our first expedition in 1983.

How long have you made a living as a filmmaker and lecturer?

I've been a freelance filmmaker, mountaineer, lecturer, and writer for more than twenty years. Before that I was a teacher but only managed to do that for five years. There were too many rules, and everything was regulated.

Everything was geared toward your pension. I didn't like that. I like freedom. It's not so safe. It's not so sure. But I like it this way.

Was it hard to reconcile such a life with being married and having a family?

Certainly it made things difficult. But I'm happy that I'm married and that I have children. One has to bring together in some way things that seem contradictory. If you only follow one way and stick to that alone, you will become limited. It's better to create a total life that embraces more, even if it makes it more difficult to follow an ambition.

Did you ever have to choose between climbing and a girlfriend or wife?

Certainly not with Julie—we both went up—but case by case it's different. My first wife, Tona, went climbing with me. We climbed difficult things like the south ridge of the Aiguille Noire. Teresa, my wife now, doesn't go to the mountains, so she has gotten used to me being gone. So I've managed to keep all these things together in some way, but it sometimes meant sacrifices from the other person, who didn't see me very often. But with Julie I climbed a lot on the big mountains, not only on K2, but on Nanga Parbat, Everest, and other mountains as well.

What was your relationship with Julie like?

We had a total understanding between us. We had an inclination to discover things, felt so good high up, and found such a satisfaction in being creative. That's why we founded our film team. We loved this life of being creative and being up in the mountains.

Why did K2 appeal to you as a peak?

When I first saw it in 1957, it was just huge and regular, but I had no wish to climb it. I don't know when exactly I got Shipton's book, *Blank on the Map,* but he wrote about K2 in a way that really brought out the magic of that mountain and enchanted me. It was not only how he wrote about K2, but how he wrote about the Shaksgam, the mountain desert north of K2 that has these big glaciers. When I was on Gasherbrum II in 1979, I looked down into this area that Shipton had written about and thought, "I want to be there." And I managed to get there in 1982. When I saw K2 from that side I was simply spellbound. I saw that the mountain had this crystal shape. I saw the four-kilometer north ridge, which I thought would be a fantastic route to climb.

And then the next year I went there with Julie and we both fell under the spell. The mountain from this side is really an incredible thing. It's breathtaking in a picture, but if you're there, it's something else. You just can't help being caught by it if you see it from there. And once the mountain has caught you, it has got you.

In 1986, when Julie and I were up on K2 with all these people, we were thinking of the north side of K2 because it is so silent. But you cannot say, "I like this person—but only from the front—I don't like him from behind." So we said, "Even if it's not a good side, if we have a chance to climb it, we will climb it. We will stay here this time, but we will look for more silent places later."

How many times did you attempt K2?

We made one attempt on the China side in 1983. And we made several attempts again in 1984 from the Pakistan side, but we didn't get high because the weather was bad. In 1986 we made two attempts. On July 6, we tried it the first time. The weather had been perfect, and six of our fellow team members got to the summit, but we were a day late because of the filmmaking. We got within 350 meters of the top and then descended as we didn't want to risk a bivouac. Afterward, the weather turned bad. If we would have had an extra day we could have climbed the peak without running into that storm later on.

We made the second attempt in the early days of August and got to the top—one day too late.

Did you have any premonitions of disaster?

A few months before we climbed to the summit of K2, we visited my daughter, who was living in a Tibetan village and studying the local religion. In this and other remote villages, people often believe that the Himalaya are the place of the gods. And there are even shamans, often old women, who speak with the voice of a mountain god. In the village where my daughter was living there was such a woman, and she said she would read our palms and then tell us something of real interest to us. The woman read our palms and then fell into a trance and spoke with a very strange voice. Julie asked the woman if she would ever climb Makalu, because Julie liked Makalu very much. And the woman didn't say much for a while. Perhaps the woman felt something but didn't want to say anything since Julie had asked her only about Makalu. Finally, she said, "It says you will go very high up." And so she did, but she died soon after.

Did the number of people on the route that year make the climbing more hazardous?

Yes, but there are two aspects. One nice aspect is the international understanding and friendship and chats that you have at base camp. That's the good side. And this good side may continue further up. You may be able to help each other fix ropes, establish camps, and break trail. But whereas at base camp it's easy to cooperate, it's more difficult higher up the mountain.

Sometimes it may work, but other times it may not because it's a different world up there.

There is a dangerous side to having many people on the route. For example, one expedition may have a slow, plodding style, while another expedition may want to go alpine style. One expedition may have a lot of time; another one may be in a hurry. And then some people get up there fast because others have broken the trail. They may not be well acclimatized, or have any experience of the Himalaya, and may just travel as if they were in the Alps. And all of this together may make a terrible mess and, combined with language problems, can create enormous danger. After my experience on K2, I would say that this negative aspect definitely exceeds the positive aspect of having many people on the mountain.

". . . IT IS NOT AT ALL ETHICAL TO COUNT ON THE HELP OF OTHERS FROM THE BEGINNING OF YOUR CLIMB."

Then there are the ethics that say you should help each other. And while there's no doubt that you help each other in emergencies, it is not at all ethical to count on the help of others from the beginning of your climb.

For example, the Austrians were warned that their tents had been destroyed up high on the mountain, but they still went up without carrying another tent and just borrowed a tent from the Koreans, even though the Koreans needed this tent. The Koreans didn't feel they could refuse—they could have, they should have—but they thought that people might say that they weren't good comrades. Thus, ethical considerations pressured people and put them into dangerous situations, and that's the last thing that should come out of ethics. There's no dispute about help in an emergency, but one should do one's own climb with one's own means. That's the real heart of the matter. Not whether you climb with oxygen or without oxygen, not whether you are a big party or a small party, but that you climb with your own means. All these systems—heavy or light, fast or slow—they all work, but they should be done independently.

The effects of altitude must have compounded these problems even further.

When people judge these things from below, they forget that the higher you go, the more limited you get psychologically. And so people are moving around within their own psychological walls. Some walls are broken down because people know each other, but in 1986 many of the people up there didn't know each other. They had collaborated going up, but when the situation became very complicated, the psychological limits became evident. If there had been an emergency situation at first, we would have just gone down together. But since that came later—totally unforeseen—we stayed up there with all our problems of comprehension. That's why strange decisions can be made at high altitude sometimes. And that's why if you go high, you should go with someone you know really, really well.

What prevented you from descending?

We were prisoners of the storm. If we could have escaped, we would have. Everybody would have.

Part of the problem was we didn't have enough wands to mark the way down. Alan Rouse and I used wands up to 7700 meters and then ran out. And when there was a white-out, you would have just gotten lost if you had tried to descend without wands. You couldn't see. And the storm was so strong that it almost knocked you down. If you had been under the same conditions on Mont Blanc, you could have taken out your compass and quietly and calmly worked your way down. But if you had done that on K2, you would have been frozen dead. So you waited—you waited till the weather opened up because then you would have won and then you would be able to go down. But under exceptional circumstances it doesn't open up.

I had been in similar situations many times before, but they usually ended after two or three days. And it was an exceptional situation anyway because Julie had died. She died in the high camp after we had gotten down from the summit. We climbed the peak on August 4, and by the time we got down to the tent we were already imprisoned by the clouds. Then the storm started. She died on August 7. [Near crying] Too long. Too long....

It's difficult to say how she died, and it probably doesn't matter. She had a fall on the way down from the summit, but she probably died of a blood clot or something.

It was not a situation that could be compared to any other. It was an extraordinary situation and it doesn't really help to talk about it. I don't like to talk about it. But one thing is sure: if we hadn't lost August 3, and therefore if by the time the storm arrived we had been down on the fixed ropes, we would have made it. We did not move on August 3, and if we hadn't lost that day, we all would be alive. That was the real reason for the whole disaster.

There have been many theories about this disaster, but they should always be analyzed in terms of the high mountains. You cannot simply apply the rules of the Alps to this altitude. And I don't think people should judge these things while they are sitting in a meadow or somewhere on the plains because it is a different world up there.

Will you continue to climb the big peaks?

Yes. I don't see any limits because of age, but one finds out. It might be harder to carry loads, but climbing without loads, I don't see much difference.

Do you have a very deliberate pace?

Yes. I go slow. There's an old mountaineering guide's proverb: "He who goes slow, he goes good, he goes far." It's a very old saying. I first heard it when I was a boy. I think it's better to go slow at high altitude. That's the right way for me.

Why do you keep climbing?

For me, the reason is to discover something. That's why I started with the crystals. And, since then, every trip has been a discovery. Sometimes it was a challenge, but even with the challenge, the discovery was paramount.

It was never simply the sport point of view. There could have been a few times when Wolfi and I said, "Oh, we have done it in eight hours." But we wouldn't start the climb thinking that we wanted to be the fastest. This was never my point of view. I would take my time. I was interested in looking around the next corner of the mountain.

Do you know why you climb?

No. It's impossible to answer this last question. It is answered by what you are doing. You are creating. You are thinking. You are feeling happy. You are feeling another person's friendship. It is simply life and you are experiencing it.

Have you recovered from the K2 climb?

Yes, I have recovered, but it has really changed my life. I lost my good friend and partner—that's the main thing—and it has changed almost everything else. The only thing that it hasn't changed is my personality and my desire to go back to the high mountains. If you are a creative person, you will continue to create. If you have lived for the mountains once, you will live for the mountains again.

▲▲▲ WALTER BONATTI

*Real mountaineering is…above all a reason for struggle
and for self-conquest, for spiritual tempering and enjoyment in
the ideal and magnificent surroundings of the mountains. The
trials, the hardships, the privations with which an ascent of the
peaks is always studded, become, for that very reason, valid tests
which the mountaineer accepts to temper his powers and his
character. In the atmosphere of struggle, of close relationship with
the unforeseen difficulties and the thousand perils of the mountains, the alpinist is shown in his true colors, ruthlessly laid bare,
both in his qualities and in his defects, to himself and others.
That alone, in my opinion, should be sufficient to convince
anyone that the mountains can be for the climber the source of
the most beautiful and exalted sentiments and the supreme test
which contributes to the perfecting of certain qualities which are
at the root of progress.*

—Walter Bonatti, *On the Heights*

PERHAPS THE FINEST alpinist of the post–World War II generation,
Walter Bonatti ushered in a new era of extreme alpinism with such
compelling climbs as the solo ascent of the southwest pillar of the Petit Dru
(1955), the solo of the north face of the Matterhorn in winter (1965), and
numerous routes in the Alps, Andes, and Himalaya. Though renowned for his
stamina and sheer technical virtuosity, Bonatti may have made his most important contribution to the tradition of alpinism by developing a psychology of
climbing. He came to see climbing not so much as a conquest of peaks as a
conquest of oneself. For him, extreme alpinism served as a path to self-knowledge,
a means of growth and renewal through contact with nature, and as a way of
maintaining balance and sanity in a society growing excessively complex and
complacent.

Born in Bergamo, Italy, on June 22, 1930, Bonatti began climbing at age

Walter Bonatti. (Courtesy Walter Bonatti)

nineteen on the pinnacles of the Grigna in northern Italy. He progressed rapidly and soon set his sights on some of the most difficult routes in the Alps, especially the Walker Spur of the Grandes Jorasses. In preparation for this grueling climb, he ascended a peak called the Adamello, made the second ascent of the Direct Route on the southwest face of the Croz dell'Altissimo, traveled to the Bregaglia Mountains in southern Switzerland for further practice, and as a finishing touch, climbed the standard route on the Grandes Jorasses to familiarize himself with the descent route. Then he set out for his objective.

He failed on his first attempt when his partner, Camillo Barzaghi, insisted on retreating. Disappointed but still determined, he teamed up with Andrea Oggioni and Emilio Villa to try again. They first climbed the direct route on the west face of the Aiguille Noire de Peuterey before returning to finish off the Walker Spur. After this baptism in extreme alpinism, he was ready to tackle the toughest routes in the Alps.

Steep, unclimbed faces exerted a powerful attraction over Bonatti, and after taking one look at the east face of the Grand Capucin, he decided to put a route up it. The face presented many difficulties, not the least of which was the unpredictable weather in that region of the Alps. After storms rebuffed him twice, he finally succeeded on his third attempt with Luciano Ghigo in July of 1951.

Though he'd grown up in the lowlands, Bonatti gradually grew disenchanted with his life there and in 1953 decided to give up a secure job as an accountant to live in the mountains and devote himself to climbing. The following year he received his certificate as an Alpine guide and thereafter made his living guiding parties up peaks.

A turning point in his life came when he was selected to join the 1954 Italian K2 Expedition. At twenty-three, he was the youngest member of the expedition, and yet despite the strict discipline enforced by expedition leader Ardito Desio, a discipline that grated against his individualistic temperament, Bonatti played a pivotal role in the expedition's success the following year. Against the odds, he managed to carry several oxygen bottles to a site near the top camp. This feat allowed Achille Compagnoni and Lino Lacedelli to reach the summit via the Abruzzi Ridge, but it nearly cost Bonatti and Mahdi, his Hunza companion, their lives. Unable to find the lead climbers' tent, they were forced to spend the night at 26,500 feet without shelter or sleeping bags. In one of the most harrowing bivouacs in the history of mountaineering, the two survived by the slimmest of margins. They endured mind-numbing cold and a raging blizzard before leaving the oxygen at the bivouac site and stumbling back down the mountain the following day. Bonatti's story of the bivouac and K2 climb is recounted in *Trial on K2* (1985).

Although he had performed with distinction on K2, Bonatti was accused of jeopardizing the expedition's success by failing to reach the top camp with the oxygen. He was quick to refute this accusation, pointing out that the high camp had not been erected in the agreed-upon site and that getting the oxygen up within the lead climbers' reach at all was an extraordinary achievement. Still, such criticism rankled and for a time took some of the pleasure out of his climbing. He sought to renew his enthusiasm for the sport by attempting to solo the southwest pillar of the Petit Dru. He accomplished this in 1955, restoring his confidence in himself and rejuvenating his zest for climbing.

Despite his dislike of expeditionary climbs, he accepted an invitation to go with Riccardo Cassin to Gasherbrum IV in 1958. After two abortive summit attempts, Bonatti and Carlo Mauri finally succeeded in reaching the summit via the northeast ridge.

Other first ascents followed in the Alps and in South America. But not all of his climbs ended in triumph. On the central pillar of Frêney on Mont Blanc in 1961, he and several of his companions got caught in a lightning storm. On the descent, Andrea Oggioni and five other climbers died of exhaustion and exposure, while Bonatti and Pierre Mazeaud managed to survive. Although he had done everything possible to help the other climbers, some journalists blamed him for not doing more to prevent their deaths. In fact, all six of the other climbers would likely have perished had it not been for Bonatti's efforts. The French government set the record straight by awarding him its highest official recognition, the Legion d'Honneur, "for courage and solidarity in dramatic circumstances."

After the dust had settled following the central pillar of Frêney tragedy, Bonatti sought to complete one last hard route before retiring from extreme alpinism. He demonstrated his flair for the extravagant gesture by selecting the 100th anniversary of the first ascent of the Matterhorn to pull off an audacious solo winter ascent of the north face in 1965. After that stunning achievement, at age thirty-four he abandoned extreme alpinism for other horizons.

Since then, Bonatti has traveled the globe, seeking adventures in some of wildest and most remote corners of the world. He makes his living writing and lecturing about these trips. When not traveling, he lives in Milan, Italy, with Rossana Podesta, a former Italian movie actress.

The interview took place in Milan at the office of Bonatti's friend Mirella Tenderini, who served as translator. In person, Bonatti is a charming, articulate man who can speak as knowledgeably about the stylish resort town of Portofino as about his routes on Mont Blanc. Despite his white hair and sixty-three years, he exudes all the vigor and vitality of youth—his strong, compact build retains the fitness that got him through some of the most harrowing incidents in alpine history, while his direct, earnest glance reveals him above all as a seeker, as a man who strives to soar beyond the daily humdrum of life toward the realms of intellectual and spiritual enlightenment.

Why did you climb so many routes on Mont Blanc?

That's difficult to answer, but I'll tell you how I consider Mont Blanc today. I consider him as a father who has taught me lots of things and who has also punished me severely. And I still go back to Mont Blanc like going to a father to whom I have something to tell and from whom I want to hear things.

Mont Blanc reminds me of all my past, and since in the life of man there is a time to go back to one's roots, I go back to Mont Blanc because he is my roots.

Have you learned all of the mountain's secrets?

No. I have not discovered all of his secrets, because his secrets are endless, and that's not what I wanted to learn. But I did learn my own limitations, my own weakness. And when I learned everything that Mont Blanc could teach me, I went to look for the same things on other horizons—the great north, the bottom of the sea, and jungles full of wild animals.

How did you survive ordeals such as your bivouac on the central pillar of Frêney on Mont Blanc?

I survived thanks to experiences I had undergone in previous years that made me tough enough to overcome ordeals that perhaps were too difficult for other people. I survived because I was strong enough after years of day-to-day experience. Also, I've always been incapable of accepting fate, and I've always refused to die, and that has helped me to survive.

> *". . . I'VE ALWAYS BEEN INCAPABLE OF ACCEPTING FATE, AND I'VE ALWAYS REFUSED TO DIE, AND THAT HAS HELPED ME TO SURVIVE."*

Did that experience leave its mark on you?

It has marked me deeply, not because of the terrible experience itself, but because of the incomprehension of people toward me.

What part does the risk of death play in climbing?

As in all things of value, there is an element of risk in climbing. But anytime I have risked death, I have kept the risk under control. Through experience and preparation, I try to reduce the risk to a minimum. But, of course, this minimum must be present; otherwise my enterprises would lose zest.

How did you get started climbing?

I was not born an alpinist, but I was born with a spirit of adventure. I lived on the flatlands, and the high mountains captured my imagination. The mountains fascinated me because they represented wild nature. At first, I dreamt about climbing, watched climbers, and then tried to copy what they did.

Were you good at it?

Yes, immediately. I started to climb on the Grigna in Lecco, and six months later I climbed the Walker Spur of the Grandes Jorasses, the northeast face of the Piz Badile, the west face of the Aiguille Noire de

Peuterey, and the Croz dell'Altissimo. They were the most challenging routes in the world at that time.

Did you have heroes who inspired you in your climbing?

At age nineteen, when I did those routes, it's natural to have heroes. As I grew up, I found out that those heroes were people I admired but who were different from myself. I couldn't recognize myself in them.

Who were those heroes?

Hermann Buhl, Riccardo Cassin, Lionel Terray. The fact that I didn't identify myself with them doesn't mean that I didn't admire them. I admired them greatly, but I found that my personality, my interior search, had not much to do with mountaineering itself. Mountaineering was a means but was not the end. Mountaineering made me a man, a complete man, with all of the virtues and faults. I had to pass through mountaineering to achieve this.

Were you driven to do your climbs?

I was driven by myself. It's necessary to listen to one's own impulses, not to be driven by outsiders. And those impulses are from my inner self and not from the outside world.

Was climbing a way of self-knowledge for you?

Yes, a way of self-knowledge and self-challenge, and on top of that there was the wonderful environment.

Did you prefer to climb alone?

As a man of adventure, loneliness is an essential condition. I've not always done things alone, but each time it was possible, I preferred to go alone, both in the mountains and around the world. Loneliness has a great value because it sharpens sensitivity and amplifies emotions.

What were your reasons for doing a solo ascent of the southwest pillar of the Petit Dru?

It was a kind of redemption after the K2 climb. It was a form of protest. It was also an anticipation of the future in climbing, although at the time nobody understood that. That climb allowed me to assert my individualism within a society based on collectivism. I did that climb as a rebellion against a society of collectivism.

The generation following mine has prided itself on doing things that I had already done with that climb of the Dru. Other people in the sixties did this kind of climbing and claimed that they had discovered it for themselves.

That's because they considered my solo of the Dru a technical achievement, an athletic achievement, whereas in my mind it was an assertion of my individuality.

So you were using your climbing to speak to other people?

I didn't mean to set an example, to give a message to anybody. I did it to assert myself. It was not a message, not a model, but a point of reference. It was a way of saying, "This is one way to live one's life or one's alpinism." If people recognized themselves in it, it could serve as a point of reference for them.

Why did you need this sense of redemption?

It was in reaction to the K2 expedition, on which I had a very negative experience. The K2 expedition was not negative from the mountaineering point of view, but from the human point of view. I found myself disillusioned with values in which I had always believed—for instance, friendship. I went through a period of disillusionment that influenced my personality, my character. So the Dru was a redemption for myself.

What influence did the K2 expedition have on the rest of your climbing?

From the point of view of mountaineering, it didn't add to my experience, whereas from the human point of view it has been very important. I learned that unfortunately I couldn't trust other people much, and I learned that my best friend was myself. I also learned I could do things by myself. It was the start of my solo climbing and my soloing traveling.

Why did you become disillusioned with the other climbers?

It's a difficult matter to summarize. I wrote a book about it, *Trial on K2,* thirty years after the episode, and in it I explain the story of the bivouac. To help my companions, I performed a miracle in bringing that oxygen bottle up to the high camp. In the process, I risked death with my Hunza companion. We survived a bivouac [at 26,500 feet].

The official statement [of the Italian Alpine Club] never admitted the facts. On the contrary, they accepted a completely opposite version. I felt myself accused and dishonored, not just as an alpinist, but as a man. The club officials have not rectified the false statements. And for that reason I wrote *Trial on K2,* which is not a book of opinions, but a book of documents and eyewitness accounts.

Could you summarize the accusations?

Very briefly, I was accused of wanting to go ahead of the people chosen to be the top team; to have been responsible for the frostbitten hands and feet

Bonatti's southwest pillar route on Petit Dru, France. (Diadem Archives)

of my Hunza companion; to have abandoned him, whereas the opposite was true; to have failed to carry the oxygen bottle to the top team, whereas I left the oxygen at a higher point than originally agreed upon, and that because the top team had moved their tent to a different place than agreed upon. So I was accused of jeopardizing the success of the expedition. I was accused of having inhaled the oxygen, which was ridiculous because I didn't have a mask.

I demonstrated that all the accusations were false. But the people who could have settled this matter were too weak to take a stand, in spite of an inquest at which I was exonerated. My version was recognized at the inquest, but official members of mountaineering institutions in Italy never bothered to rectify the truth, so the written records are still false. They should do something about this. They should straighten things out, not just for me, but for their own dignity.

Why did you go to Gasherbrum IV after your disappointing experience on K2?

Despite my disillusionment after K2, I again made the mistake of going on a large expedition. On Gasherbrum IV, the organization didn't take into account the mistakes made on the K2 expedition. On the Gasherbrum expedition, we were often in the position of trusting ourselves to chance. This doesn't make it easy to get to the top and it also can cost lives.

Why didn't you do more climbing in the Himalaya?

In the fifties I did the maximum I could do. I went to K2 in 1954 and to Gasherbrum IV in 1958. That was the most I could do because it was possible to go to the Himalaya only in big, national expeditions. Climbing in the Himalaya today is completely different from the Himalaya of twenty or thirty years ago. Back then, getting to the Himalaya required an enormous financial and organizational effort. It was something very few people were able to do. And it was not a matter of merit or capability whether you got chosen to go; sometimes it was a matter of chance.

Why did first ascents appeal to you?

In accomplishing them you feel a sense of self-assertion, of testing yourself and overcoming your limits. To have this possibility of testing myself, I set some specific rules, which I had to obey. I took those rules from the classic alpinists [directness of line, severity of style] because I recognized something of myself in those rules and in that form of mountaineering. So I had a sort of Greenwich meridian.

What did you look for in a first ascent?

I looked for routes that would challenge me. And on the most difficult face, there is usually one most logical route.

Why did you come out of retirement to solo the north face of the Matterhorn in winter?

In 1964 I said that I was finished with extreme alpinism, but I went to the Matterhorn [in 1965] out of a romantic impulse. It was the centennial anniversary of the first ascent of the Matterhorn, and I found a personal way to celebrate this event.

Why did you retire after that climb?

When I retired in 1965, I felt I could do nothing more than to repeat myself. At a certain point, conventional alpinism became too restricted for me. I was not pursuing the top of the mountain, I was using the mountain to measure myself. The mountain itself is a pile of stones, and climbing only makes sense if you consider the man. As a climber, the top is not something physical you achieve, but something spiritual. The mountains are the means; the man is the end. The idea is to improve the man, not to reach the top of the mountains.

> *"THE MOUNTAINS ARE THE MEANS; THE MAN IS THE END. THE IDEA IS TO IMPROVE THE MAN, NOT TO REACH THE TOP OF THE MOUNTAINS."*

That's why I went to explore nature, transposing what I was looking for in mountaineering into this new way of looking for adventure. I went on climbing, but I stopped doing extreme climbing because my competitiveness was transported to new things like travels, which were not as spectacular as extreme climbing, but which for me had the same meaning and represented a similar challenge.

Why do people need to climb?

Why do people need to go to the moon or underneath the sea? Before us, Odysseus wanted to go beyond the outer limits of the known world, because man has always wanted to go beyond his limits; that's his condition. Curiosity and fantasy brought man down from trees, where he was an ape.

What changes have you seen in mountaineering over the course of your life?

In my opinion, there is still not relevant development in alpinism in this century as far as the mind is concerned. The technology of mountaineering and of rock climbing has developed enormously in this century, but alpinism itself has not improved considerably with respect to the mind. Compared with mountaineering of the previous century, the technology has improved enormously but the values of mountaineering in some cases have even regressed.

Who are the younger climbers who have carried on the classic tradition of alpinism?

I thought Reinhold Messner would be the one to do it, and at the beginning he accomplished extraordinary things. Before his death [in 1989], Jerzy Kukuczka achieved what in my epoch was thought impossible, and Doug Scott is also a climber who is exploring the limits of the humanly possible with the means of today.

What makes a good climber?

The qualities of a good climber are the same qualities as for a good man. These are the possibilities of dreaming and fantasy. To use climbing, but not to make it a goal in life. To use mountains, but not to allow them to limit oneself.

In climbing, it's important not to destroy the concept of the impossible. To keep from destroying the idea of the impossible, it's important to create rules and to respect those rules. An example. If I play poker with eight aces, I am sure to win, but it's not fair play, and it means nothing even if I win. Today, the excess of technique in climbing is like eight aces in poker. If the impossible is made possible, it's destroyed, and there's no value in conquering the impossible. So they overcome the problem without really winning.

Are you speaking of expansion bolts?

Yes, because with a piton the climber used his intelligence to find the logical route. When you place a bolt, it's just a matter of muscles. It's a gesture but it's not adventure. This can be right and good and even beautiful in itself, but it's not adventure. And for me, mountaineering has always been adventure. It cannot be but adventure.

How do you distinguish between the climbers who are just using their muscles and the climbers who are adventurous? Is it the risk of death?

It's not a matter of risk. When starting out to be an alpinist, a person must know what he wants from the mountain. If he wants to perform a gesture, it's okay, but if he wants to live an adventure, he must live with the rules of adventure, which are completely different from those of the gesture. In adventure, there must be a component of the unknown.

Why do you put such a high premium on adventure?

Because, as I said before, adventure is the maximum experience in life. It is something important for every man. Man is born with the spirit of adventure; that's why man has progressed through the centuries. Life is still an adventure because there is the uncertainty of death, which will happen to everybody, but nobody knows when it will come. This is terrifying, but at the same time fascinating.

Are you a religious man?

Yes. In my own way, I am. But in my opinion religion doesn't mean doctrine. I am against doctrine. Religion for me has a very wide sense and means respecting the great, mysterious forces who created us and who rule the universe.

Were some of your most difficult moments almost transcendent, religious experiences?

I've had experiences I've called states of grace, which are a mixture of exultation and a quickening of reactions. These experiences made me believe that I could do anything and that everything was possible. We use only a slight part of our potential, and on some rare occasion when we are forced to use more of our possibilities, we succeed in performing acts that usually are regarded as miracles.

> *"I'VE HAD EXPERIENCES I'VE CALLED STATES OF GRACE, WHICH ARE A MIXTURE OF EXULTATION AND A QUICKENING OF REACTIONS."*

Have you found these experiences in fields other than mountaineering?

I've experienced the same situations when living with wild animals. In the transition from mountaineering, I went to meet dangerous animals—lions and tigers—in their own habitat, without firearms. I knew a dialogue with them would be impossible, but I wanted a contact without misunderstanding. And my conclusion was that there are no animals dangerous to man if men understand and respect the rules of the animals, if men don't treat them with human logic.

One of these trips took place twenty-two years ago in East Africa. There was a region near the Serengeti that was not a park and that was far away from human dwellings. It was an ideal ground for these experiments. I crossed that region alone, without arms. I lived through some unbelievable experiences.

At one point I encountered some lions. I went straight ahead. The lions moved, but then other lions came. I suddenly felt like two people. My present self was full of worries—there was danger because of lion cubs—but another part of myself, which was possibly a remnant of our ancestors, gave me curiosity and confidence. It pushed me ahead. I chose to follow this second self, which was instinctual. I went on slowly but steadily, avoiding any noise or any abrupt movement. The lions rose up when I went on through.

The first part of myself was scared, but the second part of myself thought it was all right. I cannot explain the situation exactly, but I lived through it. That experience was one of the states of grace I was telling you about. I think that contact with nature keeps instinct alive and helps bring back the ancient rules, which are now mostly lost.

Although instinct is often condemned, I believe that it is a part of consciousness, that it exists inside each one of us. When animals do something according to instinct, there is a reason. Man also has instinct, but it's disappearing because it's been suffocated by civilization. Our logic doesn't respond any longer to the original logic.

Is heroism still possible today?

What is a hero? The real hero in this world is the one who keeps faith in himself, his personality, his identity. But this is really difficult, and even impossible, because we live in a society of compromises.

Will you continue to seek other adventures?

I am always seeking new experiences, but I don't feel that it's always necessary to risk something. I can have new experiences even here in town. An experience can be one of the intellect. An intellectual experience can be as exciting as a physical experience, and an intellectual experience can be the goal after the physical experiences.

I consider my life as a staircase, and the intellectual experience is just the next step up. I built my life around my interest in adventure, in mountaineering first and then in other ways. People usually consider me an alpinist, but I consider myself as a man who has been an alpinist. Mountaineering is only a part of my life. When people write of me, they usually say that at a certain point I abandoned mountaineering, as if it were an abrupt ending. It's not so. It went on. I abandoned a certain way of doing alpinism, but I went on developing in alpinism. I consider mountaineering as the first step in a staircase. I'm still going up that staircase.

ROYAL ROBBINS

*A boy clambers barefoot up a tree. He does it for the pure
joy of climbing; why doesn't matter. It is exciting. New. There is
a bit of danger. The thrill of adventure in going somewhere he
has never been. He might do the same on a building or on an
easy rock cliff. And from this raw beginning springs a desire to
venture onto steeper walls, smoother ones. He would go there, but
he can't—not without boots, rope, and perhaps pitons. The game
becomes complex. But the point is still the same: adventure. For
his equipment, and the development of technique, these things
which would render his barefoot scrambles too easy, will enable
him to enter more forbidden realms and so maintain the balance
of exciting newness that he enjoyed on his first trip up the tree.*

—Royal Robbins, *Basic Rockcraft*

THROUGHOUT HIS LONG and remarkable career as a rock climber, Royal Robbins succeeded in keeping adventure and newness in his climbing by continually pushing his personal limits on some of the toughest and most intimidating rock walls in the world, challenging himself to do longer and harder routes while keeping his reliance on artificial aid to a minimum. In the process, he helped revolutionize big-wall aid climbing, paving the way for the next generation of climbers by refining the techniques that would allow them to go light and fast on big, vertical walls, thus opening up all kinds of possibilities at high altitude and elsewhere. Yosemite National Park provided an immense natural laboratory for the testing and perfecting of these techniques, and through his many climbs there, Robbins not only helped develop Yosemite Valley into a world center of rock climbing, but firmly established his own reputation as one of the outstanding figures in the history of the sport.

Robbins began climbing in the 1950s at Stony Point in the San Fernando Valley of California. He made amazing progress, leading Open Book at Tahquitz Rock in 1952, the first 5.9 route in the United States.

Royal Robbins completing the first solo of El Capitan, Yosemite, 1968. (Courtesy Royal Robbins)

Shortly thereafter, he set his sights on the granite walls of Yosemite National Park. At first he repeated some of the early test pieces, such as the north face of Sentinel Rock in 1953. Then he, Mike Sherrick, and Jerry Gallwas broke new ground by completing the first ascent of the northwest face of Half Dome in 1957, the first route climbed on that magnificent face. Thus began his passionate love affair with Half Dome in particular and Yosemite Valley in general.

Robbins bestrides the history of Yosemite climbing like a colossus. During the Golden Age of Yosemite climbing from the 1950s to the 1970s, he teamed up with such renowned climbers as Yvon Chouinard, Chuck Pratt, Tom Frost, TM Herbert, and others to tick off new route after new route: the 1961 first ascent of the Salathé Wall on El Capitan, considered to be one of the finest rock climbs in the world; the first ascent of the North American Wall of El Capitan in 1964; the first ascent of the west face of El Capitan in 1967; and the first ascent of Tis-sa-sack Route on Half Dome in 1969. He also improved the style by which routes were done in Yosemite, completing the first solo ascent of the wildly overhanging

Leaning Tower in 1963 as well as the first solo ascent of El Capitan in 1968.

Never content to rest on his laurels, Robbins continued to push the boundaries of rock climbing elsewhere in the world. He created a sensation by grabbing the Direct Route on the west face of the Petit Dru in the French Alps in 1962 with John Harlin and then followed that up with the Superdirect Route on the same face in 1965. These routes demonstrated in the most dramatic way possible that Yosemite-style techniques could be transferred to other parts of the world and that such techniques represented the way of the future in climbing. Caught off-guard by these bold new routes done in their own backyard, Europeans woke up to the fact that the upstart Americans were now at the cutting edge of climbing and that they would have to adopt these techniques if they were to catch up.

In addition to these impressive ascents in the European Alps, Robbins also pulled off some climbs of remote peaks as well. In 1964 he, Jim McCarthy, Layton Kor, and Dick McCracken journeyed to the Cirque of the Unclimbables in Canada's Northwest Territories to put up a new route on the 1800-foot southeast face of Proboscis. In 1968 he moved to mixed routes, pulling off the first solo ascent of the north face of Mount Edith Cavell in Canada. This wealth of climbing experience served him well when he came to write his two classic texts on rock climbing, *Basic Rockcraft* (1971) and *Advanced Rockcraft* (1973), the early bibles of free and big-wall aid climbing.

Though Robbins doesn't climb extensively in Yosemite Valley today, he still retains elder statesman status there, exerting considerable influence on the ethical controversies that have erupted in recent years, especially that of rap-bolting. Robbins has come out firmly against this practice, arguing that it removes adventure from climbing, thereby robbing the sport of the element he cherishes most. In this and earlier controversies, such as his disagreements with Warren Harding on bolting, Robbins has proved a principled and articulate spokesman for the ground-up style of climbing (no bolts placed on rappel) and for clean climbing in general, insisting that as few bolts should be placed as possible, and only when nuts and natural protection won't suffice.

Born on Febuary 3, 1935, in Point Pleasant, West Virginia, Robbins moved with his family shortly thereafter to Los Angeles, where he grew up. In 1963 he married Liz Burkner. They have two children: twenty-two-year-old Tamara and fourteen-year-old Damon.

Over the years Robbins has become well known for his business success as well as for his climbing achievements. The couple's outdoor clothing company, Royal Robbins, does more than $10 million in sales annually.

When not overseeing his thriving clothing business, Robbins continues to climb or goes whitewater kayaking, his latest outdoor passion. These activities keep him fit and trim at fifty-eight. A quiet, thoughtful man with a salt-and-pepper beard, Robbins becomes passionate and opinionated when the subject of climbing comes up. Taking time out from a busy schedule at his clothing company's headquarters in Modesto, California, he spoke with conviction and controlled intensity about his approach to climbing and to life.

How did you get started climbing?

When I was a kid, I liked to get out of Los Angeles and up to the San Gabriel Mountains. It was pleasant up there and made me feel good. Los Angeles wasn't my idea of a good time. What's down there if you're not a social person and you don't go to parties and you really think differently from other people? There was nothing there except traffic and noise and smog and a general flurry of people who were not particularly searching for something better. People in the mountains are searching for something better. It doesn't even matter if it's there or not, it's the search that counts: it's the looking, not being satisfied with the day-to-day squalor of existence.

So I'd get up to the mountains with my friends, or alone, and we'd find our way down canyons or up creeks, always looking for what was around the next corner—something interesting, adventure.

What got you interested in rock climbing?

Just the idea of it. When I was fifteen I saw a picture in a book called *High Conquest* of a guy on a rock face with a rope hanging out in space beneath him. I wanted to do that. I thought that was glorious. It was a romantic vision of something above the squalor of daily existence.

I started climbing shortly thereafter, mostly in the San Fernando Valley at a climbing area called Stony Point. And later on I climbed at Tahquitz Rock, which is 120 miles southeast of L.A. Those are the places where I learned to climb.

I liked climbing because it was more adventurous than hiking. The danger lent an aspect of greater adventure. It meant that you had to pay attention to what you were doing—or else. This forced you to raise the level of your alertness, awareness, of your being alive. It was life-enhancing and life-inspiring because it was dangerous—frankly.

And it was fun. Obviously, the idea is to keep danger in perspective and in control. But climbing requires that there be danger. Let's be clear about that. It doesn't require that you take risks, but it does require that there be danger. You circumvent the danger by your actions and your thoughts.

This was one of the reasons it attracted me. It gave me something to focus on. And life without focus is useless. When you have something to focus on, and you can put yourself totally into it, then you're more alive and you're doing what we're here to do, what we're meant for. Climbing appealed to me because I could fasten on it and forget about everything else, which I considered mostly bullshit. That may have been a disservice to the rest of the world, but it was my narrow point of view in those days.

Did you get a lot of pleasure out of it?

Right off, I loved the physical reward of the body moving up rock. I loved it instantly. Maybe I'm part monkey or something. It's still one of the best things about climbing for me. It feels so good to move up the rock.

When I first started climbing, I had a natural talent. It wasn't up to the standard of somebody like Chuck Pratt, who is very gifted, but it was above average. There were a number of climbers like him who were more naturally talented than me, but I usually kept up with them or in some cases excelled because I had this burning drive to go all out all the time, and they weren't driven by that particular passion.

After that, when you start making first ascents, you say, "Gee, I can make a first ascent." And it's great, because you think, "Boy, I want to make another one." You forget the pain. You forget the fear. You want to repeat the experience because it's gratifying. It makes you feel competent. It makes you feel like you can do things. And if I had felt that way about everything I did, I probably wouldn't have fallen in love with climbing. But there are few people who do everything easily and well, and I certainly wasn't one of those, and when I found something that I could excel at, I wanted to do more of it.

Why was it climbing, rather than some other sport?

Climbing isn't just a sport; it's a way of life—much more than tennis or downhill ski racing, for example. Especially in those days, and probably still, it required that you separate yourself pretty much from everything going on around you.

At the beginning I got partners by talking schoolmates into going with me. After they went once, they wouldn't go again. Then I went on a climb with the Sierra Club and met Don Wilson and, through him, Jerry Gallwas and Mike Sherrick. These guys were a little older than me. They were in college. They were smart, well educated, and quite unlike any of the friends I was normally going around with. I felt honored to be in such select company.

Climbers were a rare breed. They were all very special people. They were different from anyone else I'd ever met. Among other things, they were in general more selfless, more generous, more energetic, brighter. They seemed to have a lot of life. They seemed to be a little crazy. They didn't seem to be interested in what is taken as important in the everyday world. They seemed to enjoy such silly things as putting everything they had into an activity that most of the world thought was insane. To do that, to have that perspective, takes a particular kind of person.

In a certain sense climbers felt elite; they felt superior. I'm sure we all felt inferior in a number of ways, in the ways of the city. But there was always a certain feeling of being superior because we were after higher things, shall we say? Looking around now, I see that we were neither any better nor any worse than other people, but we were different. The things that motivated us didn't motivate most of the people in the flatlands.

You were not content for the normal career.

We were not content, right. We weren't content unless we were doing something we had a passion for. That's what everyone should do, whether it's climbing or whatever. The idea of going through life without burning, that's the living dead. You shouldn't do that. You ought to find what you love and give your life to it.

Once you began to get involved with climbing, did it require that you put a lot of other things aside?

I never had the thought of putting things aside. I started climbing and I quit high school when I was sixteen. I went to work at a ski area in the winter, and I had odd jobs in the summer. I climbed as much as I could around that. When I wasn't skiing—which I would do in the winter a lot—I was climbing. Those were the days when I was climbing at Tahquitz Rock.

I was inducted into the army when I was twenty-three, and I climbed a lot while I was in the army. When I got out, I decided I would devote my life to what I really loved doing, which was climbing. In the summer, myself and guys like Chuck Pratt, Tom Frost, TM Herbert, Dick McCracken, and Glen Denny just camped out, watched our pennies, and scrimped by. We did a lot of hitchhiking in those days. We didn't have much money, but we had a lot of freedom. That was the choice we made.

Were you ambitious about climbing?

I wasn't ambitious in the sense that I said to myself, "I'm going to become a world-famous mountain climber. I'm going to become the best mountain climber." I was ambitious in the sense that I wanted to be as good as I could at whatever I did. As a matter of fact, I've come a lot further in climbing and everything else than I'd ever dreamed.

Later on, when I became known as a leader in American rock climbing, that felt good, and ambition crept in. Insofar as it does, you have to be careful, because ambition is founded on pride and can start interfering with doing your best job.

But in the early days, I quit regular working and took up climbing because that's what made me feel alive. That's what gave me personal rewards. And that was the motivating influence of all the other climbers I knew. Some of them were interested in fame, but it was a pretty rare climber whose main motivation wasn't climbing first.

Was the climbing competitive in the fifties?

It was competitive very early. In 1950, I remember I heard about this guy Yvon Chouinard who had been to Stony Point and had climbed all these things. We had our little competitions among ourselves, but this was the first outsider to enter into them. I pictured him as some superathlete, a tall guy with blond hair and everything. Yvon's short, has dark hair, and he's a very good athlete, but it's his mental attitude and mental approach that make him stand out, not his natural talent as an athlete.

Yvon would do something that I'd been trying, and then I'd do something that he'd been trying. Before I met him there was this competition going. But our competitions were mostly fun and good-spirited. They were the sort of competitions you have when you're playing cards or baseball.

> *"YOU SHOULD ALWAYS GO OUT OF YOUR WAY TO MAKE SURE THAT EVERYBODY'S CLEAR ABOUT THE AID YOU USED. IF YOU STEPPED ON A PITON, YOU DON'T OVERLOOK IT."*

Sometime after that, especially when going for new routes in Yosemite, the competition was more in earnest, and then the danger arose of mean-spiritedness creeping in. Good competition is where it's fun, where people do better because they're competing against one another, where the meanness is kept out. There's no need for it if you're competitive. You do what you can to excel. If somebody beats you at the game, you face it; you don't start telling stories about not stepping on a piton when you did.

One of the things that happens, of course, is some guys go up and set a speed record. And if you happen to know that they did it by methods that they aren't admitting, like the second guy climbed the rope hand-over-hand, then the competition becomes a little dishonorable.

That happened at times. It's very hard not to say, "Yeah, they did it really fast, but...." Sometimes the "buts" were genuinely a point and sometimes they were niggling and shouldn't have been raised at all because then they can start souring relations, which is unfortunate.

Certainly, we should always declare the aid. This is fundamental. You should always go out of your way to make sure that everybody's clear about the aid you used. If you stepped on a piton, you don't overlook it. If you used devices that previously hadn't been used on a climb, you don't pretend that you did it better, without at least admitting that you had these devices. Because then if you do that, people can't say, "Oh, yeah, but...." And then you're being honest.

In some areas this is important for safety. If you climb a certain route and you use something like a hook to get up, or you use a bolt and then chop it, and you tell somebody that you did it free, that's setting somebody else up for something dangerous. That's not right. So it's just doing the right thing and being honest. Competition is fine as long as those things are being adhered to.

When you arrived in Yosemite in the early fifties, who were the leading climbers?

Allen Steck, John Salathé, Chuck Wilts. Steck was probably the principal leader there.

Did these guys have a style you admired?

Yes, I'd say so. Salathé in particular. That's why we named the Salathé Wall after him. He set certain standards of style instinctively that distinguished him. When he climbed these big walls in Yosemite, he used as few bolts as he possibly could, so there was a style there that I admired.

Was that the beginning of a particular Yosemite style of climbing?

Yes. Salathé did everything from the ground up, with as few bolts as possible. He was a great early leader and a shining example for us. We repeated his routes and, boy, we had a hard time getting up them. We had to use every bolt he placed, and we had a lot of trouble climbing between them. He was a very skilled climber; he was also a very principled one.

Salathé was a key figure in developing my climbing philosophy, which is based on a triad of exemplars. The first was Geoffrey Winthrop Young, with his philosophy of sportsmanship in climbing, the key element being the way you do something, not just getting to the top; the second was Salathé, who applied that sort of philosophy to modern rock climbing in Yosemite; and the third was John Muir, with his wilderness ethics and respect for leaving things the way they are.

Why did Yosemite appeal to you as a place to climb?

If I'd have been in New York I probably wouldn't have gone to Yosemite, but it seemed natural here if you were a Californian. But frankly we didn't look at it and say, "Hey, this place should be a world center of rock climbing. Let's start inscribing our names here." In retrospect, we had very little imagination. If we had seen what Yosemite was to become, we would have done a lot more climbing there.

Back then, climbing wasn't a big deal in the United States. If we did a new route and we did it well, only a few people heard about it. So we earned the respect of those we had respect for. People outside climbing could have cared less. Mostly they were saying, "What are those fools doing?" That suited us fine. We didn't want any more than that. We were happy with people thinking we were crazy. We didn't care.

There must have been amazing possibilities for new routes at that point.

Yes. We were lucky because we were there during the Golden Age, and the Golden Age translates into a lot of opportunity. The routes were sitting there. All we needed was the gumption and the skill and the imagination to tackle them. What's interesting, looking back, is that it took us a comparatively long time to tackle them. We approached them with a lot of trepidation.

When you say "Golden Age," what do you mean by that?

I mean the period starting with Salathé's and Anton Nelson's ascent of the Lost Arrow Chimney [1947]. That was the beginning of the Golden Age. There's a major separation between that and the routes that were done before—routes that didn't require the commitment, the equipment, or the skill that these routes of Salathé's required. The commitment was the main thing. These were multiday climbs; they were long and difficult; they were really separate from anything that had been done before.

What were some of the first routes you climbed in the Valley?

When I first went to the Valley, I remember looking over at the north face of Sentinel Rock and thinking, "Gee, I'd sure like to repeat Salathé's route on that wonderful face some time." I didn't dream that the very next year [1953] Jerry Gallwas, Don Wilson, and I would make the second ascent in good time [two days] and good style. Afterward we felt really good and started wondering about first ascents.

And in the summer of 1956 we [Robbins, Warren Harding, Don Wilson, and Jerry Gallwas] made a half-hearted attempt on the northwest face of Half Dome. We didn't get anywhere. We started up the wrong crack system and ending up thrashing.

We came back terrified. Nobody had ever been in a place like that before in circumstances like that before. We were venturing into the unknown. There was a big overhang at the top; we didn't know if we could get over it. We didn't know Thank God Ledge was there. We might have had to rappel all the way down, and nobody had rappeled all the way down a face like that before. There was a traverse in the middle. What if we couldn't make the traverse back across? Et cetera, et cetera.

In 1957 we got the gumption to be serious about Half Dome. As it turned out, we needn't have been so terrified, but we didn't know that. You look back and you see that for us kids it was a good adventure.

Why had you set your sights on Half Dome rather than El Cap?

Because it was obvious. We wanted to do Half Dome or El Capitan because these were the two biggest faces; everything else was secondary compared to them. We thought we could see a route on Half Dome, and it's 2000 feet instead of 3000 feet. It seemed like the next step. After that, maybe start thinking about El Cap. But it didn't seem logical to jump to the 3000-foot monolith when the 2000-foot climb hadn't been done. Even after Half Dome had been done, El Cap simply awed us all. It looked like too much. Looking up there, we didn't find continuous cracks. We didn't see a line. We would look at El Capitan and we would say, "No, it's not worth it, because you're going to have to do so much expansion bolting."

That's what we told ourselves, and we believed it, but the truth was that we were finding reasons not to do it because we were misperceiving it. If you really want to climb it, you start looking for the ways that you can do it; if you don't really want to climb it, you start looking for the ways you can't do it. And that's what we were doing.

Warren Harding was looking for the ways he could do it. Because he hadn't been on the Half Dome climb, and wanted to be a hero, he took on El Capitan. He showed more imagination and more gumption than we had and got the first ascent of that wonderful route [the Nose, 1958]. He used more bolts than we thought should have been used on any climb, but the truth is that if we had been really eager to climb it, we would have got up it with fewer bolts, or we would have found another way, which we did on the Salathé Wall, where we used only thirteen bolts. We were just awed, scared, and didn't have the balls for it at that time.

After Warren showed what could be done, we made the second ascent in seven days because the bolts were in. We said, "You can actually climb this [El Cap] without sieging it." So we started looking for lines that would lead more naturally to the top without crossing big blank areas. And that led us to the Salathé Wall, which to this day is the best rock climb I've ever done. It's certainly the best first ascent, because it's so beautiful, and the rock is so good, and it has different problems, both aid and free, and pendulums and wonderful ledges to spend the night on—it's got everything. And we used only thirteen bolts making a 3000-foot climb, compared to 125 that were used on the Nose.

Salathé Wall on El Capitan, Yosemite. (Photo by Tom Frost; Diadem Archives)

So you were concerned even then about using too many bolts?

I don't know if we knew in our minds what was too many in terms of ethics, but we did have in mind what was too many in terms of what we wanted to do. We hated placing bolts.

We didn't consider bolt-placing climbing. It was a way to connect climbing, but in itself it wasn't climbing. We used twenty on Half Dome, and that was a lot of work. We just couldn't face placing 125. It just didn't seem right. A bolt was to be used only in terms of absolute necessity, because anybody could place a bolt, and bolting was not climbing. But we were willing to use bolts if it made possible a route otherwise impossible that was worth doing. We had a sense that there was a point of too many bolts, but we didn't know what it was. We just wanted to avoid them if possible. If you could do a 3000-foot route on El Cap with only thirteen bolts, that was good. But if you had to use 300 bolts, we wouldn't have considered doing it.

When you say "we," to whom are you referring?

Chuck Pratt, Tom Frost, Dick McCracken, Glen Denny, Steve Roper, TM Herbert—these are the people I did most of my climbing with then.

I wasn't climbing with Yvon in those days because Yvon didn't spend much time in the Valley. He spent most of his time in the Tetons. It was only later, when Yvon began to sense the importance of Yosemite as a climbing center, that he started spending a lot of time there. And he always had this love/hate relationship with the Valley—mostly hate—because it was quite different from the Tetons, which are more relaxed. The Valley was intense and competitive and that turned him off.

But you as a group agreed on these principles?

I think we were all very close about it. As a matter of fact, nobody really disagreed much except Warren Harding and a guy named Ed Cooper, who came into the Valley from the Pacific Northwest and immediately started climbing a new route on El Cap [Dihedral Wall, 1962] without becoming familiar with the Valley or without learning about it. He sieged the route, putting up lots and lots of bolts, which we thought was history.

Did you and Warren Harding get along?

He and I hit it off right away because we both were genuinely passionate about climbing. In fact, I made an early attempt on the northwest face of Half Dome with Warren. He was a typical burning climber and one of the more distinctive characters I've met. He was very much an individual. He had his own way of doing things, his own mind, his own approach. And he didn't care much for following what other people did. This set him apart as a pioneer and maverick.

We didn't always agree on the way to do things, but that's one of the things I liked about Warren. Warren and I have always been good friends. We've differed pretty strongly on our philosophy—I'm a moralist and he isn't—and some people think for that reason that we don't like each other, and that's never been true.

When did the friction between the two of you begin to heat up?

After he did the Dawn Wall route on El Cap [1970]. I didn't find fault with the Nose, although I didn't want to be a part of that, because for one thing it was his party, and for another I just didn't want to do a climb requiring siege methods and that many bolts. In retrospect, I was overly fussy. It would have been nice to have been on the first ascent of El Cap.

But later I was put off by Harding's active seeking of fame and publicity, which started with his Dawn Wall ascent. Because of the nature of the climb and the way they [Harding and Dean Caldwell] did it, it attracted a lot of attention. And he seemed to be grandstanding and doing climbs more for the public than for himself. That was what caused the beginning of the difference in our philosophies. Harding's philosophy seemed to be to select the blankest place he could find and put in as many bolts as necessary, and ours was to avoid bolts.

So it was both a question of personalities and of rock-climbing technique?

Yes. And Harding's approach was more of a spirit thing between him and the mountain, and in a way, the blanker a route was, the more challenge it was, and the more concentration and dedication and effort it might take; because bolts, after all, don't take any skill, but they take a lot of work to place. And so bolting allowed him to bring his tenacity and fighting spirit to bear on the climbs he did. The actual skill-level stuff interested him less.

And I worried that if his approach became accepted, it would be very bad for Yosemite and American climbing. And so I fought it on that basis: fine for him, but generally destructive of both the rock and of climbing standards.

And this came to a head on the Dawn Wall, where you erased his route?

Yes.

Was it your idea to erase that route?

Yes. A bunch of us were talking about it, but it was as much my idea as anybody's. I perceived that if anything was going to be done I'd have to do it because everybody else was just talking.

Did you later regret doing it?

I regretted that I'd started it since I didn't finish it. I decided partway up that it was a mistake. On the other hand I didn't feel any remorse. My position was simply that if you have the right to place bolts, anybody else has the right to remove them.

What effect did that have on climbing in the Valley?

It's arguable that it did a lot of good. After that, nothing worse [than the Dawn Wall] has been done, and climbers on the whole have tended more toward my way of doing things, or the way of doing things that I am a part of, than Harding's way. We haven't seen any more Dawn Walls as far as I know.

> "WE CONVINCED A GENERATION OF CLIMBERS TO ADOPT CLIMBING METHODS THAT MAKE CLIMBING MORE DIFFICULT."

If you hadn't been in the Valley, do you think that people would have done pretty much the same routes that you did?

It's hard to say for sure. I don't know if people would have perceived going up the Salathé that way—making that traverse, dropping down, and doing a pendulum, or whether they would have waited until they used more bolts and could go up straight from the bottom. A few things might have been done differently, but the routes are pretty much there and they would have been done. Our goal was to do the routes in the best possible style—no fixed-roping, as few bolts as possible, only using aid if you can't do it free.

What were the techniques that you helped develop in Yosemite?

In free-climbing techniques, not very much, but I did develop the arm or elbow lock to climb off-width jam cracks. I had to do that to climb these things that Chuck Pratt climbed, because he was a master of that stuff, and that was a way of coping with the difficulty of these off-widths; so I developed that because I had fairly flexible arms, and I could get my elbow up around there, and that was, I think, a contribution.

The other thing I guess I'll take a little credit for is developing the hauling method that we used. I was tired of the brutal methods we'd been using up till then that were just killing us. That was a pretty good idea.

And then my major contribution outside the climbs I did was to introduce in a serious way artificial chockstones for protection in climbing. I pushed them strongly, and Chouinard was an early convert and made a big difference with his catalogue in changing the ethos. Together we accomplished something pretty amazing. We convinced a generation of climbers to adopt climbing methods that make climbing more difficult. Placing nuts requires better judgment, intimacy with the rock, and a lighter touch.

Plus it doesn't harm the rock.

That, of course, is a big part of it. But for both stylistic and environmental reasons, climbers chose to raise themselves rather than raise their technology.

What did your generation of climbers in Yosemite contribute to the history of climbing?

High standards in aid climbing is the big contribution. Americans developed big-wall rock climbing to a significantly higher pitch than anyone in the world because we had the training ground and we had the values and also because we were isolated, which led us to develop our own ways of doing things.

What were the key elements in developing big-wall aid climbing?

There were two main things in big-wall rock climbing in which we were leaders. One was the development of equipment and the ability to use it with skill, figuring out ways to make pitons, malleable smashees, hooks, or whatever stick to the rock to avoid bolts. We hated bolts so much that we did everything we could to avoid them.

The other part of big-wall rock climbing we helped develop was the logistics of it, which include getting people and a lot of gear up steep, hot rock. This was more of a challenge than most people realize. They see the steepness, and the difficulty of placing pitons, and the fear of a bunch of them coming out, and things like that. But in fact the most dangerous thing about that sort of climbing is its complexity. Especially when you have a team of, say, four—you've got ropes all over the place, you've got carabiners all over the place, you've got bags hanging everywhere, you've got pitons in, and so forth, and this opens up the possibility of a mistake.

You must be clear all the time, for example, that your knot is still tied in your own rope, which may seem like an obvious thing, but I know of two world-class climbers whose ropes came off them in midpitch. You have to make sure that you really are tied in, and that what you're tied to is truly secure, and that it's doubled up to something else, and that nobody comes along and in the process of undoing something undoes you. It's an extraordinarily complex matter, and it gets tiresome, but you have to be thinking all the time, because mistakes can cause deaths.

When did the Golden Age of Yosemite climbing end?

In 1970 the Golden Age might be said to have ended or transformed, because the glory of doing first ascents up big walls was not there. I was still doing new routes and climbing at as high a standard as I ever had, but somehow the focus changed. Doing the big routes became less important, and free climbing and speed ascents became very important.

Did speed ascents interest you much?

Oh, yes. Sometimes I'd go out to set a speed record for the fun of it, for the competition, for the feeling of climbing well and efficiently. You don't want to take that kind of thing too seriously, but it's fun. It's just like trying to do routes free where there has been aid before. It's a challenge.

On the other hand, you want to be sure that whatever you do when you try to climb a route fast is fair, is understood, and that you're honest about it.

When did the rest of the world begin paying attention to Yosemite?

About 1965. That's the year we did the North American Wall. There was a movement toward the out-of-doors in general, and the interest in climbing picked up as part of that. People started seeing climbing as a legitimate expression of the outdoor experience, instead of something that freaks associated with the Sierra Club did.

Back in the days when we started climbing, people thought climbers were nuts; they also mostly had the same opinion about people in the Sierra Club. These were fanatics, goofballs, geeks, whatever, spending all their time talking about the wilderness. The outdoor passion was held by comparatively few people, and of those few, the passion of climbing was held among the very few. We were all grouped together as weirdos. That began to change with the growing appreciation of the outdoor experience in the general populace that took place in the sixties with, unfortunately, a lot of other stuff.

And then climbers elsewhere began to realize the potential of a place like Yosemite?

Yes. And American climbers went to Europe about that same period and did new things in the western Alps. That certainly got some attention. It showed that American techniques and equipment had something to offer. And so we started getting visits from the Continent around that time.

What routes did you do in Europe?

I made new routes up the west face of the Petit Dru [Direct Route, 1962; Superdirect, 1965], which is one of the Aiguilles around Chamonix. These were major routes; one took three or four days and the other took five days. They were necky routes; doing that sort of climbing in the French Alps, with the weather they have, is serious. But we were able to get major first ascents in the Alps, of all places, and this was a coup.

Did this create a stir?

It created some interest, and rightly so. It wasn't our superior climbing ability, it was the fact that we had certain techniques developed in Yosemite that we could apply, and we had certain equipment that they didn't have.

Putting these things together enabled us to do routes that they hadn't conceived of. But it wasn't long before they were up on that stuff. They're doing all that stuff themselves now.

Why did you want to leave Yosemite Valley and climb elsewhere?

Variety and challenge. We got to where we weren't terrified of the walls anymore. We felt that if we approached them in the right way and used our heads, we wouldn't get killed. That's the way it is in rock climbing. If you get hurt or killed, it's 100 percent your fault. You've got to take all of the blame. You can't say it was chance. It's all your decision—whether you're going to get in over your head, your paying attention or not paying attention in those crucial moments.

So one can climb pretty well under control in very hard rock climbing, but doing that in an area where the weather and rockfall and avalanches are also part of the game is a bigger challenge, and that attracted us. That's why we went to the Alps and to South America and to the Rockies and to Alaska and so forth. We had to prove to ourselves that we could do it in a tougher environment.

So the techniques you developed in Yosemite could be transferred to routes elsewhere, such as Chris Bonington's route on the south face of Annapurna in 1970?

Yes. That's why he had Tom Frost along on that climb; Tom brought that to the climb. But it's easy to overstate that. The amount of Yosemite-type climbing they did on Annapurna wasn't so great. It was still mainly slogging up a big mountain.

On smaller faces, the first real experiment took place in 1964, when Jim McCarthy, Layton Kor, Dick McCracken, and I—using a $500 gift from the American Alpine Club—drove up the Alcan Highway in a Volkswagen bug with all of our gear. We drove from the Tetons to the Northwest Territories and were flown into a place called the Cirque of the Un-climbables—which actually are climbable. We did the southeast face of Proboscis, which was almost a replica of Half Dome—1800 feet, dead vertical, and cold and windy and snowy.

That was the first expression of Yosemite-type climbing in an alpine environment. After that, you started seeing more of it. And eventually, of course, you started seeing it in the Himalaya. But you see it a lot less there, because the other problems are so great.

What are some of the problems that remain to be done in Yosemite?

I don't know if I should let them out; I'm still considering them myself. There are a couple of bizarre things that might be done—even by an old man—because they're different, nobody's thought of them. Outside of that,

I don't know; you'd have to ask the young climbers up there. It's their vision that's going to shape the future of Yosemite climbing, not mine. I'm sure there are a lot of new things to do, however, whether it's first ascents or whatever. I'm sure there are a lot of places people haven't climbed where somebody can, and I'm sure there are a lot of different ways of doing things.

Should Yosemite be kept a traditional climbing area?

Yes. My position is that sport climbing has a place and it's not in Yosemite. Unfettered sport climbing and unfettered rap-bolting are totally destructive of the adventure ethic in climbing. If we start having rap-bolting on routes that supposedly can't be done any other way, pretty quickly you're going to see bolts on routes that can be protected but only with difficulty, and then you're going to see bolts alongside perfectly usable cracks.

> " . . . *WHAT WE'RE SEEING NOW IS A COLLAPSE OF ANY ETHICAL STYLISTIC STANDARDS IN FAVOR OF GYMNASTIC PLEASURE IN CLIMBING.* "

This has been the evolution in the Alps in France, Italy, and Switzerland, and it's happening in Yosemite already. There are two instances of this happening on the Cookie Cliffs.

Some of the rap-bolters, such as Mark Chapman, are saying, "We have the same values as you and we're against placing bolts anywhere they aren't needed," but it's happening, and what are they doing about it? Nothing. They're like liberals, who don't have the backbone to stand up to the excesses of the left. It's the same way with these guys who are rap-bolters with adventure climbing credentials, who've opened the door and don't know where to set the limits. So they're responsible for creating the opportunity for the lowering of standards and everything else to come.

Whereas our generation had a clear definition of how to play the game: the way you do it counts; you avoid bolts whenever you can; any bolts placed are from a natural stance; the rock is sacred, so you don't change it, you don't chip holds. These standards guided the actions of Yosemite climbers since the forties, and what we're seeing now is a collapse of any ethical stylistic standards in favor of gymnastic pleasure in climbing.

What can be done to counteract this?

We've tried to raise the issue repeatedly. We've tried to paint those who are leaders in this area as being bad guys. I think they should be ridiculed, ostracized. In some cases the chopping of bolts is a possible alternative. But it really turns on the reactions of most climbers. So right now the battle is for the hearts and minds of the majority of climbers.

Do you think that this is something that should be settled in the climbing community?

Yes. And I think the climbing magazines have a big responsibility that they are not discharging. They want to have it both ways. They don't want to estrange the people who pay the bills, but on the other hand they are not fulfilling their responsibility to tell the truth and to support the values that got them where they are in the first place, which are the values of adventure climbing and the importance of keeping that alive in American rock climbing.

Is there a consensus on this issue yet?

No, there's no consensus whatsoever. What's essentially happened is that traditions are being overturned. They were fine the way they were. They preserved standards and ethics and the best in American adventure climbing. Then sport climbing came in and set a tone for athleticism over adventure. This is fine as far as it goes, but you have to ask, "What have we lost?" You've lost something pretty precious. You've lost adventure, something that requires courage and all those hard elements of self-control and coping with fear and discipline and judgment and all the personal growth things that you have to develop to be a successful rock climber in the old sense. You don't need to develop these qualities with bolts everywhere, and so you've lost something. Adventure rock climbing in America is seriously threatened by the sport-climbing wave.

Is Yosemite still at the cutting edge of current climbing?

Well, it depends on how you define that area. In sport climbing, definitely not; it's not a sport-climbing area—yet. And the hardest sport climbs are being done elsewhere. But if you take what I call real rock climbing, where people are doing a variety of climbing with great skill, then I think Yosemite is still one of the centers. People like Peter Croft are doing things that astound everybody in the world. I put his accomplishments above any that I've seen in rock climbing and that's going on in Yosemite. He's head and shoulders above these guys who are doing 5.14s. I don't know if he can climb 5.14 or not, and it's irrelevant because the things that he does require far more mastery of the whole person.

He's flashed 5.13s.

That's fine, but that's not the point. It's not his ability to win a climbing contest or to climb at a very high technical level, because that's not so unusual; you've got people doing that all over the world. But you don't have people soloing Astroman. You don't have people climbing El Capitan twice in twenty-four hours, and all of these various levels of mastery that he is showing, plus a character that is head and shoulders above a lot of petulance and nay-saying and faultfinding that even I'm involved in.

What have you learned from your many years of climbing?

One of the things I learned was the importance of tenacity—that hanging on and not saying die until you're really beaten causes you to win a lot of the time. I learned that if you keep trying, even if you think you're not going to make it, then that increases the chance of success enormously. And even if it doesn't increase it enormously, if it makes a marginal difference, that marginal difference is all the difference in the world.

Does this apply to the clothing industry as well?

Yes. Running a business is like a climb, only it's a very long climb. Sometimes you want to say, "We're not going to make this climb. A storm is going to come in. I know it is. So maybe we ought to start rappelling now." Instead you can say, "We can climb another pitch, and even if the storm looks certain to break and force us down, and it will be more difficult and more miserable, we will still get down okay. We can still climb another pitch, and by climbing another pitch, if the storm doesn't break, then we have a chance to go for the summit." That's the difference.

And you can apply that in business. You don't get discouraged; you steadfastly go after what you're after. That makes the difference. Not brains, knowledge, money, experience, friends, but tenacity.

That's one thing. The other is faith. You have to have faith in what you're doing. You have to have faith that a certain approach is the best one, that it's going to give you the best chance of getting what you're after. For example, I had the faith that if I devoted myself to climbing, other things would work out. I couldn't easily justify it—I couldn't say, "Well, when I get to be sixty, I will have achieved this, this, and this, which will ensure that I enter my dotage okay, financially"—but I didn't care. I just had the faith that if I devoted myself to what I loved, then everything else would take care of itself.

▲ WARREN HARDING

Why do people climb? How the hell do I know? Answers to this perennial question range from Mallory's rather facetious (I think) "Because it's there" to (again) Mallory's enigmatic "If you ask the question, there can be no answer."

Personally, I dig another version of Mallory's statement. Like, "We climb because it's there and we're mad!" How else could you explain freezing your ass off, battling heat and thirst, scaring yourself to death just to get up some rock face or mountain peak.... In some ways climbing is similar to golf. It is a game (equally absurd in its basic concept). But climbing has an element of personal danger. It's virtually impossible for a person to be injured or killed playing golf. (Well, he could starve to death trying to make it as a pro or be done in by a wife who had become a golf widow.) However, it's not unheard of for a climber to have very bad things happen to him. Conversely, it's damned rare for any climber, no matter how good he might become, to make a great deal of money from climbing. Risk your life or bodily injury for nothing? Insane.

—Warren Harding, *Downward Bound*

ONE OF THE PIONEERS of big-wall climbing in Yosemite National Park, Warren Harding, alias Batso, earned the reputation of being an "outlaw" in Yosemite Valley by his frequent use of expansion bolts and his iconoclastic attitude toward climbing, an activity he regards as essentially absurd and therefore worthy of satire. His offbeat sense of humor is best evinced in his book *Downward Bound: A Mad Guide to Rock Climbing* (1975) and his very occasional climbing journal, *Descent,* which spoofs straight-laced climbing magazines and pokes fun at the self-proclaimed "hard men" of the climbing world. Harding believes that climbing should be enjoyable: it's not something to take too seriously.

Though he delights in mocking climbers and climbing, Harding cannot be written off as a clown. In his prime he pulled off some of the most impressive climbs in the history of the Valley. On November 12, 1958, he, George Whitmore, and Wayne Merry made the first ascent of the face of El Capitan, an imposing 3000-foot granite monolith that towers over Yosemite Valley. It took them thirty-seven days spread out over a year and a half to fix the ropes, haul the hardware, and finally complete the route, which they dubbed the Nose. In all, they used 675 pitons and 125 expansion bolts, an amount of artificial aid criticized by climbers who claimed that the bolts defaced the rock. But, in fact, no other climbers at the time possessed the temerity to put up such a bold, ambitious route, and given its length and difficulty, the tactics seemed justified.

From the early 1950s to the early 1970s, Harding pushed the boundaries of what was considered humanly possible on rock walls. With doggedness and determination, he spent days, weeks, and months if necessary to establish new routes up Yosemite's sheer granite walls. In addition to his first ascent of El Cap, he pioneered such routes as the south face of Mount Watkins in 1964 with Chuck Pratt and Yvon Chouinard; the first ascent of Liberty Cap southwest face in 1969 with Galen Rowell and Joe Faint; the first ascent of the south face of Half Dome in 1970 with Galen Rowell; and the first ascent of the Dawn Wall of El Cap in 1970 with Dean Caldwell.

A short, wiry climber with incredible stamina, Harding showed that it was possible to live and work for extended periods of time on vertical or overhanging rock walls. Because of his willingness to stay committed to long, difficult routes, Harding succeeded where other climbers failed. His strength and tenacity commanded the admiration of the Valley's climbing community, but his climbing style eventually came under criticism. Some climbers felt that he placed more expansion bolts than necessary, that he sieged routes that could be done alpine style. These climbers believed that his techniques took some of the sport and adventure out of climbing.

Despite the criticism, Harding remained true to a philosophy of climbing elegant in its simplicity, namely: start from the bottom and go to the top. In other words, it doesn't matter so much *how* you get to the top, as *whether* you get to the top at all. Since Harding did most of his ascents during the early years of climbing in the Valley, such a philosophy provided all the uncertainty a climber could ask for. And indeed, it was precisely because of his ability to face up to uncertainty that he figured so prominently in the development of Yosemite as a world center of rock climbing.

Over the years, Harding has come to epitomize the climber as individualist, responsible only to himself and his climbing partners and unbounded by any external rules and regulations. It was this approach that fueled disagreements between Harding and climbers such as Royal Robbins, who called for a new style of climbing in Yosemite Valley, a style that emphasized free climbing over aid

Warren Harding. (Photo by Galen Rowell)

climbing. These differences of opinion eventually came to a head when Robbins, to protest what he considered Harding's excessive use of bolts, took the unprecedented step of erasing part of one of Harding's routes.

The controversy erupted in the fall of 1970, when Harding took aim at what he considered the ultimate climb in the Valley: the Dawn Wall of El Cap. He and Dean Caldwell began climbing on October 23, but, battered by storms, promptly fell behind schedule. On November 11, the Park Service, realizing that the two climbers had planned to be on the wall no more than fifteen days, sent a rescue team after them. Believing that they still had a chance to complete the climb, Harding and Caldwell turned down the rescue, creating a sensation in the local and national media. The two went on to finish their route and were greeted at the top by a crowd of reporters and television camera crews.

Shortly after the first ascent, Robbins, angered at the style in which Harding had completed the climb and the attendant publicity, repeated the route with Don Lauria. On this attempt Robbins brought with him some unusual gear: two cold chisels with which he intended to remove the bolts Harding had placed, thereby erasing the route. Robbins chopped the bolts on the lower end of the route, but the higher he climbed, the more he became impressed with the quality of Harding's and Caldwell's aid climbing. Eventually, he gave up on erasing the route and simply climbed it.

Both Harding and Robbins are quick to smooth over past differences, but they represent opposing philosophies of climbing that are still in conflict today. When, where, and how should expansion bolts be used? Do they scar the rock more or less than pitons and other hardware? Should routes be climbed continuously, or are fixed ropes needed on some climbs? These are just a few of the issues Harding and Robbins wrangled over, issues that still confront climbers today.

Born in Oakland, California, on June 18, 1924, Harding is a witty, self-deprecating individual with graying hair and a wicked grin who bears an uncanny resemblance to Mephistopheles. He grew up around Downieville, California, and later moved with his family to Marysville, in peach orchard country. He worked as an aircraft mechanic during World War II, after which he drifted into surveying.

As a young man Harding excelled at track and cross-country in high school. Later he turned to auto racing but discovered he didn't have the necessary dedication. Eventually he became interested in scaling rock walls and in 1952 began climbing in earnest. Shortly thereafter he went to Yosemite, where he began a long and illustrious career as a rock rat.

Harding has been married once, to Connie Frank in 1948. They divorced after several years. In the late 1960s he took up with Beryl Knauth, alias Beasto, who illustrated *Downward Bound,* and was a competent climber herself. Today Harding lives in Moab, Utah, with Alice Willie-Flomp, his companion of several years. "We're somehow still together," he says. "She threatened to murder me last night, but nothing came of it." He has no children: "I've always steered clear of that. I can barely manage myself, much less anyone else."

The interview took place in a Chinese restaurant in downtown San Francisco. Over a couple of Tsingtao beers, Harding recounted his climbing stories with characteristic wit and flair and gave his side of some of the controversies surrounding the early climbing history of the Valley.

Is climbing a ridiculous activity?

Oh, absolutely. But so is football, auto racing, skiing, warfare.

What are the benefits of climbing?

In spite of the fact that I ridicule and lampoon it, I think it's a great thing to do. It gets you out-of-doors. You have some tendency to get in great shape. You develop a great mental attitude. And for me, the greatest thing is the people I've met.

What kind of mental attitude do you develop climbing?

You just put yourself above many things. I can't articulate it very well.

Why were you so determined as a climber?

I don't know. I suspect that shows a darker side of my personality; being a small person I like to try hard. Even in backpacking, I take great delight in forging ahead of the bigger and stronger people, then putting down my pack somewhere and coming back and offering to help.

So you have a strong will?

I guess, or maybe it's stupidity. I have the uneasy feeling that that could be a factor. Or maybe it could be that it didn't seem that hard to me.

How did you first get interested in climbing?

I was always kind of a would-be Walter Mitty type. I liked to think of myself as being very heroic. When I went to work for the California Division of Highways, there was a guy who would go off on weekends climbing mountains. I thought he was nutty, but I also thought, "Maybe he'll take me with him." I started going off with him and I really got interested. I started reading things like *The White Tower* [a climbing novel by James Ramsey Ullman]. I acquired gear. One thing led to another.

And basically I was pretty good. It was about the only thing I ever was good at, although I was good at running in high school.

How old were you when you started climbing?

Twenty-eight. That's later than most people. I don't know what I did before that. I was interested in racing sports cars, but I wasn't that good a driver.

When did you first go to Yosemite?

I didn't go to Yosemite till the fall of 1953, just for a few small climbs.

What were your first impressions of the place?

Pretty damn awesome. Standing under El Cap really takes you down to size.

Who were some of the other climbers who were around back then?

Mark Powell, the Dolt [Bill Feuerer], Frank Tarver, Allen Steck, Jerry Gallwas, Don Wilson, and Royal Robbins, of course.

What was the climbing scene like?

The clubs were pretty active—the Sierra Club rock-climbing section, the Stanford Alpine Club. They'd come in groups and do things. There was a park regulation at that time that you had to sign out for these climbs, and it was required that a qualified leader from a recognized climbing club was in the party. I never joined any clubs, but I just talked my way into it.

Were there climbers who lived in the Valley permanently?

Yeah, there were quite a few who would just hang out in Camp IV and try to climb as much as they could. I wasn't quite that dedicated. I'd go off and work and come back for a period of time.

What kind of work did you do?

I started out doing survey work with the California Division of Highways, but then I moved to the Division of Architecture. They had a pretty liberal vacation policy, and I was able to get a leave of absence if I wanted to be off for a while.

In 1956 I went to Alaska and worked construction, which was even better. The pay was a lot better, and it was fairly acceptable to take off for a while.

Construction surveying is essentially what I've done ever since. I retired two or three years ago. But I've always worked. I was not a romantic climbing bum.

Was the climbing competitive back then?

It was getting to be. In the spring of 1954, Frank Tarver and I did the first ascent of the north buttress of Middle Cathedral, which was what people were vying for at that time. It was the hottest thing around. We got up that rather handily.

After that, the northwest face of Half Dome seemed to be the next step. I went up with Royal Robbins on one exploratory trip in 1956. We got a third of the way up in three to four days. The leader of the group [Don Wilson] thought we weren't moving fast enough, but Royal and I wanted to stay and go higher anyway. But it was decided that we'd go down.

I really never felt comfortable around Robbins. He seemed too intelligent, too serious. Besides that, he was a much better climber. So I hooked up with Mark Powell and Bill Feuerer. I was more compatible with Mark and Dolt. We were really serious wine-drinking buddies.

We came into the Valley in the spring of 1957 to do Half Dome, and— "Oh, look at that"—Royal and his new crew were just topping out. So being rather egomaniacal, we stomped around and said, "El Cap." We started up that, knowing that we wouldn't make it, but we'd just see how far we'd get. We got up about a thousand feet in seven days, came down, fixed ropes, and yo-yoed back and forth for a year and a half. That story is well-documented.

Why did you choose the Nose route for the first ascent of El Capitan?

Because it's the best-looking line on the whole face. To me that's very important, the look of the line. Also, it had ledges.

How many days did it take you to get up that?

Thirty-seven working days spread out over a year and a half.

Was a lot of that time spent fixing ropes?

A lot of work just fixing ropes and hauling stuff up to previous high points. The final push in November of 1958 took twelve days, but three days were spent reaching our previous high point.

So it was more like an expeditionary climb?

Definitely. We even called the ledges camps—Camp I, Camp II, et cetera.

Were you criticized for taking such an approach?

Oh, yeah. There's always somebody who'll find something wrong with what you're doing. But we just did what we did.

And they criticized you because you used too many bolts?

People who had never been up there said it just sounded like a lot of bolts. I don't know how anyone would know unless they'd been there. Going up in 1989 I noticed that there were a hell of a lot more bolts than we ever put in.

You couldn't have climbing without controversy, but I don't enter into these things, except to do what I do. If somebody doesn't like it, the hell with them.

What effect did this climb have on rock climbing in Yosemite Valley?

The first ascent of the Nose had a big effect. It was a very significant step in popularizing climbing in Yosemite. Watching climbers became an important feature. A lot of people come there just to watch climbing, especially on El Cap—there are always half a dozen parties on El Cap. People bring spotting scopes.

When did you first meet Royal Robbins?

That was back in 1952. Royal and I did a climb on Tahquitz Rock and we got along fine. He was just starting out, but was absolutely brilliant. He was so much better than anybody else. But as I say, personality-wise we were so far apart. He

> *"IF SOMEBODY DOESN'T LIKE IT, THE HELL WITH THEM."*

liked to play chess and do intelligent things, and I was a serious drinker and nonthinker. So it's just as simple as that. Different personalities.

What were his strengths as a climber?

He was strong. He tried hard. And he was smart, very smart.

Were you the two leaders in Yosemite?

Two of the leaders. Layton Kor from Colorado did some smashing things in the sixties. Royal was definitely the leader in his group. The others in his group were Tom Frost, Chuck Pratt, Joe Fitschen, Mike Sherrick.

How was your group different from Robbins's?

For one thing, I seemed to be about ten years older than everybody else, and maybe they [Robbins's group] were just going through some idealistic phase. There was instant criticism of my using of fixed ropes on the Nose, even though some of these people did the same thing to a lesser degree on other climbs. They thought I was using too many bolts, and this and that.

To succinctly answer your question, I was more of an individualist, while they had a stronger herd instinct. I did what I felt was right—right for me. If it wasn't right for somebody else, screw 'em—as long as I wasn't spray-painting the rock or anything that bad. It's a matter of individualism over collective thinking.

They seemed to have a real philosophy of climbing. Did you have one too?

Yeah, I just wanted to get up. It wasn't particularly important how I did it. In the old days it was, "Can I do it at all?" It wasn't, "How well?"

Did your philosophy of climbing differ from Royal Robbins's?

Definitely. He wanted to excel in everything he did. I didn't give a damn whether I was considered good or not; I just wanted to climb. It's different strokes for different folks. But I'd never condemn him for his efforts.

Was there a rivalry between you?

Some rivalry did develop when we took a shot at El Cap to get a foot in the door. We got about a third of the way up.

So there was a competition for routes?

Oh, absolutely. But nobody went up and pulled our ropes down, or anything like that, even though they didn't agree with what we were doing and thought it was unethical. Everyone was still pretty much of a gentleman in those days.

When you decided to climb something, how did you go about scouting it out?

Sometimes I'd bring my surveying transit up and scope the thing out. In the case of the Dawn Wall, Dean Caldwell made a photographic strip map of $8^1/2$-by-11 glossies over the projected route so that we could keep track of where we were. It's entirely possible to get lost. I'd scope it out, see what was there, and think about what I'd need to get up this utterly blank section. "Better bring a lot of drills. If it looks possible to climb it free, we'll try that too."

How did you decide which parts would be free climbing or aid climbing?

On most of the things I've gotten into there's been very little free climbing, even for my level of ability, which in those days was 5.8 at best. Most of it was nailing [aid climbing]. This was before nuts were even invented or popularized. I'd just go, ready for anything, because I'd feel downright silly getting partway up and, "Oh, gee, we don't have this size of piton. Oh, we don't have any more bolts."

Some people consider that unsporting or lacking in adventure. Again, I say, "You do it your way and I'll do it mine."

Do you think that these disagreements represented a conflict between generations?

No. That's been part of climbing as long as the British climber Frank Smythe claimed he'd rather die than use a piton. Well, it came to that one day. He did use the piton. I'm sure he was scarred forever. So I just don't take anything that seriously.

Did you have to get psyched up for routes like the Dawn Wall of El Capitan?

We had to get sobered up. I don't get psyched up. Sobered up—yeah.

Were you and your buddies heavy drinkers?

Oh, absolutely. We had a group who had sports cars. We loved to go screaming around, wearing out tires, going to wineries in the Napa Valley. Drinking was very much a part of the thing.

How did you decide on the Dawn Wall route?

Glen Denny and I went out one day in 1970 armed with a jug of wine looking for what we thought would be the ultimate rock climb in the Valley. We were rather pompous assholes. We settled on the area between the Nose and the North American Wall. Our idea of the route differed from what other people had been looking at; they wanted to go up the right side of El Cap Towers. I wanted to keep this totally separate from anything on the Nose.

Glen never got on it, and I had this accident in the fall of 1969. My leg was demolished when I blundered out into a line of traffic and this pickup caught me. I really couldn't handle my construction job, so I was working in a sports shop in the Valley.

I met Dean Caldwell, who'd just come back from South America. We were instant drinking buddies and bullshitters. He had a bad ankle, so he couldn't climb, and neither could I; so we knew we were safe. But we went ahead and developed special equipment like haul bags for this Dawn Wall thing. Finally, my job was over, and in about mid-October we got on the rocks.

Were you looking for a particular line?

No, just an area. It [the Dawn Wall route] took off with cracks leaning up this way, and from our map we saw that just short of this dark water streak we'd want to turn left and go out across a blank area to a dihedral system that went straight up to the top. We just assumed that there'd be a good crack pattern in the back. That didn't prove to be the case, but we were there, so we kept going. That's one of the reasons it took as long as it did.

We got all kinds of flack on this—"No climb should take that long." Well, it did for us.

It was just a little hard-core elite group that seemed to suffer from the delusion that they were the voice of all climbers. This just wasn't true. The majority of climbers I meet seem to think, "Hey, Harding, you did a good job." So I don't feel that these people particularly know what they're talking about. I'm not impressed with anyone, to the extent that they're going to tell me, "Now, here's how it are, Harding." I figure my mind's just as good as anyone's.

How long did it take you to climb the Dawn Wall?

Twenty-seven days.

Did you plan to spend that much time doing it?

We had planned for an absolute maximum of fifteen days. By day fifteen we were less than halfway up. But we could communicate quite well by notes and shouting. We let it be known that we thought we could do it. So we kept going. But totally unbeknownst to us, the Park Service had been worrying. The Park Service had actually consulted some medical people, wondering if anybody who had been on a rock wall for twenty days would still be in mental shape to conduct their own affairs. And the consensus seemed to be, "Maybe not." So they went ahead and launched this rescue, which we just flatly turned down. We didn't have anything to do with that.

Did the rescue group actually climb down to the ledge where you were?

No. On day twenty, Dean and I reached a nice ledge about four feet wide and eight or ten feet long. We named it the Wine Tower, since we were semisponsored by the Christian Brothers Winery—they gave us wine to take. When we reached this ledge, we had Christian Brothers brandy with us, and we also had a nice bottle of Cabernet Sauvignon and a crystal glass. We were running low on food, but we still had a little salami, cheese, bread. We were having kind of a party there, and we heard this voice from below, and I thought it sounded familiar. It turned out to be TM Herbert.

He yelled, "What the hell are you doing up there?"

"We're climbing. What are you doing?"

"We've come to rescue you."

"What?"

We'd noticed helicopters and fixed-winged planes flying around in increasing numbers during the last few days. It came as no surprise that something big was up. So right away Dean and I started yelling, "No—we're not going to be rescued." Looking up, we could see ropes being lowered. With a lot of screaming and shouting we finally got them to knock that off.

So you obviously weren't much interested in giving up on the climb.

Oh, God, no. If you put that much effort into something and you're feeling great, you're not going to give it up.

And it took you seven more days to get to the top?

Yeah, it was quite an experience.

You must have been very low on food.

We'd ration very stringently. We'd split a can of sardines for a whole day's meal. Practically nothing. Water wasn't a problem, though. We still had half a gallon when we got to the top. We'd run out of brandy. It was so good in our bivvies. We'd just take little tiny slurps. We made one fifth last twenty-five days.

Did you get delirious from lack of food?

Naw, we never had any problem. When we got up I felt great.

Did you realize that there were television cameras and reporters waiting at the top?

Not at first. Dean led the last long rivet pitch—a full pitch of rivets and bolts—and it put him about sixty feet below the rim. Then there was a series of nail-up overhangs. By this time there were all kinds of people hanging over, looking. They said, "Hey Dean, don't come up tonight." It was getting late in the day when he got there anyway.

And he said, "Why not?"

"There's a hell of a lot of people up here and it would really screw up their television cameras."

That kind of prepared us for what was at the top. The next day I led the last little sixty-foot nail-up. I was shocked when I saw what was up there. It was a real circus. All the media people were there asking questions. Then they got their stuff and headed out to phone in their stories. And a helicopter picked up their film.

After they left, we had a hell of a party with the forty or so people who'd come in. I ate and drank too much and was barely able to make the hike out. Beryl Knauth was there and we cracked open a bottle of brandy and started walking down the trail. We were both kind of crocked. We got somewhere and tipped over—we had real heavy packs. I didn't have sense enough to slip my arms out of the pack straps. We were just lying there on the trail. People came back looking for us. Fortunately we were only a couple of hundred yards from the roadhead. So technically I was rescued.

Did your ascent of the Dawn Wall cause a lot of friction with Robbins?

He was definitely miffed that Caldwell and I got on the Dawn Wall ahead of him. He somehow had come to believe that that was his area. When he found out that we were up there, he got very upset. I don't know what goes on in his mind—it's such a powerful mind that who knows?—but he just decided that he had to erase the route by going up and chopping out all the rivets and bolts, which some people seemed to think were excessive. I don't know how they thought these were excessive; they weren't there.

Did this bother you?

No, I thought it was funny. But what he did on the Dawn Wall was utterly stupid, and does he ever know it. It's just different personalities, and I don't think there's any way of saying who's right and who's wrong. Since then, the route has been put back together. It's considered one of the standard El Cap routes.

How was Yosemite important to the development of rock climbing elsewhere?

For a long time it set the standard for rock-climbing development, both with aid and free climbing. It still may, technique-wise, but the best rock climbing now has gone on in the higher elevations and the Himalaya—the real heavy-duty, serious stuff. But I imagine the people doing that would want to get very good in Yosemite first.

Do you consider Yosemite the rock-climbing center of the world?

Yeah, if there is one. It's like a pilgrimage to go there. Everybody wants to climb El Cap because it's the most prominent thing, and with the equipment and general techniques available today, almost anyone can do it.

Does that surprise you?

Not really. It's like comparing the lap speeds at Indianapolis in 1954 with what they're doing today.

What do you think of what's happening now in climbing?

It's absolutely amazing, and whether it's good or bad, I just get the feeling that these people don't have as much fun. There's a superemphasis on high-level free climbing and speed. It's almost like everyone's trying to be an Olympic athlete.

Are you against bolting on rappel?

No, but it puts the climb in a different category, and not a very high level one. To carry it to extremes, it would be like retro-bolting the Nose. That's essentially what these guys [Todd Skinner and Paul Piana] did on the Salathé Wall. They spent about a year checking out every pitch and putting in what protection was necessary. It seems like an awful lot of work for what they accomplished [the first free ascent of Salathé].

Do think that there's a progression, a development, in climbing?

No doubt about it, but it's like anything. The four-minute mile is down to what now? Everything improves, numerically speaking anyway.

How does that apply to Yosemite?

The climbing is being done all free. I don't particularly think of this free-soloing as necessarily an improvement. These guys have got so little to gain and so much to lose. If that makes them feel superimportant or something, fine; it doesn't matter to me.

Have you ever taken a serious fall?

In thirty years of climbing I've taken six leader falls. On a couple of them I managed to grab a rope and have it burn through my fingers, and in another case a rope looped through some fingers and squished them. Once I got hit on the head with a rock on Leaning Tower. As it turned out, except for the scalp wound, I wasn't hurt at all. The doctor said, "You might have brain damage, but with you it's difficult to tell."

So you've been lucky in avoiding serious accidents.

I've been very fortunate. I've had a couple of what I call glitches—where I've screwed up in my rope management—which could have been disastrous. But I was having a good day, and nothing happened.

About the weirdest thing that ever happened to me occurred on the first ascent of the Nose. We were camping, if you could have called it that, on Sickle Ledge. We'd been working up above, and we came back and I flopped into my little spot. I was really beat. I thought, "I'll lie here for a few minutes and then I'll get myself into the bivouac bag."

But I fell asleep. I was dreaming that I was there [on Sickle Ledge] and that I was also slipping over the edge. It was a real narrow thing. In the dream I thought, "No problem, I'm anchored. I'll just slip on over [the edge] and the anchor will catch me."

All of a sudden I woke with this terrible start: I was slipping over and was not anchored. I think that's possibly the weirdest thing that's ever happened to me.

Did it bother you to be up on those rock walls?

No. I feel really comfortable up there. I had to get used to it, but I was not acrophobic, because I became accustomed to it very quickly. You have to get used to heights or you're not a happy camper. I've heard of a few climbers who never did succeed in overcoming this and they were not happy. That's a dreadful feeling.

Now that you're retired, what do you do for recreation?

I drink a lot; I'm a pseudo-alki. I watch soap operas. I write. I'm writing a climbing soap opera. I've got four episodes written.

I go out in the La Sal Mountains outside of town and traipse around. I sometimes go out for a full day's walk. I like to get up into the hills and rocks, picking up trails, or going cross-country to join up sections of trail.

Are you still climbing?

In November of 1989 I went to Yosemite to do the 31st anniversary climb of the Nose and basically jumared up. I really haven't done much climbing in ten years. I keep thinking that I'll get back into it, but I don't know whether that's true or not. I'm reverting back to being a relaxed mountaineer type, which basically I've always been. I don't have to be doing a world-class performance to enjoy myself. It's nice just to be in the mountains.

▲ CHRIS BONINGTON

*In organizing a big expedition to Annapurna or Everest,
one sometimes loses the stark simplicity and romanticism of
mountaineering, becoming involved in the maze of finance,
public relations, commercial exploitation. Yet there is a fascination in this—at least there is to me. This also is a game—to be
played as a game. It is serious; it is exacting. There are more
pitfalls than on any mountains, but surmounting these pitfalls
has its own special thrill and challenge. And in the end you come
back to the mountain.*

—Chris Bonington, *The Next Horizon*

I N THE DIFFICULT and dangerous game of expeditionary mountaineering, few
climbers have proved as proficient as Chris Bonington. One of the most
celebrated expedition leaders of the post–World War II period, the ebullient
Englishman brought superb technical climbing ability and a genius for organization to bear on some of the most technically demanding faces ever attempted in
the Himalaya. His expeditions to the south face of Annapurna in 1970 and the
southwest face of Everest in 1975 stand out as some of the most formidable
mountaineering achievements in history.

Born in Hampstead, England, in 1934, Bonington grew up as the only child
in a one-parent family, his parents having divorced shortly after his birth. A quiet,
shy, adventurous boy, he learned to be self-sufficient while his mother was away
during the day working as a copywriter in an advertising firm. At school he was
a conscientious student, attending the University College School in London and
the Royal Military Academy at Sandhurst, where he became fascinated with
military history.

During his summer holidays in the Wicklow Hills of Ireland and Snowdonia
in Wales, he got his first glimpse of mountain scenery and began to dream of being
a climber. He started rock climbing at sixteen and progressed rapidly, reaching the
top of the existing grade [Extreme, 5.9] while still in his teens.

Chris Bonington. (Photo by David Breashers)

After graduating from Sandhurst, he was commissioned in the Royal Tank Regiment in 1956. He spent three years in northern Germany commanding a tank crew and then two years at the Army Outward Bound School as a mountaineering instructor. It was during this period that he first climbed in the Alps, making the first British ascent of the southwest pillar of the Petit Dru in 1958 with Hamish MacInnes.

In 1960 he wangled an invitation to accompany the army's British-Indian-Nepalese Services Expedition to Annapurna II (26,041 feet) and reached the summit, further boosting his confidence. Expedition leader Jimmy Roberts served as a role model for Bonington, demonstrating how to integrate climbers into an effective team and how to organize the logistics so that everything ran smoothly and efficiently. Bonington learned much from Roberts that he would later apply on his own expeditions.

After returning to Europe, Bonington continued to push the grade. In 1961, he, Don Whillans, Ian Clough, and Jan Djuclosz grabbed the first ascent of the central pillar of Frêney on the south side of Mont Blanc, one of the most sought-after climbs in the Alps at that time.

Finding his army career too confining, he left in 1961 to join Unilever Ltd. as a management trainee, but after nine months of selling margarine he realized that he could never reconcile a conventional career with his love for mountaineering. He decided to try to scratch out a living as a professional climber and in 1962 got some sponsorship at least partly as a result of completing the first British ascent of the north wall of the Eiger.

After several years of working as a photojournalist and doing shorter routes, Bonington decided to try for something bigger. In 1968 he began to organize an expedition to the imposing south face of Annapurna. At that time no major Himalayan wall had been climbed, and tackling steep rock and ice on a 12,000-foot face at that altitude was a step into the unknown. Bonington assembled a strong, cohesive team for the attempt and put his army experience to use in planning the logistics of the climb. The team succeeded in putting Dougal Haston and Don Whillans on the summit on May 27, 1970.

Buoyed by the success of the Annapurna expedition, Bonington turned his attention to an even more intimidating route, the southwest face of Everest. His 1972 expedition was beaten back by high winds and bone-chilling cold, but Bonington didn't give up on the route. He returned to England and made preparations for another attempt in 1975. This time Doug Scott, Dougal Haston, Peter Boardman, and the Sherpa Pertemba reached the summit.

Two years later, he and Doug Scott joined forces again to make the first ascent of the Ogre in the Karakoram Himalaya. After reaching the summit, Scott skated off some verglass and broke both legs at the ankles, turning what had been a enjoyable expedition into a survival epic. In helping Scott descend, Bonington cracked some ribs and had to endure excruciating pain the rest of the way out.

Aided by Mo Anthoine and Clive Rowland, the injured pair descended through a blizzard and managed to reach base camp, where, starving and exhausted, they discovered their companions had given them up for dead and had abandoned the camp. The four of them stumbled back down the mountain, eventually catching up with their astonished friends.

In 1978, Bonington led a small team to attempt the previously unclimbed west ridge of K2. The group made good progress until Nick Estcourt, one of Bonington's best friends, was killed by a huge avalanche that swept across their route. After Estcourt's death, the team members abandoned the expedition.

When China opened up its mountains to Westerners, Bonington wasted no time in applying for a permit. In 1980 he made a reconnaissance of Mount Kongur, a remote, unclimbed mountain in the western Xinjiang Province. He returned the following year with Peter Boardman, Joe Tasker, and Alan Rouse to climb the peak.

In 1982, he, Peter Boardman, Joe Tasker, and Dick Renshaw attempted the unclimbed northeast ridge of Everest. Renshaw retreated after suffering a mild stroke, and Bonington decided that since he was moving much slower than Boardman and Tasker, they should go for the top on their own. They disappeared shortly thereafter, marring what up until then had been one of Bonington's happiest expeditions.

In 1983, Bonington set his sights on a lower but technically more difficult objective, the west summit of Shivling (21,330 feet) in the Gangotri Himalaya in India. He and Jim Fotheringham made a five-day, alpine-style ascent of the peak. Later that same year, Bonington traveled to Antarctica with an American team to climb Mount Vinson. Battling subzero temperatures and fifty-mile-per-hour winds, he reached the summit by himself, the other members of the team having turned back. A few days later he helped support his companions in their successful attempt.

In 1985, Bonington was invited to join the Norwegian expedition to Everest. Despite a spontaneous promise to his wife, Wendy, that he would never attempt Everest again, the lure of the world's highest peak proved too great. After gaining her approval he accepted the invitation and later that year fulfilled a lifetime's ambition when he set foot on the top of the world.

It would have been understandable if, after summiting on Everest, Bonington had retired from the sport, but his love of climbing continued to lead him even further afield. In 1988 he led an expedition to Menlungtse (23,450 feet), one of the most beautiful and technically difficult unclimbed peaks in the world, and claimed the first ascent of its west peak.

In 1991 Bonington sailed to Greenland with Robin Knox Johnstone to climb in the Lemon Mountains. In 1992 he co-led an Indian-British expedition to Panch Chuli II (22,600 feet) in the Kumaon Himalaya, teaming up with Graham Little to make the first ascent of the peak's west ridge. Later on the same trip, Stephen Venables badly broke his leg in a rappelling accident, and on the way to get help, Bonington took a 400-foot tumble on steep snow, fortunately suffering no injuries. He pressed on to Madkot, where he organized a rescue that soon helicoptered Venables out. Despite the close call, Bonington has continued to climb, planning trips to Greenland, the Caucasus, and other areas of the world.

Today, Bonington lives in the Lake District of northern England, where he is within an hour's striking distance of a number of crags. He and Wendy share a beautiful Beatrix Potter–like cottage surrounded by rolling hills and green pastures dotted with sheep. The Boningtons were married in 1961 and have two sons, Daniel and Rupert. Since 1962 the Boningtons have both made their living doing freelance work—Chris as a writer, photographer, and mountaineer, and Wendy as a teacher of the Alexander technique.

The cottage's rustic exterior gives little indication of its high-tech interior, which is a kind of company headquarters for Bonington Ltd. and contains computers, elaborate electronic gadgetry, an extensive slide library, and a book-lined study, where the interview took place on a sunny Sunday morning in mid-August. Although an exceedingly gracious and hospitable man, Bonington was clearly more interested in actually going climbing than in talking about it and occasionally darted a look out the window to make sure that the unpredictable English weather wouldn't ruin his chances of getting in a couple of routes that day. A tall and sturdy fellow with bright blue eyes, a gray-brown beard, and an energetic, irrepressible manner, Bonington clearly will never be content with his elder statesman status in climbing but will always be avid for new routes, new climbs, new challenges. Rather than looking back on a long and illustrious career, he will always have his eye firmly fixed on the future.

Was your military background helpful in organizing expeditions?

Definitely. In the Royal Armoured Corps I was in charge of a tank crew, and I very quickly learned that if I was an autocratic leader and depended on the pips on my shoulder, I got very little out of my men. A tank crew is very much like four people on a rope—you're confined in the little tank and you're dependent on getting the three people under your command to do what you want them to do. In other words, the effective military leader is someone who says, "Right, I'm going to put my military rank into a box and lock it away, and I'm going to capture the respect of the people under me purely out of myself." And it's only when the leader has done that that he can get the best out of his crew.

Did being a respected climber in your own right make it easier to lead expeditions?

Yes. On the big expeditions that I led in the seventies, I was at the peak of my own climbing career. There was no doubt that in 1975 Dougal Haston and Doug Scott were stronger, but I was right behind them, and I was probably stronger than most of the other members of the team. So it was very much a peer group. You don't want to lead an expedition from base camp; the Herrligkoffer [German expedition leader] style of leadership doesn't work. You want to be right behind the lead climbers.

On an alpine-style expedition, say as on Kongur, I was in theory the climbing leader, but there the decisions were totally by consensus, and the initiative very often came from Pete Boardman or Joe Tasker. You need someone who is actually going to conduct the discussion, and I was, if you like, the chairman figure within that group, and to do that I needed to keep up.

Did you find it hard to subordinate your desire to summit on Everest or Annapurna to your duties as expedition leader?

No. Because if you've conceived of a plan and you're totally committed to it, the success of the concept as a whole is actually bigger than your reaching the summit.

Isn't it quite difficult to think in those terms?

No, I've never found it remotely difficult. Both on Annapurna and on Everest, I felt that the important thing was for the expedition as a whole to succeed. On both climbs I phased myself in for a second or a third summit attempt, and in both instances circumstances made it impossible.

On Annapurna south face, Ian Clough and I went up to join Don Whillans and Dougal Haston for the first push to the summit, and then we were hit by a storm. It was obvious that Don and Dougal were a stronger pair, so Ian and I just dropped back into support once again. So it's being realistic about yourself and, much more importantly, saying, "This expedition is important. I want to make it work. And therefore I will do what is most likely to make this thing succeed."

Do you think your expeditions were successful because you were able to get the members to think in those terms?

Yes, I think so, and because I was able to use the people effectively. Dougal, for instance, wanted to get to the top of that mountain, and he was only happy in that position. Nick Estcourt, say, was the kind of person who was prepared to adopt a support role. So I would use people in the most effective way. And if your fellow team members recognize that you, the leader, are making decisions that are for the good of the team as a whole and not for the good of you personally, then you've got the moral high ground.

For instance, on the 1972 [Everest] trip, Mick Burke and Doug Scott hit real problems at the foot of the rock band and hadn't been making much progress. I wanted Dougal and Hamish MacInnes to finish the job off, but Mick and Doug felt this was their bit of the climb. We had a long argument/ discussion. And I was able eventually to get them to let Dougal and Hamish have a go because I wasn't arguing for myself, I was arguing for the group as a whole. So it was much easier for both Doug and Mick to accept.

How did you get started climbing?

I took up climbing when I was sixteen because it sounded like an exciting, adventurous thing to do. I found the sheer physical sensation of climbing immensely satisfying, and I was a natural from the word go.

Why were you a natural?

I was light, agile, and progressed very fast. Within the first year I did my first Extreme, which was very close to the top of the existing grade. And I was doing Joe Brown routes within two years. I relied on technique rather than strength and I'd come unstuck when I got into real overhanging situations where I would need a lot of arm strength, which I've never had.

Who taught you to climb?

I was, to a degree, self-taught. I got a friend of the family to take me to Harrison Rocks [a sandstone outcrop near London]. And later he arranged with his friend Tom Blackburn to take me climbing in Wales. Tom wasn't a good climber, so I had to lead him up things. When Tom went home I met up with an old schoolmaster, who took me under his wing. He taught me the basics of rope management and used me to lead his schoolboys up routes. So I was leading from the word go. The first Very Severe [5.5–5.6] I ever climbed was one I led, which is a very healthy way to go. You're very lucky if you're shown the absolute basics of climbing and then find out the rest for yourself.

Who were some of your early climbing partners?

I did some of my best early rock routes with Geoff Francis. We went off to Scotland together and climbed a lot in Wales. When I went to Sandhurst I got to know Mike Thompson, who is one of my oldest friends. We did a lot of new routes together in the Lake District. Mike and Geoff and I were involved in opening up the Avon Gorge. Then in 1960 I climbed with Tom Patey, who of course was one of the great characters of climbing. I had one of the best climbing holidays I've ever had in Scotland with him. We put up ten new routes in ten days.

And I bumped into Hamish MacInnes purely by accident. I went up to Scotland for my first winter climbing in 1953 and Hamish was there at the hut. He was already very much an established climber in Scotland. We did the first winter ascent of Raven's Gully. I was very much taken up by Hamish, and from that time on we have climbed together over the years.

How did the routes of your generation differ from those previously done?

The difference was actually in technology. In the prewar period, you had only a hemp rope and mimimal protection. The average climber took along only a couple of slings with a couple of carabiners. So you only had about two running belays on any pitch. And immediately after the war you had the introduction of nylon rope and thin nylon slings, which you could put around small flakes of rock. And then very quickly people saw that you could slot pebbles into cracks. And that was the precursor of the nut. With this protection, you could fall off with slightly greater sanguinity, and so the standard was pushed up because of that.

> "SO WE TRIED
> A NEW ROUTE ON IT.
> IT WAS A BASTARD.
> IT WAS DIFFICULT.
> IT WAS GREAT."

The hardest prewar routes in the Lake District—Eagle Front and so on—were Very Severes. And then immediately after the war the Extreme rating came in. There wasn't a huge jump in standards, but there was a significant difference in steepness. And then Joe Brown and Don Whillans came along and pushed the standard. They were the major innovators of that postwar explosion. They were going into places never thought possible. They were both geniuses at climbing.

When did you start going to the Alps?

In 1957 I arranged to meet Hamish there. He was much more experienced than I was and so he accentuated my progress. We went to the north wall of the Eiger, but the moment I saw it I knew that it was way out of my league. So we went to Chamonix. We were originally going to do the Walker Spur of the Grandes Jorasses, which in 1957 hadn't had a British ascent. But the weather was bad, and then Hamish noticed the Aiguille de Tacul, which is on the other side of the Leschaux Glacier. He said, "Let's climb that." So we tried a new route on it. It was a bastard. It was difficult. It was great. So my first route in the Alps was a new route.

Did climbing in the Alps prepare you for the Himalaya?

Yes. That was the natural preparation. In 1960 I had the first opportunity of going to the Himalaya, to Annapurna II. And then because of my Alpine background and reputation and what I'd done in the Himalaya, Don Whillans invited me to go on the Nuptse expedition. So that's how my Himalayan climbing started.

Did you learn a lot on those two early expeditions?

Yes, an immense amount. On Annapurna II, Jimmy Roberts was a very good expedition leader. A military approach to expeditioning is quite a sound one, not from the military discipline side, but from an awareness of logistics. Climbing a mountain and fighting a war are very similar. Your success in climbing a mountain depends on having the supplies in the right place at the right time. Even if you're on an alpine-style push, having the right amount of supplies with you and rationing them out correctly is what helps you.

And having a team working together in an integrated way is important. Jimmy Roberts knew how to integrate the Sherpas and how to integrate the climbers, and I learned an immense amount from that.

And Nuptse was years ahead of its time; it was a very steep, technical climb. There we had very little unity amongst ourselves; we were arguing like hell most of the time. And yet somehow, at the end of the day, all of us managed to subordinate our boisterous egos, managed to work together, and we climbed the mountain as a result.

So Jimmy Roberts taught you a lot about leading expeditions?

Definitely. And I learned from Nuptse that you need a structure within an expedition. We climbed the mountain, but I don't think any of us were totally happy with the achievement because there had been so much backbiting. If you can work together harmoniously, you end up enjoying the experience a lot more and you're more likely to succeed.

So certain elements of military strategy apply to climbing?

Yes, if you can forget the war-mongering side of it. And the vast difference is that in war people are pushed to take risks that they might not want to take. In climbing people choose to take risks. If you're an expedition leader and you ask someone to do something, and if that person says, "No, I think it's too dangerous," you must accept that absolutely. There's no question of either persuading him or despising him for not wanting to do something he feels is too dangerous. Climbing is a game; there's no point in climbing a mountain except for your own personal satisfaction and your group satisfaction.

The leader's job is to create a situation where everyone can work harmoniously to achieve their own personal expectations. The leader's role is to enable that group to achieve its own focus. The leader's role is not to impose his will onto the group.

So a climb should be organized like a democracy rather than a dictatorship?

It's not a democracy in the sense that everything is put to the vote. I don't think that works in a large, siege-style expedition where apart from everything else you have people scattered in different camps up the mountain.

But I would talk to a lot of people within the group so that I got a general feel for the consensus, then make a plan, submit that plan to the group, ask for comments, and if I got good suggestions I would incorporate them into my plan. I would therefore work within the consensus but would not have a formal vote at every stage of the expedition. In a group of four or so, it's different, and the leader becomes the chairman of the group. You reach decisions by discussion in a completely democratic way.

On the other hand, if you come to an absolutely fundamental question on a big expedition like K2, when Nick Estcourt had died, and it was a decision whether to go on with the expedition or not, every single individual has the right to have a say in what we did; so we did that with a democratic vote. I was in favor of going on, and so was Peter Boardman, but everyone else wanted to call the expedition off; so the right decision was to call the expedition off.

So it depends on the circumstances?

It depends, yes. As with life, it's very dangerous to have fixed rules. But as a general trend, I think an organization needs to work within the consensus of the group and the leader's role is to interpret the consensus. However brilliant the leader's plan, if the group doesn't think it's a good plan, it's not going to work. It's also important that the group be involved in the discussion and in the decision-making process. But this is done in an informal way, rather than having a vote at every stage, which some expeditions do. They have the complete democratic process; they sit down and discuss every decision. And the danger of that is that you spend most of the expedition sitting around in a circle talking and you don't climb the mountain.

So your expeditions weren't organized according to a strict military chain of command?

No, definitely not. And at the end of the day in the military, the officer can say, "Right, I am the officer. I have been appointed from on high. My word goes." The leader of an expedition can never do that because you've only got the leadership of that expedition as long as you have the actual acceptance of the group. You're as dependent on the group as they are on you.

What was the first expedition that you led?

Annapurna south face.

How did you come to be leader of that climb?

It was really by default. I'd never really thought of myself as a leader or a particularly good organizer; I was a failed lieutenant in the army. We'd all been talking about going off to the Himalaya together, but nobody ever did anything. I hadn't been on an expedition since 1961 and it was now 1968. I'd gotten fed up with my photojournalism and I wanted to get back into expeditioning.

Originally we were to go to Alaska and it was going to be Dougal, Nick, Martin Boysen, and myself. The Himalaya had been closed. And then we learned that the Himalaya had opened up. And Dennis Gray showed me this photograph of the south face of Annapurna, and I thought, "That would be a lovely thing to climb."

So we changed our objective, added more people, and started looking for sponsorship. And I plunged into expedition organization and leadership simply because I was the person who was prepared to grasp the hot iron and make it happen.

Did you have a lot of organizational ability?

I think I had that latently, and then my experience in the army and on photojournalistic trips helped. But I made a lot of mistakes on the south face of Annapurna. In a way, sitting down and writing a book is a very good discipline. If you try and write an honest book, then you have to do some self-analysis. After Annapurna south face I was thinking, "Terrific. We were successful. We climbed the mountain." But then I went back and read other people's diaries and everything else. I saw the mistakes I made. And then, having seen those mistakes, I made many fewer mistakes in 1972 on the southwest face of Everest. And in 1975 I made even fewer.

What were some of the mistakes you made on Annapurna?

I spent too much time out in front. And because I was unsure of myself, I allowed myself to be swayed too easily into changing plans. One of the critical times was when Tom Frost and Mick Burke were out in front, making heavy weather of it. Don, Dougal, and I were sitting watching them through the binoculars, saying, "Why the hell are they taking so long?" It's very easy to think the people out front are taking a long time while you're sitting in base camp. And then Dougal proposed that he and Don go straight up. Without thinking of the consequences, I said, "Yes, sure. Move straight up." And then all hell broke loose over the radio because Nick and Martin felt they'd been overridden, and Mick and Tom felt that they'd been overridden. I changed something in midstream that shouldn't have been changed. By holding back it might have slowed things up a day, but it wouldn't have mattered, and the transition would have been smoother. So that was a mistake on my part, and at the end of the day it came out right, but there was a row over the radio that was unnecessary.

On Everest in 1972, I thought I'd give everyone clear roles so that they would know what they had to do, could accept it early on, and then could get on with it. And so, for instance, Nick and Dave Bathgate had the job of making the route across to the foot of the right hand of the rock band. Doug and Mick had the job of actually climbing the rock band. And Hamish and Dougal were going to make the first summit bid. And the problem there was that things never go like that, but having given Doug and Mick the rock band, they became territorial about it. And so I had a snag.

In 1975 I was very careful to keep things closer to my chest and to give people very short-term objectives. I would give, say, Doug and Mick the job of putting the route out to Camp III. Nick and Tut Braithwaite had the job of putting the route out to Camp IV. Dougal and Hamish had the job of putting the route out to Camp V. And what might happen after that, I didn't worry about. There was no point in thinking about it. You try to plan too far, then you get into problems of disappointing people.

And on all three expeditions, there was always a very strong caucus of people who had been with me before. They had learned what to expect from me, and I'd learned what to expect from them; so we had a pattern, a *modus vivendi* going, which was important.

And they were your friends too.

Yes. There was a strong element of friendship, which is important, even where sometimes there was an element of conflict. You get this with all climbing relationships, the Brown/Whillans partnership finally foundered because of this; Joe Tasker and Pete Boardman were very, very close partners, but there were signs that that partnership had reached a conclusion, and probably they'd have remained good friends but gone off to do different things. And certainly after the Ogre, there were stresses between Doug and I because Doug is a powerful leader himself and has a different style of leadership from mine. There was conflict beginning to grow on the K2 expedition between the two of us, simply because he wanted to mold the group one way and I was molding the group another way. In fact, K2 was the last expedition we were on together, and yet we have maintained the friendship and a very warm mutual respect. But there was a time when Doug needed space to develop his own leadership. He has developed an expedition style that is very successful for him.

Route climbed by Bonington on the South Face of Annapurna, 1970.
(Photo by James Roberts; Diadem Archives)

How would you characterize the differences between your style and his?

Doug likes to work on a system where in theory everyone does their own thing and in practice everyone does what Doug wants them to do. I think, interestingly enough, Doug's style is more centralist than mine. I like to have a structured expedition that enables the consensus to come out. By having a clear-cut plan, and giving people jobs and roles, and leaving them to get on with that role, you have a system of delegation that works for me. And the kind of people who work well with me—for instance, Joe and Pete—are also the kind of people who like that system. They also were goal-oriented and had a very structured way of doing things, and so we climbed very happily together.

But Doug likes to do things himself. Most of the organization of his trips he does himself. He puts the whole thing together, and when he lets someone do something, he tends to change it because it's been done in a different way. And he has a group of friends who fit within his system. It's not a matter of one system being better than another system, it's that one system works for one group of people and another system works for another group of people. There are quite a lot of people who wouldn't fit so well into my system and would fit very well into Doug's. And vice versa. So it's a matter of having different groups of people working well within different systems.

But it's very important to make sure that people understand the system under which they work and that they are comfortable within it. Then you've got the makings of a happy expedition. If, on the other hand, you get a group of people who are not happy with that kind of system, you get clashes and people become frustrated because they're working within a system that doesn't suit them.

But isn't it inherently difficult to set up a system that will suit climbers, who tend to be an individualistic lot?

I think it is. For instance, Annapurna south face and the 1972 and 1975 Everest trips were good expeditions, but there was friction. Within every system there will be friction. Climbers per se are strong individualists, and therefore you'll always have some conflict; but interestingly enough, as I've gone on, there has been less and less friction. On the 1975 Everest expedition there was quite a lot of frustration early on. I had split the team into two groups going out, simply because it's more comfortable traveling in a smaller group. But inevitably the group that was away from me felt that decisions were being made by "the leadership" without their being involved. That sorted itself out, and by the end of the trip we had a happy expedition, but it was such a large group that there were still frustrations. Because I had left Hamish out of a summit team he was disappointed. And because I made that decision when I was at Camp V and Hamish was at base camp, I wasn't able to explain it to him in the way I should have or could have. So there were those kinds of frustrations.

I'd say the 1982 Everest expedition was one of the happiest trips I've ever been on because we were six very like-minded people. There wasn't a row throughout that expedition. There were some heated discussions, but they were always within a format of mutual respect. And they always ended up in a decision by consensus; the person in the minority—it might have been Pete one time, another time me, another time Dick—said, "Right, okay, the majority has decided this. Let's go with it."

It sounds as if you got along very well with Peter Boardman and Joe Tasker.

Yes. I really enjoyed climbing with them. They were very realistic. They believed in organization. They believed in a plan. And they were rational, which I am.

So you're more rational, less intuitive?

Yes.

Doug talks a lot about how his intuition guides him in his decisions on a mountain. Do you have the same kind of intuition?

> "... *I AM SLIGHTLY SUSPICIOUS OF THE GUT FEELING.*"

Yes, I have my intuitions. We all are intuitive. But I am slightly suspicious of the gut feeling. We all have gut feelings, and you translate that gut feeling as being right if you're alive at the end of the day, and not if you're dead. Therefore, if you have the gut feeling to go on, as Ian and I did on the north wall of the Grandes Jorasses when the weather was lousy and sixteen people turned back, we were right because the weather didn't break. But if there'd been a great storm and we'd been wiped out, then we'd have been wrong.

And it was the same with us on Kongur. At the end of the four-day storm we had practically no food, but we had a gut feeling to go on and so we went on. If we'd been hit by another storm on the top of Kongur we'd have probably been killed. On the way down Pete was hit by a stone, and if that stone had been a millimeter to the left so that instead of being slightly concussed, he'd actually had a fracture of the skull, we would have had an appalling rescue operation in which Pete probably would have died and we might have died in trying to get him out.

So very often the gut feeling is the self-congratulation of hindsight. I respond to gut feelings just as every climber does, but at the end of the day I believe that there is a strong element of luck in survival. It's very easy to congratulate yourself, whether you're Doug, or Messner, or me, but at the end of the day, I'm sure each of us is just lucky.

There must have been many times when Messner was unbelievably lucky to be alive. When he went solo on Everest and he fell down that crevasse, he landed on a snowbridge. If he hadn't landed on a snowbridge he might have been very dead.

When Doug went off the end of the rope for the second time on the Ogre, he managed to grab another rope in passing; if he hadn't done that he'd have been very dead. On Menlungtse I pulled out a snow stake and went out of control, and if I hadn't just grabbed the rope in time, I'd have been dead. On the north face of the Grandes Jorasses Dougal had clipped improperly into his abseil device and did a couple of somersaults before managing to grab a rope as he went past. That wasn't intuition, that wasn't skill, that was luck.

So pushing the limit at altitude is very, very dangerous. When Pete and Joe were going for the Pinnacles [on the northeast ridge of Everest in 1982], they were obeying their gut feelings, but the gut feeling didn't happen to be right that time. And when you look at the number of people who get killed in this kind of altitude game and analyze the number of narrow escapes the survivors have had, I think it comes down to luck.

So it isn't just experience or savvy?

No. I think that in extreme climbing at altitude you're exposing yourself to a huge number of risks. Now, okay, if you haven't got skill, if you haven't got savvy, if you don't listen to your gut instinct when it says, "Go back down," you're exposing yourself to a few more.

Why do you continue to take such risks?

Because I enjoy climbing; it's a big part of me.

What does it add to your life that you couldn't find elsewhere?

Adrenaline, excitement, a whole series of very strong sensations. The risk game is very addictive. And it's not like going into a terrifying situation; it's actually the command of risk. And I suspect that these sensations provide a special kind of cocktail in your body. And I think it's been proven that there is a whole series of chemical, hormonal changes that make the person addicted, and that is why climbing and similar activities have such a strong hold on the people who take part in them.

So does that mean that you have to keep searching for harder and harder lines to keep up the level of risk?

Not really, no, because I find now that my love of climbing is as great as it ever has been. I want to go to the Himalaya again. I want to go and explore again. But it's not to climb harder and harder lines; it's just going out into a mountain environment that I love and the excitement of going for an unknown peak where there is going to be an element of risk. If you're a person who needs to go harder and harder and harder and harder, apart from anything else, you must come to a point where you either are dead or you can't actually push it any further.

Have the deaths of friends and acquaintances in climbing accidents ever led you to question the value of the sport?

No, because you know right from the word go that climbing is dangerous. And if you're going into high-altitude climbing, you know that risk is an inherent part of the game. So you've got to accept it. It doesn't reduce your sadness at the loss of a friend, but even there the tragedy is not for the person who got killed on a climb; it is actually for the wife, the girlfriend, the children, the parents. It's the people very close to that person who are bereaved and lost and left without him. The individual who gets killed has had a full life. He has gone out right on top, doing something he enjoys doing. And so the tragedy isn't within him; the tragedy is within the survivors. I feel a terrific sense of loss for Nick and Pete and Joe because I enjoyed their company. But it is my loss. They went out having a great life.

What about on the Ogre? Did you think you were going to die there?

I wondered about it, yes, after I'd broken my ribs, and we were caught by a bad storm, and I knew I had pneumonia coming on. And gosh, another couple of days of that and I could have been dead. But then, you know, then one curled oneself up into a little ball and concentrated on staying alive.

You've climbed many magnificent peaks—the Ogre, Everest, the Eiger and many others. How do you choose your routes?

The unknown quality and aesthetic beauty are very important to me. For instance, both the south face of Annapurna and the southwest face of Everest were superb lines and steps into the unknown. Before we ever set out on Annapurna's south face I'd wake up in an absolute cold sweat and think, "What if we get to the foot of that mountain and it's absolutely impossible?" So the south face of Annapurna was the biggest step into the unknown of them all, because no big Himalayan face like that had ever been climbed. The challenge of an unknown problem is fascinating to me—looking at something that seems impossible and then using your experience, your knowledge, and your intellect to turn the impossible into the possible.

It was the same with the northeast ridge of Everest. I was going to organize a large expedition to go back to the northeast ridge of Everest, and then Brummy Stokes got in front of me and they climbed the unclimbed section. And the moment that section had been climbed, I lost interest in that route. There was no point in organizing a huge expedition to climb something where everything was known.

How do you go about financing your expeditions?

I become something of a salesman. I go out and sell my expeditions. I enjoy it.

Are there times when commercial motives get in the way of the climbing?

I think the important thing is that you don't allow them to get in the way. And you do this by explaining to the sponsor what the objective is and then by being very, very careful that you don't allow the sponsor to change that objective. You tell the sponsor what you want to do, and you ask the sponsor, "Are you prepared to support what we want to do?" If the sponsor says, "Yes, but…" you've got to start asking questions.

I've never thought, "I can't do this because the sponsor wouldn't want me to." On K2 we decided to give up the expedition right at the beginning, and the sponsor was totally behind us and said, "You made the right decision." If you strike the right relationship, the sponsor becomes supportive and helpful rather than a threat.

Why did you go back to Everest in 1985?

I suppose the desire to get to the top of Everest was there latent in my mind. And it was going to be by the south col route with masses of Sherpas, a relatively safe operation. And so I decided it would be lunatic to refuse Arne Naess's invitation.

What was your role on that expedition?

I was, to a degree, Arne's chief of staff. My contribution was to do the background logistics, advise him on the number of Sherpas to employ, and run the actual logistics in the early stages of the expedition. It worked very, very smoothly.

Did you think that it would be your last chance to climb it?

It probably was. I wasn't getting any younger.

How did it go as a climb?

It was great. But even with oxygen I was stretched. At one stage I remember going up toward the south summit. I felt absolutely knackered, and I lay there thinking, "I'll never make it." And then Odd Eliassen said, "C'mon, Chris, you're going to do it." And then Odd—and this was the kind of spirit we had on that trip—dropped back behind me, just to give me the encouragement of having someone behind me. It was a great experience.

Do you see expeditions as microcosms of the world in general?

Yes, very much so. And one of the attractions of climbing is that we remove ourselves from the incredibly complex world with a whole series of very vague objectives and enter the very simplistic world of climbing. There you have an absolutely clear objective—climb that mountain. You have a group of people with nothing else to do but climb that mountain. You have much more leisure than you have at home because you've stripped everything away so that all you have to do is climb the mountain. And even climbing the mountain is comparatively simple. And so you've got the time to read books, play games—it is a very simple business.

Is that why you climb?

No, that's a bonus. I think the reason for climbing is much deeper than that. Rock climbing is a combination of the physical and sensual. It's the physical satisfaction of feeling yourself climbing and then the sensual appreciation of the surroundings. Then going out into the Himalaya, you get an extra dimension. I enjoy the feeling of being amongst a different people, a people living a much simpler kind of life. I love sitting above a small Himalayan village at night, smelling a wood fire, feeling the beauty of it. It's a romantic combination.

> *". . . ONE OF THE ATTRACTIONS OF CLIMBING IS THAT WE REMOVE OURSELVES FROM THE INCREDIBLY COMPLEX WORLD WITH A WHOLE SERIES OF VERY VAGUE OBJECTIVES AND ENTER THE VERY SIMPLISTIC WORLD OF CLIMBING."*

When you go to the Himalaya you've got the whole thing much more broadened. You've got the planning of the expedition, the fascination of the country, going up a little rolling hill on the Tibetan plateau by yourself, and you've suddenly got this great mass of air around you, distant mountains, the huge emptiness of it, the sheer, utter, empty beauty of it, so that the impact is that much greater. So this is the real reason, and the little microcosm, that's an extra attraction.

So have the best moments of your life been reaching the summits of some of these peaks?

Not necessarily. On the 1975 Everest expedition, the high point for me was on the way down after putting Doug and Dougal into the top camp. I sat down in the snow and knew that we'd done everything we possibly could, that it was up to them now, and that they were in a very good position to make it. And I just had a terrific sense, I suppose, of love, for the whole team. Everyone had worked to achieve this one end, and I just found a vast sense of contentment that this had been done.

And in 1985, when I got to the top of the mountain, there was a sense of confusion, of exhaustion, of the loss of friends [on earlier trips], and everything else. I was very content to get to the top of Everest, but that feeling came afterward. The 1985 trip was a super trip; there was no anger of any kind on that trip. I liked and respected every single member of the team, and therefore there was this terrific sense of contentment with what one had done.

The best trip I've ever had was on Shivling, which I climbed with Jim Fotheringham. That was the purest alpine-style thing you could ever have—we hadn't planned it, there was a very high level of commitment, we were climbing very well together; but the moment of getting to the top was dampened by the thought of "How on earth are we going to get back down again?" And so the feeling of contentment about that experience came some days later.

Your feeling about an expedition comes quite a bit later, and it's after you can reflect on it and look at the whole and see how you personally performed. It's how you related to the people with whom you climbed, how much you gave as well as how much you took. And if you actually succeeded in getting to the top of the mountain, but also gave a lot to others, then the satisfaction is considerable.

DOUG SCOTT

*Many mountaineers would concur that facing up to
potentially dangerous situations, at all levels of ability, is central
to the pursuit of the sport. Without an element of danger lurking
around the corner, mountaineering must lose its unique appeal.*

—Doug Scott, *Big Wall Climbing*

I<small>F CONFRONTING AND OVERCOMING</small> dangerous situations is the essence of climbing, Doug Scott surely qualifies as one of the sport's purest practitioners. The intrepid Englishman has courted danger at every step of his career, from the early days in Derbyshire, where he climbed with the aid of a clothesline, to extended epics such as the southwest face of Everest (1975), where he and Dougal Haston were forced to bivouac just below the summit and managed to survive without even suffering frostbite.

Scott has thrived on risk for some three decades, taking on increasingly difficult high-altitude routes and somehow finding a way to return home to tell about them. In a sport where the margin for error is slim to none, he is one of the few high-altitude veterans who is still alive and climbing, and his greatest worry seems not to be his own mortality, but what new route to do next year.

He credits this longevity to a well-developed intuition that guides him in his decisions on a mountain. This intuition helps him to decide when to take it to the limit on a peak and when to retreat and try again next year. For an alpine-style apostle like Scott, this sixth sense makes all the difference between success and failure, life and death, on an extreme route.

The son of a policeman, Scott was born in Nottingham, England May 29, 1941. He began climbing at age twelve on the Black Rocks at Cromford, a nearby crag-climbing area. By fourteen he had ventured off to Wales and Scotland; by seventeen he had made his first visit to the Alps to climb Mont Blanc and other peaks in the Chamonix area; by twenty-one, he had traveled to the Atlas Mountains of Morocco in search of even more adventurous routes.

Working as a schoolteacher in the early to mid-sixties, he spent his summers making trips to such exotic locales as the Tibesti Mountains of Chad in 1965, Kurdistan in 1966, and Koh-î-Bandaka in the Hindu Kush of Afghanistan in 1967. Shortly thereafter, he gave up teaching to devote more time to climbing.

Doug Scott. (Photo by Chris Bonington)

The gamble paid off when he was invited to join the 1972 British expedition to the southwest face of Everest. After returning from this unsuccessful attempt on Everest, he was asked to write articles and give slide shows and talks on the expedition, activities that have provided the bulk of his income ever since.

Working hard on his chosen craft, Scott developed thereafter into one of the world's leading high-altitude climbers, pioneering routes in 1974 on the east ridge of Changabang with Chris Bonington, Martin Boysen, Dougal Haston, and others, and on the southeast face of Pik Lenin (23,406 feet) with Paul "Tut" Braithwaite. The following year he gained international renown when he and Dougal Haston summited on the 1975 British Everest Southwest Face Expedition. With Everest behind him, Scott turned his attention to lesser-known but equally necky routes, such as the south face of McKinley, completed with Haston in 1976, and the west ridge of the Ogre (23,900 feet), climbed with Bonington in 1977. Overconfidence got the better of him on the Ogre, however: he carelessly slipped on rappel and pendulumed wildly into a wall. The impact broke both his legs at the ankles, requiring that he endure one of the most hellish descents in mountaineering history. With the help of Bonington, Mo Anthoine, and Clive Rowland, he crawled most of the way back down the Biafo Glacier to safety.

In the course of these and other climbs, Scott began to gravitate away from the fixed-rope, siege-style tactics characteristic of big expeditions and toward a stripped-down, alpine-style approach that relied on the experience and resilience of individual team members rather than the logistics of a large organization. The pivotal climb in this regard proved to be the north ridge of Kangchenjunga (1979), where he, Joe Tasker, Peter Boardman, and Georges Bettembourg did most of the route alpine style. He, Bettembourg, Alan Rouse, and Brian Hall successfully employed the same strategy later that year on the north face of Nuptse.

In recent years, Scott has refined this lightweight approach, adopting a multipeak style of acclimatizing in which he books a number of peaks, ascending the smaller ones in preparation for his major objective—all attempted in one sustained, committed push. This approach first bore fruit in 1981 on the east pillar of Shivling, which he climbed with Bettembourg, Rick White, and Greg Child, and then again in 1982 on the sheer southwest face of Tibet's Shisha Pangma, which he ascended with Roger Baxter-Jones and Alex MacIntyre. Scott continued to pursue this alpine-style approach on such peaks as Lobsang Spire in 1983 with Greg Child and Pete Thexton; Baruntse and Chamlang in 1984 with Ang Phurba, Jean Afanassieff, and Scott's son Michael; and Jitchu Drake, in Bhutan, where he, Victor Saunders, and Sharu Prabhu pioneered a new route in 1988. In 1989 he attempted Rimo II, in the Indian Himalaya, where he, Prabhu, and Laurie Wood reached 22,000 feet. In 1991, he, Prabhu, and Nigel Porter ascended the south ridge of Hanging Glacier Peak South in Nepal. Scott's enthusiasm for climbing shows no sign of flagging, and in the future he plans to concentrate on first ascents in remote mountain ranges of the world.

Married at age twenty, Scott and his former wife, Jan, have two daughters, Rosie and Martha, and a son, Michael, who has accompanied him on a number of climbs. The couple divorced in 1989. Scott now lives in the Lake District of northern England with Sharu Prabhu, his companion of several years and also an accomplished climber.

Scott is tall and squarely built, with his full beard, unkempt brown hair, and round, wire-rim glasses giving him a strong resemblance to the late John Lennon, one of his favorite lyricists. A phlegmatic, introverted man, Scott speaks slowly and precisely, often describing the most harrowing adventures in the wry, dry, understated style that has been a hallmark of English climbers since the days of Eric Shipton and H. W. Tilman.

The interview took place at Scott's friend Steve Swenson's house in Seattle and at several other locations around the city as Scott made calls at several of the outdoor equipment companies that help underwrite his climbs. Throughout the course of the day, Scott gave the impression that, although these duties were necessary enough, all in all he'd much rather be out climbing.

How did it feel to climb Everest by a new route up the southwest face?

It felt fantastic. We arrived at six in the evening, the sun filtering through the layers of cloud and bursting out again. It was a magnificent sunset; you could see a good 400 miles. You could see the curve of the earth. Obviously we were quite euphoric. Both Dougal Haston and myself had spent nine months of our lives trying to get there; that was the third expedition for us both. So it was nice to get it finished.

And then you don't quite know what will happen on these trips. They never work out as you think. The most significant thing from the point of view of my future climbing was spending the night out just below there in a cave, without sleeping bags and oxygen, and surviving the night without frostbite. If you're a climber, you can see that that would really widen the range of what you might do next. Assuming you can spend a night out there, there's a good chance you can spend at least one night out anywhere, as long as you can get out of the wind. So that gave me a lot of confidence to try other things in more lightweight style.

Did this experience teach you your limits?

I don't know if I've ever gone to my limit sheer endurance-wise. As for putting up with the cold, I think I reached it on the top of Everest.

What got you through that night up there?

Knowledge that other people had slept out on Everest lower down than us, and nearly all of them had gone back to have fingers and toes cut off. So it wasn't survival that was worrying us as much as the quality of survival; we didn't want to lose any of our digits. So we worked hard at keeping the blood flowing. We didn't go to sleep; we just rubbed and rubbed our toes and fingers.

How did you and expedition leader Chris Bonington get along on that climb?

Chris was very good at organizing expeditions and seemed to need to be a formal leader, which I found difficult at times. But the southwest face expeditions were good trips. It was just a matter of rationalizing those differences, which we did. We still go rock climbing in Britain together.

Mount Everest from the west. (Photo by Doug Scott)

So he had a more organized approach?

He seemed to like a more structured expedition, which obviously worked for the southwest face and other things he's done since. But it did tend to get bigger than I would have liked, and we used to get very involved in sponsorship and that sort of thing.

Do you think that style of climbing is necessary for certain peaks or certain routes?

You can never say that anymore since Reinhold Messner soloed Everest without any backup at all, apart from his girlfriend at base camp. So it all depends on the team, their experience, and so on. I don't like to lay the law down, but as far as I'm concerned, the smaller the expedition, the better. You don't have to get so involved with your sponsors and the media. You don't end up having all these peripheral activities taking place that can get between you and your climbing—filmmaking, men from the newspapers, people writing books.

The crux of the problem is if you decide to take oxygen, because that weighs so much—say, thirty-six pounds for two bottles and regulators and everything—then you've got no room in your rucksack for anything else. And so you've got to have people to help you get into position, which means having a lot of Sherpas. And to get the oxygen into position, you've got to rig up a fixed rope as a supply line that you can jumar up or abseil down. It acts as a safety rope as well, in that if there's ever a storm or someone is ill or just exhausted, it's easy to clip on the friction brake device and scuttle down to safety.

> *"YOU HAVEN'T REALLY LEFT THE GROUND WHILST YOU'RE IN THE VICINITY OF THAT FIXED ROPE. ONLY WHEN YOU GET TO THE END OF IT AND TAKE OFF DOES THE CLIMBING BEGIN."*

So that rope takes the commitment out of the climbing. You haven't really left the ground whilst you're in the vicinity of that fixed rope. Only when you get to the end of it and take off does the climbing begin. Only then can you get that wonderful feeling of being out on a limb, going for it, feeling a million miles from home, and taking responsibility for yourself and your partner. Up to that point, there is no real commitment. That's the trouble with big expeditions.

Fixed-rope climbing is just like a construction job—logistics, exercising the leader's plan. No one feels that involved. People absolve themselves from all responsibilities to this Freudian father figure who's working through this master plan, which was punched out on the computer back home. That's not climbing; that's more like running a business.

Do you think that that was a necessary stage in the development of climbing?

It's still going on. The Japanese nearly always climb that way and yet they are very strong and brave climbers. A lot of climbers from other countries too. To get to the summit is most important to most people, not how you get there.

A few years after the southwest face of Everest, four of us went to Kangchenjunga climbing semi-alpine, and we made the third ascent of Kangch by a new route. It was a far more satisfying achievement because we did that without oxygen and without Sherpa support after the north col.

That always stands out as the most satisfying thing I've done. No big 8000-meter peak had ever been climbed alpine style at that time. That was in the spring of 1979. It was stepping into the unknown. We were always wondering if we were getting in over the top. How we would cope if someone got edema? But it all worked out in the end.

How did you get started climbing?

My father was amateur heavyweight boxing champion of the U.K. in 1948 and he used to encourage me in sport. I used to do a lot of middle-distance running when I was a lad at school.

Climbing had nothing much to do with school or my father; it was just something I found for myself when I was out with the scouts, seeing climbers in action on the local rocks about twenty-five miles from my home.

Was this outside Nottingham?

Yes, a place called the Black Rocks in Derbyshire. We would cycle out from school for the weekend. That's how we got started. We had a clothesline for a rope. We just watched a few of the climbers to see what they were doing and then made mistakes and learned our lessons as we went along. This was before mountain schools and education got into climbing.

What appealed to you about climbing?

It was as much getting out of the city and away from home and school as it was climbing, just being out in the countryside, being on our own, making our own decisions, taking responsibility for ourselves.

Did you have heroes who were climbers?

No. Never really understood how people can have heroes. Some people impressed me, obviously—Shipton. I read *Upon That Mountain* very early; I liked that. I also admired Lionel Terray, whom I noticed went on three expeditions a year. I thought that was a good idea.

Did you climb mostly around Nottingham?

Yes, mainly on Derbyshire gritstone and later limestone. At fourteen I went off to Wales, to the hills there, to climb a mountain called Tryfan; then the Lake District the year after; Scotland the year after that; the Alps when I was seventeen—this was all with friends from Nottingham. I've been to the Alps every year since. The Mont Blanc region still offers the best combination of climbing you can get—rock and ice, sensible but proportioned.

When did you get more serious about climbing?

From about twenty-one onward I couldn't think of much else I wanted to do. We'd had these seasons in the Alps but always took off for more exotic places—the Atlas Mountains in 1962, the Tibesti Mountains in Chad in

1965, Kurdistan in 1966, the Hindu Kush of Afghanistan in 1967.

Did climbing interfere with your teaching career?

Yes. I began teaching at twenty, and at first the headmaster was sympathetic, so I used to get leaves of absence without too much trouble. But in 1971 I had to go off to Baffin Island for six weeks, and he finally said, "It's either your career or your climbing." I said, "I better resign." And so I did. I finished teaching in 1971.

Was it difficult to make that decision?

No. I quite liked teaching, but I couldn't put everything into it that I wanted to. I was putting too much strain on the rest of the staff, who had to cover for me when I was away. It was always a bit awkward when I got back. But I used to take the kids out on weekends from time to time on various trips to make up for it. But really, I'd come to the end of the line. It's a very exhausting job anyway. You don't have much time for yourself.

Were you able to make a living from climbing?

At first I did building jobs, construction work, roofing, houses, that sort of thing. And then suddenly, out of the blue—as so often happens when you place yourself in a position of insecurity—interesting things come your way. The phone rang, and Don Whillans asked me if I fancied going with him to Everest in the spring of 1972, which I did with the German/European Everest expedition.

I came back from that having gotten myself up to 26,000 feet. Then Chris Bonington asked me on his first Everest trip in the autumn of 1972. After two trips to Everest, people starting ringing me up to talk about my climbs. I suddenly found I could come up with some money from lecturing and a little bit from writing articles. And that just carried on.

It happened by chance. I didn't stop teaching to become a professional climber. It just came about. I've always had reservations about that. I never wanted earning a living to affect how I climbed. I always wanted to put the climbing long before making money out of it.

I did toy with the idea of trying to climb all the 8000ers, or at least visit them; but it seemed that that would limit me to just one type of climbing, and I'd much rather not impose that on myself, but go here, there, and everywhere. I did make a decision after visiting Makalu not to go back to the 8000ers while they're so crowded. So I'm back to looking for interesting peaks in more remote areas. I'd like to go back to Bhutan, but that's so expensive. And, of course, there are a lot more interesting mountains in Tibet, but dealing with the Chinese authorities is so stressful that it's not so attractive.

Do you acclimatize quickly?

No, I don't acclimatize quickly, but once I have acclimatized, I seem to get along well. I have to allow myself a good three weeks before I feel like climbing reasonably, before I feel anything like climbing.

I don't know anybody who won't benefit from three weeks of acclimatizing. That's how long it takes for our physiology to match that of the Sherpas. We have the same blood count as them after three weeks there. People can dash about, but they'll never enjoy it as much as if they give it about three weeks.

Because I'm getting older and a lot of my friends have died, I'm climbing with younger people, and it's very hard to put this over to them, because it all looks so easy, relative to the Alps, or what they've done in Alaska or the Rockies or something. The nature of the routes is usually a lot less technical, and all the young guys just want to get there and get on with it. And that's one of the problems I have—trying to talk them into taking it more slowly.

To help that along, I got into this multipeak style of climbing or acclimatizing whereby you book smaller peaks, climb those, and then go straight on to the main thing, rather than going up and down the same peak, which is boring and tedious.

So that's the technique you mainly use now?

I have since autumn of 1979, after Kangch. I booked Everest, and to acclimatize for that I booked Kussum Kangguru north summit and then Nuptse north buttress, both of which we climbed. We never got to Everest, but it worked out all right as far as it went.

Then the next year we went to Makalu. Again, we did a similar thing—climbed four peaks between 20,000 and 23,500 feet, then climbed Kangchungtse (25,000 feet), and then went on to the southeast ridge of Makalu. We almost did it, but Georges Bettembourg was sick with a pulmonary embolism and there were bad storms; so we had to descend.

In 1982 things also worked out well. First we climbed Nyanang Ri and Pungpa Ri. After a long rest, we went straight up the 9000-foot southwest face of Shisha Pangma—up and down in four days. That's where this multipeak approach came to fruition.

After you'd climbed Everest, did these other peaks still seem like worthy goals?

Worthier. Sensible. You could enjoy them, without the oxygen and everything on Everest.

Do you ever tire of going on expeditions?

I get a bit fed up these days with the organization—two or three months of chasing gear around, booking flights, and the rest of it. Sometimes I think,

"What am I doing?" but they are always fairly interesting. There's always something new to learn about climbing, myself, and everything else in the world.

What do you learn about yourself in the process of climbing?

A lot of problems will arise between members. Climbing is no different from the classroom, the office, the factory floor; there will always be some degree of backbiting or argument—somebody feels that they're not getting recognition for what they're doing. The only difference is that when you're climbing you can't walk away from it. You can't go home and forget it. You can't go down to the pub and drown your sorrows. You've got it twenty-four hours a day, so you do have to sort things out. Climbing does give you a chance to come to terms with yourself. What you find out about yourself just comes as a gift.

> "CLIMBING IS NO DIFFERENT
> FROM THE CLASSROOM,
> THE OFFICE, THE FACTORY
> FLOOR. . . . THE ONLY
> DIFFERENCE IS THAT
> WHEN YOU'RE CLIMBING
> YOU CAN'T WALK AWAY
> FROM IT."

Everyone comes back changed from a long expedition to the high mountains. You're never quite the same person you were before. I feel more in touch with myself and close to my friends, feel more compassionate toward all those back home after I've taken it to the limit on an extended climb. It's got a lot to do with having slowed everything down, not being besieged with anxieties and worries.

What's the ideal size for a climbing team?

Four. If it's two, and one's ill, you're stuck. If it's three, two can be company, three can be a crowd. If it's four, then two twos independently equipped but moving together can be very supportive on big peaks. And if you're really good friends and you don't mind crowds, then six is all right.

When you organize an expedition, how do you go about choosing the other members?

These days, with so many expeditions happening, people will play the field a bit, which might mean simply that they look for the one that's least expensive or fits in with their time frame or interest. So you end up asking quite a few people, and in the end a small group comes. Occasionally everyone comes and you've got a huge group, but it's not like the huge group all climbs on one rope or one route.

There is something to be said for taking a lot of people because a lot of people share the unique costs, such as the liaison officer, the food to some extent, local staff, cooks. But there are a lot of problems with taking a lot of people because you end up with too many points of view and you don't get much done, unless you're fairly ruthless. Generally, you want people who are easygoing but still can acclimatize and climb.

What are the essential qualities that make a mountain climber?

Physically, they come in all shapes and sizes. I think they've got that curiosity to see around the next corner, to discover all the secrets of the mountain, to keep pressing on. They probably all found out early on that when they're back in the mountains they feel more at home than they do in the city, and that by risking their lives they actually do come alive.

Is it that sense of risk that allows you to feel more alive?

Yes, or just the hard struggle, going without food and enforced fasting. It all helps to change you, to give you a new awareness. You're slightly reborn, like after a long illness, especially one involving a fever. You come out from that feeling like everything's new again. I suppose a lot of it is just being back in the mountains, being in touch with natural processes, having to pay attention to the seasons and the elements.

Is there a real need for that nowadays?

You wouldn't think so, would you?—with the number of people that cram into towns—but I certainly need it. You can't be out there all the time, but the memory of it affects all that you do. It remains a reference point as to where you can be.

Would you want to be out there all the time?

I suppose I do enjoy the contrast, though I actually do live twenty-two miles from a town, way out in the sticks.

How do you choose your routes?

If I can find a face or main feature on a mountain that no one has ever looked at, written about, photographed, fixed-roped, then I'm interested—if it's reasonably safe. The beauty of the Himalaya is that there are more unclimbed ridges and faces. And since climbing is all about facing the unknown, and therefore pioneering new routes, that's the place to do it.

I quite enjoy climbing peaks like Shisha Pangma. No one had ever walked in the valley to get to that side of the mountain; so not only did we have an unknown face, but there were no remnants of half-hearted attempts from fixed-rope expeditions. We just had everything to find out about that one. So that was really appealing.

It was the same with Nuptse north face. No one had done that before.

Did writing the book Big Wall Climbing *help to define your own approach to the sport?*

It was good for me to understand the traditions of the sport in some depth, to talk to the old climbers and see how enthusiastic they were. What we're doing now is just an ongoing tradition. It does worry me how climbing will end up now that the traditional reasons for climbing are changing. Many climbers are coming into it from school; it's part of the curriculum, a school activity. I'm not certain that physical-education teachers will keep the old traditions alive. Bringing it to a child on a plate might change things.

Are you disappointed in the direction climbing seems to be going?

I'm somewhat worried about the effect of education classes on climbing, of the effect of climbing walls, of the explosion in the outdoor market, the number of magazines coming out, how quickly information is passed, how fast personal psychological barriers erode because you know that what is possible for other climbers is potentially possible for yourself.

And there does seem to be a change in attitudes to climbing. This obsession with 8000-meter summits is new, and the lengths to which people go to climb one. A lot of deaths now occur not by falling off, or getting caught in a storm, but with climbers who climb themselves into the ground, who die of exhaustion or mountain sicknesses such as cerebral edema or pulmonary edema. A lot die now because they're so gung-ho, so obsessed with summits.

A few years ago on Makalu, a Mexican climber reached the summit and then was found in the snow, delirious, about to die. Two Poles went to the summit, leaving the Mexican to fend for himself, refusing to help him. He was rescued by a Spanish team that fortunately had brought bottled oxygen.

They [the Poles] went to summit, and only one came back. The one who came back said he didn't know where his friend was. I can't imagine that. I can't imagine how you could go home and tell relations—wives, families, and whomever—that you really don't know what happened to your partner.

Marcel Ruedi, the Swiss climber, went to Makalu a few years ago desperate to get his last three 8000-meter summits done, to be the first climber of the fourteen 8000-meter summits. He had himself helicoptered to base camp, and within a week or so of leaving Zurich he was on the top of Makalu. He died of altitude sickness on the way down. He was totally obsessed—a nice chap, but crazy, crazy to let himself get to that position.

Haven't climbers always been trying to get to the summit at all costs?

There's always been some of that, and we've all gone through it, usually in our late twenties or early thirties. But it seems to be more prevalent now than ever before. There's not always that camaraderie between teams and countries that you used to see in the mountains. It was always good to see another team, share base camp, entertain each other. But I discern a certain hardness creeping in.

Where is mountaineering going now that the highest Himalayan summits have been climbed?

The main summits and the main features on the more popular peaks, such as Everest, have been climbed, but the rest of the Himalaya is just wide open. It's still like the Alps were in the 1890s or early 1900s. There will be more technical climbing higher up, though that will be at a slower rate because of the lack of oxygen. There probably will be more traversing of mountains, or a string of mountains, as the Russians have been doing in the Pamirs.

> *"A LOT OF DEATHS NOW OCCUR NOT BY FALLING OFF, OR GETTING CAUGHT IN A STORM, BUT WITH CLIMBERS WHO CLIMB THEMSELVES INTO THE GROUND."*

I hope to see more alpine-style climbing, simply because those teams are usually smaller, have less effect on the local people, cause less disruption to the local economies, and leave the mountain in a better state, not fixed with rope everywhere. But that probably won't happen because about half the climbers who go to the Himalaya are Japanese, and they're nearly all fixed-rope expeditions. I don't know why they do that. It must be something in their national character, the need for security or something.

There are some great climbers in Japan—winter climbers who face exceptional cold and difficulties—but always the fixed rope. They're afraid to cut off and go for it. They like to stay within the organization. That's the characteristic impression I suppose everyone gets of a Japanese person—get in a big firm, cushioned from all the problems of life, selling themselves to the firm for security. They seem to apply that to the mountains, with big teams and hierarchies of organization.

Who have been some of your favorite climbing partners?

Georges Bettembourg from France, Dougal Haston of course, Roger Baxter-Jones, Mick Burke, Nick Estcourt, Chris Bonington, Peter Boardman, Joe Tasker, Paul "Tut" Braithwaite, Ray Gillies, Alex MacIntyre, and Greg Child.

Have you done much soloing?

Only bouldering on rock in Britain, doing easier routes. Not any Himalayan solos. I certainly admire Reinhold for doing Nanga Parbat and Everest solo—fantastic achievements.

What is it that makes you a successful climber?

I've never been an exceptional rock climber. The hardest moves I've ever made are Yosemite 5.11. But in Himalayan climbing I was naturally fit, born with a big pair of lungs and reasonable circulation, and just by keeping at it I slowly developed my trade. And if everything's right, I can usually stick to it and stay committed to the route.

My criteria for turning back dates to March of 1976 when I was on McKinley south face with Dougal Haston. We were in a storm for two days, and on the third day it was still very bad weather.

I said to Dougal, "What do you think?"

And that hard Scotsman looked at me and said, "You haven't got frostbite yet, have you?"

"Oh, I see, right. We just climb until we do. And hopefully get to the summit before we do get frostbite."

I'll stay committed until my body starts to suffer—frostnip coming on, or I start to get double vision, cerebral edema, or a bad chest cold that sounds like it's developing into something nasty, like pulmonary edema—then I'll scuttle down as fast as I can.

Are you able to tell when that kind of thing is happening?

I think I've learned to mind myself. When you're above 26,000 feet, it's not always the case that you can rationalize your position. I seem to rely more on a feeling within my chest as to whether it's right to continue. I rely on an intuitive process. What my sixth sense, or intuition, is telling me—that is the governing factor. That's very powerful. It might tell you to go up. It might tell you to go down. There's no way you can not pay attention to it when it comes on strong.

Has it shown itself to be right a lot of the time?

Every time. That's why I'm still here. But I don't think you get in touch with that if blind ambition's driving you, you've got your blinkers on, and all you can think about is the summit, oblivious to all else. You take your chances then. I think it's vital not to be too ambitious if you want to survive for long in the Himalaya.

Did your intuition allow you to survive when a lot of your friends have died?

I'm not saying that they died because of their ambition, I'm just saying that my intuition has certainly helped me. There's nothing wrong with being ambitious as long as you're aware of the dangers. I hope I've learned at least that.

I don't know why some of them died. A single stone comes down the south face of Annapurna while Alex MacIntyre is resting, hits him on the head, and kills him.

So many times when the lads have been killed, it turns out that anyone who was really close to them—wives, mothers, girlfriends, close friends—all had some strong premonition that something nasty was going to happen.

I later found out that when we were walking in to K2 in 1978, Nick Estcourt had a vivid dream that I was poking around in the snow looking for his body. As it turned out, Nick and I were avalanched. I survived. The rope broke and left me right on the edge of the avalanche, looking down that 4000-foot mountainside. Nick ended up at the bottom, buried in all this avalanche debris. As it happened, I was the only one to go and poke around in the ice blocks, making sure his body was well covered, not open to the elements or the birds.

So I get very fatalistic about it. It just reinforces my feeling that a lot of this is already written out.

Why did your accident on the Ogre occur?

It was me being too gung-ho for the summit. After Everest, I was led to believe I was invincible. I took it all too lightheartedly.

I was abseiling down in the evening and wasn't paying attention. I put my Vibram soles against the rock, tensioning off to retrieve some climbing gear; but meltwater on the rocks had turned to verglass, and I skated off. I went swinging across this void, about a 100-foot swing. Suddenly all these rocks were rushing toward me. I just managed to get my feet up in front of me and—splat—I went straight into them. My glasses shot off. I lost my ice axe. I found myself dangling on the end of the rope. I discovered I broke both legs at the ankles. It was eight days going back to base camp through a five-day storm, four days without any food.

How did you get through that?

With the help of Mo Anthoine and Clive Rowland. They obviously couldn't carry me, but they broke trail, fixed the abseils, and kept an eye on me. So did Chris Bonington until he broke two ribs abseiling down. He was probably in more pain than me after that. It's awful abseiling down with two broken ribs. And then he got pneumonia and was coughing up this yellow liquid.

What were you thinking as all this was happening?

Just took it as it came. I didn't think too much about the whole thing, but I hallucinated a lot. Going without food does that. On the sixth day, I got interesting insights into myself, a lot of them bizarre, but quite interesting.

And it had its lighter moments. We didn't have any food, but we had a tape deck and plenty of batteries and five Doctor Hook tapes. We played those a lot.

I remember Chris had told us he thought he was dying. An hour or so later he croaks from his tent that he just had a brilliant idea. He was going to make our fortunes for us. I asked him how he'd manage that. He said he was going to write a book about it—60 percent to him, 40 percent to us—which caused a laugh at the time because it seemed like we'd never get out of it.

Was that one of your worst moments in the mountains?

It was the most extended, most embarrassing worst moment. I'm sure anyone who was up there would have done the same thing, crawl on your knees, just keep going.

After experiences like that, why do you keep climbing?

Just to see another place, to see how I do this time. I keep thinking the next one will be the time that tells me I'm getting too old for it, but so far it's just gotten easier in the Himalaya. I have no problem acclimatizing or keeping going.

How does climbing fit in with the rest of your life?

It's quite disruptive really. Usually before I'm going away, I don't really want to go. I get the feeling to go in the winter, but by the time I've finished organizing everything, I start to wonder what it's all about. And there's so much left undone at home, I almost wish I wasn't going. But as soon as I've walked around the valley a bit, and have got into the mountains and it all opens out, then I heave a big sigh of relief and wonder why it took me so long to get there. Because I forget just how good it is.

Are you still competitive about climbing?

I don't think so. I don't think I was ever that competitive about climbing; I was only ambitious for myself. But I still get pissed off if someone does a climb I've set my mind to. There's always competition for the route, not competition against someone else.

Do you want to climb Everest again?

Probably not.

What other climbs would you like to do?

I'd like to spend more time in Bhutan, but so far they won't open up any more mountains. I might get back to Afghanistan.

I'd like to get some of my thoughts down on paper—books and things—find time for that.

What kinds of thoughts?

I'm amazed what has come my way without me really expecting much. I've always been full of self-doubt and all that, but when I've been really ambitious to do something, and it suddenly seemed like it wouldn't happen—the weather was bad, or the people I was with were ill or I was ill, or the team just wasn't getting on well enough to justify climbing any further—I'd have to let go of that ambition. And once I'd done that—totally giving it up, thinking I'd come back in another year—so often events changed: weather or snow conditions improved, the team suddenly seemed to feel better toward one another, people felt strong after illness. And then we'd go for it and achieve what we set out to do, but more humbly, without ambition driving us. And what we achieved then came as a sort of gift, like we'd been allowed to go there, to reach our goal, like we were being helped somehow.

▲ Voytek Kurtyka

The philosophical-religious traditions of the East created a very vivid and apt conception called The Path. The Path means a particular way of living and behaving conditioned by a code of ethics and by a system of technical instructions governing different aspects of practical everyday life, such as diet, methods of fighting, meditating, breathing, etc. Observing the rules of The Path was supposed to help in achieving the higher levels of wisdom, or in the case of determined yogis and monks, the final insight into the nature of the human self and the surrounding world.

I dare to express the conviction that mountaineering, by reason of the remarkable qualities it contains, may turn into a precious method of physical and spiritual growth. Referring to the tradition of The Path, I would like to call this method, "The Path of the Mountain."

—Voytek Kurtyka, "The Path of the Mountain,"
published in Canadian journal *Alpinism*

For Voytek Kurtyka, mountaineering is not so much a sport as it is a religious activity, a means of testing and perfecting character, a way of experiencing in a short, concentrated time the extremes of human emotion—the extraordinary joy in being alive and the abject terror of confronting death—thus providing a glimpse into the essential truth of life. In Kurtyka's conception, The Path of the Mountain begins at the physical level with the sheer animal exuberance of ascending rock, moves to the psychic satisfactions of doing longer and harder routes, and culminates in the spiritual epiphanies accompanying some of the most demanding climbs in the Himalaya and elsewhere. For him,

Voytek Kurtyka. (Courtesy Voytek Kurtyka)

mountaineering is a multidimensional activity that allows for the fullest expression of all aspects of his personality, whether physical, psychic, emotional, or spiritual. Rather than being a mere recreational activity, it is for him a way of life.

His passion for mountaineering began at age twenty-one when he made his first trip to the Tatra Mountains of southern Poland in 1969. The following year he went to the Alps, where he repeated such classic routes as the Walker Spur of the Grandes Jorasses and the American Direct on the Petit Dru and opened up new routes on the north face of the Grandes Jorasses as well as the north face of the Petit Dru.

Kurtyka's first high-altitude climb took place in 1972, when he accompanied a Polish group to the Hindu Kush of Afghanistan. He broke away from the main group to make an alpine-style first ascent of the north face of Acher Chioch (23,000 feet). That climb whetted his appetite for alpine-style ascents of high-altitude objectives and two subsequent unsuccessful expedition-style trips—the 1974 Polish Lhotse South Face expedition and the 1976 Polish K2 east ridge expedition—only confirmed his desire to employ alpine-style techniques exclusively. In 1977 he put this philosophy into practice once again when he ascended the 8000-foot northeast face of Koh-î-Bandaka in the Hindu Kush with English climber Alex MacIntyre and the American John Porter.

Thereafter, he eschewed the big 8000-meter peaks such as Everest in favor of lesser known but aesthetically appealing lines, including a new route on the south face of Changabang (1978), which he climbed with MacIntyre, Porter, and Polish climber Krzystof Zurek, and the east face of Dhaulagiri (1980), which he completed with MacIntyre, Ludwick Wilczycznski, and René Ghillini.

After MacIntyre's tragic death (he was killed by stonefall on Annapurna in 1982), Kurtyka paired himself with Jerzy Kukuczka to form one of the most formidable teams in the history of Himalayan mountaineering. These two experts at "the art of suffering," as Kurtyka refers to Himalayan climbing, succeeded on some of the most committing routes ever done—the southeast ridge of Gasherbrum II (1983), a new route on the southwest face of Hidden Peak (1983), the traverse of Hidden Peak and Gasherbrum II via a new route (1983), and finally, the first complete traverse of Broad Peak (1984). Their partnership ended in 1984 when Kukuczka entered the race for the 8000ers; Kurtyka demurred, preferring to follow his own path on less crowded and more aesthetic objectives.

The gleaming white pyramid of Gasherbrum IV had long fascinated him, and in 1985 he made a bid for its west face with Robert Schauer. It proved a beautiful but dangerous line. Both men nearly died on the climb as the weather deteriorated, forcing them to spend more time on the route than anticipated and causing them to run out of food and fuel. They managed to push their way just short of the top, but deep snow put the summit out of reach, and so they retreated, thankful to have gotten off the mountain alive.

Kurtyka's routes often exhibit a quality of aspiration, and this is especially true of his breathtaking line on the east face of Trango Tower (20,500 feet). In

1988 he and Erhard Loretan succeeded in scaling the twenty-nine-pitch route, finally topping out after three attempts and fourteen days on the obelisklike peak. Since Trango, the two have teamed up with Jean Troillet to make one-day ascents of the west face of Cho Oyu (1990) and the south face of Shisha Pangma (1990).

In addition to these impressive high-altitude achievements, Kurtyka has completed many hard rock climbs over the years and is presently working to put up a four-pitch 5.14 route in the Tatra Mountains.

Kurtyka was born on July 25, 1947, in Skrzynka, a village in southwest Poland, moved to the village of Trzebieszowice, and then to the city of Wroclaw. His father was a professional writer, quite well known in Poland under the pseudonym Henryk Worcell. His mother was a housewife, caring for his father, himself, and his two brothers.

Kurtyka has been married once and divorced. In 1989 he married his present wife, Halina, and they live with their son, Alexander, in Zabierzow, Poland. To make ends meet, he and his wife run an import business specializing in Indian clothing.

The interview took place in a meadow beneath the imposing 3000-foot south face of the Marmolata, a peak in the Dolomites of northern Italy on which he had come to do, as he put it, some "leisure climbing." Leisure climbing for Kurtyka consists of one-day ascents of Grade VI rock climbs, mere walks in the park when compared with the spiritual purgatories of Himalayan peaks.

In person, Kurtyka is a cheerful, energetic man with the lean and sinewy build of a middle-distance runner. He manages to appear nervous, quirky, confident, concentrated, intense, patient, irritable, imaginative, pragmatic—all in the space of a single second. After two weeks of climbing in the Dolomites, his habitual nervousness had subsided somewhat and he could give his full attention to the questions. He took great pains to answer them carefully, narrowing his piercing blue eyes, rocking his tensed body back and forth, twirling a purple wildflower between his fingers, and expressing through the musical, lilting quality of his voice the complex personality of one of the boldest and most imaginative high-altitude climbers in the world today.

Why has Poland produced so many great Himalayan climbers?

The first thing is that the Poles are quite an adventurous people, and the second thing is that the history of Poland encouraged a kind of tough behavior. We lived in very hard political conditions for centuries. We had problems all the time, either with the Germans or the Russians. For over a hundred years we lost our independence, from the end of the eighteenth century to the beginning of the twentieth century. And for generations the Poles behaved in a patriotic way, and one of the first duties was to be strong, to be tough, not to step down, not to let yourself be beaten. Even Polish kids were taught to be tough. If you were not tough, you were weak and you were a bad boy.

In Poland this attitude developed because we had to be ready always for another uprising, for another hard struggle. This attitude was shifted to the mountains so that the Poles would think three times before coming down. And if they did come down without success, defeated, they were totally different people from a French or American expedition coming down defeated. The Poles came down with a bad conscience, as though they had done something wrong. They came down with a psychological hangover. "You were beaten. You are weak. You are not strong enough. If you lose, you are something inferior. You're not really a man."

So Poles would be willing to endure a lot so as not to be defeated?

Yes, this is at the root of Polish mountaineering attitudes.

This attitude must be especially useful in the Himalaya.

Yes. You've just got to be tough. Here on the Marmolata, on the rock, you've got to be tough and very skilled. But in the Himalaya you've just got to be tough, because in most cases there are no great technical difficulties. You just have to fight the cold, the weariness, the hunger, the thirst, and the sense of danger. You're not supposed to retreat before the danger.

And Poles are good at Himalayan climbing because they're used to dealing with danger, privation, suffering?

Yes. I like to describe Himalayan climbing as a kind of art of suffering. Just pushing, pushing yourself to your limits.

What were you like as a boy? Were you tough?

I was a typical young boy, very lively. I liked to play games, wander through the forest, look for mushrooms, things like that. Possibly the most distinct feature of my personality is that I had an extreme love of nature from the very beginning. I remember my childhood as a very happy life within nature.

We lived in a mountainous village with beautiful hills covered with forests near an excellent river. It was a kind of natural paradise. I loved to play in this natural paradise, and I had some fantastic experiences climbing on the walls of a castle and some very small cliffs and trees.

When I was ten we moved to the big city, and this was possibly the most important feature of my childhood. When we moved to the city it was a personal disaster.

Why was it a personal disaster?

I had a terrible longing for nature. I remember myself crying, remembering the happy past years of living in nature. We lived in the downtown part of Wroclaw. There was a nice park close to my house, but it was a typical city park, with nothing of the wilderness, nothing of unspoiled nature; it was something that I was scared to touch or to tread on.

When did you start climbing?

At age twenty-one. Some people invited me and my girlfriend to go climbing and I just touched the rock and I knew from the very beginning that this was exactly what I loved. And I was pretty skilled at climbing from the very beginning, so immediately I became part of the climbing community; there was no problem with being introduced to people or places or routes. It was very spontaneous. In the spring we went rock climbing, and then in 1968 we went to the Tatras, Polish high mountains where people do mountaineering.

> *"I LIKE TO DESCRIBE HIMALAYAN CLIMBING AS A KIND OF ART OF SUFFERING."*

What about climbing appealed to you?

It was just a kind of animal instinct. And to be in the mountains reminded me of my happy childhood in nature. When I went to the mountains I found it absolutely fantastic. I liked nature and I liked moving on rock, so two elements of my personality combined in a way.

What's the climbing community like in Poland?

Well, things are changing extremely in Poland. Everything is changing because we changed the [political and economic] system. It looks like the functioning of the climbing clubs is moving into a totally different pattern. We used to have gatherings two times a week; now people come less and less to club gatherings. The clubs were financially backed by the government; now there is nothing like this. The mountaineering community life now tends toward more private groups of people who develop some personal inclination toward one another. Of course the clubs still exist, but it is difficult to say how they will turn out. I can't say how it will end up.

And, formerly, all Polish climbers belonged to a club?

Yes, all Polish climbers belonged to a club. Most came to the club gatherings once or twice a week. The good climbers got some help and some sponsorship. There was no expedition that wouldn't be sponsored by the Polish association of mountain clubs or the climber's own club. It was very well organized as a result of the Polish political system. Everything was organized to be under the control of the government. So if you did well, you could go to the Himalaya or other mountain ranges. But the climbing community was always politically very rebellious, and they made up a big part of the Polish dissidents. A lot of them belonged to the underground movement. For this reason, mountaineering, although sponsored by the government, was always treated like an unruly child.

Is climbing a popular activity in Poland?

It is. Again, it's changing. The tendency right now is that most people are interested in free climbing, climbing on cliffs. And a lot of people still go to the Alps. However, within the last three or four years there's been a very serious decline in interest in the very high mountains like the Himalaya.

The first reason for this is that maybe 80 percent of the best high-altitude climbers have died. So there are not the climbers who could be the driving forces, who could pull the Polish climbers toward the Himalaya, experienced people who have both organizing experience and proper mountain experience and fitness and everything. The experienced ones, the strong ones, the ones who knew the routine, died.

The second reason is that the political system changed, the financial system totally changed, and people can't expect to be sponsored or to make expeditions the way it was done in the past, which meant taking out a lot of goods produced in Poland, selling them in India or Pakistan or Nepal, getting the currency, and then going to the mountains. This way won't work anymore because Polish prices are approaching western European prices; if you tried to sell Polish goods in India you would lose money.

On the other hand, people earn much more money now in Poland. Before, a month's salary was about $20 or $30 a month, and for this you could live in Poland. But to go outside Poland, this was nothing. Now the average Polish salary is about $150. For some people who are in business, going to the Himalaya might be easy, but for the young guys who are just starting the alpine experience, it's actually harder than before. And this is the second reason we are seeing a decline in interest in the Himalaya. For the young guys it is very hard to get enough money to go to Nepal.

And so sport climbing is the most popular kind of climbing?

Yes, there is a big interest in sport climbing. People construct artificial walls. We don't have a lot of natural rock like you have in the States, but we have some good limestone and sandstone rocks. So 90 percent of the people are just interested in sport climbing; some 30 or 40 percent of the young climbers would be ready to go to the Alps; and maybe 5 or 10 percent of the climbers would go to the Himalaya.

When did you first begin climbing in the Alps?

In 1971. I did the classics—the Walker Spur [of the Grandes Jorasses], American Direct on the Petit Dru, Petites Jorasses, Les Droites—and also a new route on the north face of Petit Dru and another new route on the north face of the Grandes Jorasses to the right of the Croz Spur.

Were these climbs harder than the climbs you'd done in the Tatras?

Yes, they were harder, they were longer, they were more exhausting.

And the following season, in 1972, I was in the Hindu Kush. I was lucky to do an exceptional alpine-style ascent. We did a very fine big-wall climb on a 7000-meter peak [north face of Acher Chioch].

So already you were thinking of doing alpine-style ascents at high altitude?

Actually, I wasn't thinking about it so much as just clinging to the habits from the Alps. I stood before the wall, it was big, and I considered it reasonable to do it exactly the way I would have done it in the Alps. I was the driving force for using these tactics. I said, "There's no reason to put the camps here. We just acclimatize somewhere and then we go and make it with one or two bivouacs." And we made it with two bivouacs.

And after this first experience I decided that never in the future would I like the traditional style. I later went with big expeditions three times, but it was something very strange and artificial for me. I felt totally alien to the idea of a big team, with distributed functions and jobs.

Does that have something to do with your personality?

Definitely. I'm generally quite rebellious. I like being left alone with the things I do, not being interfered with, just concentrating on what I'm doing. And I have this extreme liking for nature. I like to be in more intimate conditions with nature. So being with a big team with logistics and tactics spoils everything.

And you like to go climbing with friends?

I don't like to be in very casual partnerships. Partnership is very important to me. If I am with a person I like, then I'm ready to take much greater risks. If I am with a partner I don't like, there would be no chance that I would go into a risky situation with him.

Who were some of your partners?

Alex MacIntyre, Jurek [Jerzy] Kukuczka, Erhard Loretan, Jean Troillet— these were the people who made the biggest impression on me and who remain with me today.

Was Alex MacIntyre your first good partner?

I had some very fine partners when I was climbing in the Tatras. But since I did my first three big climbs in the Himalaya with Alex—Koh-î-Bandaka, Changabang, and Dhaulagiri east face—it's natural that I came to know him quite well. We were together on four expeditions, and I can't say I was fed up with him.

How did you both get along?

In a lot of ways we were very similar. We had the same inclination to fall in love with a particular mountain or face. And then that state of being in love with some particular mountain gave us amazing motivation. It was the same thing as being in love with a woman—you do things that you would not be able to do normally. In this way we were psychic brothers.

It was very fortunate that we managed to fall in love with the same objectives. I had just seen Bandaka in pictures, and Alex had never seen it; but on the train I managed to persuade him to climb it. When we came to the face we were so stunned by what we saw, there was no question that we would try. We were

> *". . . THAT STATE OF BEING IN LOVE WITH SOME PARTICULAR MOUNTAIN GAVE US AMAZING MOTIVATION. IT WAS THE SAME THING AS BEING IN LOVE WITH A WOMAN. . . ."*

terribly afraid of the wall. It was the most dangerous thing I've ever done. There was a lot of rockfall, and there was a serac barrier at the top. The most dangerous thing was rockfall. There were two sections where if you tried to cross in the morning hours you'd surely get hit. It was not just some chance, but a sure thing that you'd get killed. Fortunately we understood this, and so we crossed the first section in the afternoon. And the second one, the huge chimney we called Cyclotron, was trembling with stones till noon, and in the afternoon it was quiet. So we waited a half-day before climbing through it.

What kind of routes did you fall in love with?

It's hard to describe the particular impression that is appealing to you. It might be the beautiful rock section. It might be the beautiful shape or just the general look of the face. In the case of Trango, it's obvious. When you are underneath it, you can't believe how beautiful it is. Here it is beautiful, but looking at Trango Tower is something that is three times better than looking at Marmolata.

In the case of Changabang south face, again it's obvious—that is a very impressive rock face. Gasherbrum IV is again so fantastic, even just looking at the pictures. But in other cases, some other aspects appealed to me—for example, long traverses like the three Broad Peaks [north, central, and main peaks], or being extremely quick on a very beautiful face, a very obvious line like on Cho Oyu or Shisha Pangma.

But it's mainly the beauty of the line that motivates you?

Two aspects are most important for me: the aspect of adventure and the aspect of aesthetic beauty.

And that's why you don't have much interest in the 8000-meter peaks?

Yes. I don't think I would find enough motivation to take all those pains and go through those dangers. But if I really admire something, then it's much easier. My routes are quite carefully chosen.

Did you and Jerzy Kukuczka fall in love with similar objectives?

Yes. I gave the ideas, I found the things to do, and since they were the objectives that I wanted very much to do, I was very motivated. And I managed to convince him to go for those things too. He agreed that I was the man of ideas for our team. And in him I found a very confident personality who helped me very much. He brought great calm, and with this calm I was also more peaceful and had fewer doubts and uncertainties.

We were very different personalities, totally different, but we made up the differences between us. I represented some values, and he represented some other values, and together we made a good team.

How was your personality different from Jurek's?

I'm sensitive to dangerous situations, especially after years of experience in the high mountains. These situations worry me; I'm very conscious of so many dangers. And it might be harder in the coming years to accept big risks in the high mountains because so many friends have died. The people who pushed the limit all died. There is no escape. On the other hand, it's amazing, but I never had a single accident in the mountains. Never a single person in my company suffered anything—not even a scratch.

That's amazing considering the kind of climbs you've done.

Yes. I'm conscious of this. But with both Jurek and Loretan, I was the person who was restraining them in dangerous situations.

Is it necessary to have one person in the partnership who is especially safety-conscious?

Yes, because the very inspired climber when he is at his peak will go for anything. I did it myself so many times, being in love with some huge wall, not hesitating, just going for it. I somehow survived it, but most climbers like this die. At my age and with my experience I will not accept just going blindly for something; it's very important to know when to refrain.

Did Jurek take too many chances?

Oh yes. Jurek was taking too many chances, definitely. I did not think it was proper. And the basic proof is that he lost something like five partners. While he was climbing with me, we never had a problem. We were quite lucky. But later, when we parted, he started losing partners one after another.

What was Jurek like as a climber?

He was very quiet. He was very confident in what he was doing. I think it had to do with his religious background. He believed in God. He thought he was fair in his life, that he was just in living, that he was following the general principles of religion. And so, since he was fair, he expected God to be fair with him. This is what he told me. So if he was defeated on the mountains he would ask God, "Why? What did I do wrong? Why this treatment?"

So it was obvious that he suspected that God's justice is like human justice. I do not believe in God's justice. Just have a look at what He did with the Poles or the Jews. There's no explanation for those things, or why kids have to die, or why women are raped.

Why did you nickname Jurek "The Knuckle"?

We called him "The Knuckle" because in Poland there is a dish made of pig's feet called knuckle. And he just loved pig's feet. So we called him that for fun.

In English that nickname would imply that he was really tough.

Maybe it's an excellent nickname in English too, because he was really incredibly tough. I've never met a person who was so incredibly tough and so psychically motivated. He was a phenomenon. I doubt there was anybody else like him in the mountaineering world. After two months of extreme danger, of extreme doubt, of extreme bad weather, he would still go for the summit. Everybody else would be fed up, and he was ready always to take another huge portion of risk and another huge portion of suffering. He was always ready to take a lot of suffering.

What motivated him?

I'm not sure. Some people have a kind of animal drive to push forward— the conquistadors, for instance. Alexander the Great had the same stuff; he was just pushing, pushing blindly. With a few soldiers he was taking over huge armies. He was just pushing.

Jurek was the astrological sign of the ram, and Alexander the Great was also the ram. These are people who without discrimination hit an obstacle with their head. And they hit it until they break it or they break their own neck. He was this kind of animal. He was just pushing. He was just hitting something until he would crush it—without consideration, without thinking, just pure energy pushing on.

Was it inevitable, then, that he would die climbing?

No, but I would say that it was predictable. I knew him very well and I was afraid of him. He was personally very lucky, but the people who were with him were not lucky; they were dying. He was luckier, but you suspected that one day he would end up like them.

And, of course, you know how he died. It was a typical dead-end situation. He was on a single, very thin, six-millimeter rope, pushing up a very high part of the south face of Lhotse. There was no way down. As long as he could make the next step, he would continue. However, there was always another step of unprotected ground, practically without belay. So after something like sixty or seventy meters of this he fell off, and of course the rope broke. [Kukuczka died in 1989.]

There was no retreat for him. Retreating for him was the worst imaginable disaster. He would never back down. He was this kind of person.

What effect did his death have on your climbing?

It had a bad effect on the climbing. For a couple of years I had second thoughts about whether it was ethical to put myself through such dangers in the mountains. Any life is a life, whether it is yours or somebody else's; the life has a value in and of itself. Definitely, you cannot risk somebody else's life. But even if it's your own life, I'm not sure you've got the right to risk it. But on the other hand, if you decide not to risk your life, then you may slowly die as well. You may die psychically.

Does risking your life allow you to live more fully?

Yes, definitely.

But is it even harder to justify the risk now that you have a child?

Yes, harder. On my last expedition, definitely. I thought a lot about Alexander and it was not easy.

Have the deaths of many of your friends and partners also made you more conscious of the risk?

Yes. Fortunately, none of them died while climbing with me. But anyway they died.

Did their deaths make you question the value of climbing?

I've written an article about this called "The Path of the Mountain." That means the way of living and the way of looking for your own truth through an instrument, which in the case of mountaineers is climbing mountains. And, of course, I tried to justify why the mountains and why the climbing. What is particular in the mountains and in the climbing that justifies considering it an instrument of some mental or some psychic searching? And through mountaineering can you expect to find out something about yourself and the world around you? I believe that climbing is, in a way, a religious experience for me, because climbing is the activity through which I find out the best truth about myself and the surroundings of nature.

So climbing is a way to come to this realization?

Yes, yes. It's very difficult to talk about it, to serve you some portion of mystical experience, but definitely my climbs in the mountains are mystical experiences for me. And they are extremely positive. They make it easier to accept all the negative aspects of life—getting older, getting weaker, getting ill from time to time.

Why do first ascents appeal to you?

Because they are more adventurous. They are totally unknown. And they are much more creative, which gives you a lot of joy and pumps up your ego.

Is this one of the reasons that the west face of Gasherbrum IV appealed to you?

When I tried Gasherbrum IV it wasn't very famous. There had been three or four attempts, but it was nothing like Lhotse south face, where a number of teams just followed one after another. Between climbers, everyone knew about it, but there was no real chase for this. With Gasherbrum IV it was a case of personal love; it was just beautiful.

Did it take you a long time to figure out how to climb that face?

Well, it was so obvious. It was just a mistake by the other parties. There was a huge gully, and then there was a big barrier; but the initial gully gave access to the heart of the wall, so there was no reason not to use it. So I attempted the line starting on the right, instead of the left line following the big spur, which was dangerous.

Were you lucky to survive that climb?

Yes, that was the hardest mountain experience for me. We spent four days without food, three days without drinking—a very long time. Everything

Kurtyka's route on the West face of Gasherbrum IV.
(Photo by Januz Onyuszkiewicz; Diadem Archives)

that could go wrong on a big wall went wrong there—everything. We found ground with very poor protection, with a dubious retreat. Then we ran out of food and fuel. Then, in the last section near the summit, we met terrible snow conditions—steep snow, sometimes up to your waist. We could travel just 200 meters a day. And a breakdown in the weather—the worst thing that can happen on an alpine-style expedition—happened just before the summit. We spent two nights just sitting, being unable to crawl out and stand up. Of course, we were also without food and water. So everything that could go wrong on an alpine-style ascent of a serious wall went wrong there.

Was it hard to keep going?

No. Actually, after the second day, it was obvious that we were going to have to continue to go up. So there were no doubts; there was no thinking about retreat. However, on the last part just below the summit, when the weather was terrible, it was the one time in my life I was conscious that I might die. And I decided that if the weather would not clear, then I would get out of the bivouac sack and I would try to descend. I would have wanted to die standing, not lying down. It's better to move than to sit and slowly die.

Did your mind play tricks on you on that climb?

Yes. I even tried to classify them. Possibly the most striking was the sense of the presence of a third person. And what was possibly the most amazing thing about this is that both I and Robert Schauer had them at the same time. It was so striking, so tangible, this sense of a third person, that at one moment I tried to talk about it with Robert, and the moment I started, I could not express myself, I just said something like, "Robert, I would like to tell you something, but it's very strange."

"I know what you mean," he said. "You sense him, the third person."

"Yes. Do you too?"

"Yes."

This was very strange. And a similar thing happened with Robert on that very dangerous bivouac when I had thoughts of possible death. Actually it was a good experience, being very clearly conscious that I was going to die, being unable to do anything about it, and since I knew that this was possibly the moment when we would die, it seemed to me that this was a very important moment, possibly the most important moment in the life of a man. And it seemed to me so absurd that Robert might not know this. He might not be conscious that in just a couple of days or hours we could be absolutely stiff and dead. So I thought, by God, he should know this. He must know this. If he doesn't know this, it's terrible. It was so urgent for me to share this knowledge with him. So I started talking about it, and again, he understood what I was going to say. He said, "Yes, I know what you mean. I'm ready. I'm prepared. Don't worry."

Was it disappointing not to climb Gasherbrum IV to the very top?

Of course. Right after the climb I was very disappointed, but everybody admired it very much, and although I didn't accept it as being done completely, everyone else accepted it as being done. And now it doesn't matter much. Lately I think it's very important to be defeated sometimes. A person who is just winning, winning, winning, is losing something. He just wants to possess more and more. I think losing is very important also.

What can you gain from losing?

> *"YOU MUST KNOW THE SENSE OF FAILING, AND IF YOU ARE WISE ENOUGH, YOU MAY APPRECIATE THE STATE OF LOSING. . . ."*

There is something good in losing, but it's so difficult to grasp what it is or describe it. Maybe it's the sense of the fullness of life, maybe the ultimate acceptance of the total shape of life. You must know the sense of failing, and if you are wise enough, you may appreciate the state of losing, which makes you humble and more relaxed. And if you are just winning, then there is no understanding that finally you will lose. You will grow old. You will grow weak. You will lose everything. It's a big mistake to forget it. This is the way of the middle path. You should know the sense of both winning and losing.

So climbing becomes a metaphor for life?

Yes. You experience in a short time what life is. For instance, you experience either a euphoric success or a terrible disaster. Or you may sense very painfully that you are growing older. You may be conscious that your fitness is passing away. I haven't noticed this yet. Each year I do harder and harder rock climbs. And I don't think that when I was younger I would have been able to do ascents of 8000-meter peaks in one night and day [Cho Oyu and Shisha Pangma]. So what I do is still better and better, but I'm very conscious that at any moment I will feel the decline of fitness. So through mountaineering, in a very drastic way, you may experience what it is to grow older. And in thinking about it, you must find a way of accepting that you are not as strong as you were. So again, mountaineering becomes a metaphor for life.

Was it gratifying to succeed on the east face of Trango Tower after failing on K2?

Yes. I had been thinking about Trango Tower for a long time. I saw it for the first time in 1976, and even then I was thinking about climbing it.

Was it an adventurous climb?

Yes, but not as adventurous as some others. What is the essence of adventure? The essence of adventure is being put in an unknown position from which you don't know what will happen. The unknown is the essence of adventure. And on Trango Tower the aspect of adventure was not as great as on Gasherbrum IV or on the Broad Peak traverse, because we fixed 500 meters of rope for the descent. The ropes were there, so it was not a position of being completely unknown. This possible escape route eliminated an aspect of adventure.

But another aspect of adventure is facing up to the unexpected, and this happened a lot on Trango Tower. We never knew what the next pitch would be [they aided many of the twenty-nine pitches] or if the weather would hold. So in this sense it was an adventurous climb.

Were you exhausted after the climb?

Yes, but definitely less exhausted than after Gasherbrum IV.

Are climbs like this cathartic for you?

Yes. And what is catharsis? It is a purification. But purification from what? Purification from the neurotic effects of everyday life—being preoccupied with small, stupid things, busying your mind with unnecessary things that are totally untrue, as in the case of neurotic behaviors. The huge psychological and physical stress of a big mountaineering experience sweeps out of you all the unnecessary rubbish. It's quite common that people get a sense of being refreshed and renewed after a climb. So in a way your climbs also serve other people because you're a normal person when you come back to normal life. You're not a neurotic animal, mad and crazy.

So is this your motivation for climbing?

I wouldn't say I do this for this or that purpose. These are just effects; they are just a part of it. One part of it is just being in the mountains; another part is feeling the pleasure of movement; another part is having an adventure; another part is discovering the best truth of yourself. This is The Path of the Mountain. Just being on your path. For one person the proper path is being a philosopher. For another person it's being a worker. For me it's staying in touch with the mountains and climbing. This is the way I find the most of life and the most truth of myself. My understanding of life is definitely shaped by mountaineering.

JEAN-CLAUDE DROYER

*It is common to see climbers on our rock faces using a piton
for resting or a foothold on routes which are regarded as "free
climbs." For some this has become habitual, no longer even
questioned, and their progress on these "free" routes is a series of
more or less rapid movements, interrupted by periods anchored to
a piton, which has thus become a kind of lifebuoy. Now, one
should understand that this cannot really be considered as "free
climbing," as examination of the following definition clearly
shows: "the free climb is that in which the climber uses for his
progress only the natural roughness of the rock." It follows that
artificial aids such as pitons, wedges, rope slings and the like
must be used only as safety precautions.*

—Jean-Claude Droyer, "Free
Climbing—Some Ideas for a More
Rigorous Conception," in *La Montagne*

J EAN-CLAUDE DROYER'S definition of free climbing doesn't sound like fighting
words today, but when he introduced it to France in the mid-1970s, it proved
the alpine equivalent of throwing down the gauntlet. For years, continental
climbers had grabbed and pulled on pitons, ropes, bolts, and carabiners so as
to scratch and claw their way to the top of a peak. The suggestion that they eschew
these artificial aids and climb using only the natural roughness of the rock met
with nothing less than shock, outrage, and undisguised animosity. Undismayed
by this hostile reaction, Droyer persisted in his free-climbing crusade, writing
articles, eliminating aid from existing routes, and pushing the standard on his own
hard free routes. By the late seventies a group of young climbers had gathered
around him, and by the early eighties he had pretty much convinced French
climbers that his concept of free climbing offered the best chance for keeping
challenge and commitment in the sport. Droyer's efforts helped set the stage for
the current revival of free climbing in France and paved the way for such

Jean-Claude Droyer. (Photo by Kathrin Neuhauser)

pioneering figures as Patrick Edlinger, Didier Raboutou, Jean-Baptiste Tribout, François Legrand, Catherine Destivelle, and others. For these reasons he is rightfully considered the father of modern free climbing in France.

Like many French climbers, Droyer got started climbing on the boulders of Fontainebleau outside Paris. He first visited the area at age sixteen and spent a season or two there honing his skills before moving on to the Alps. After struggling up easy Alpine routes, such as the regular route on the Aiguille du Grépon and the south ridge of the Aiguille du Moine, Droyer eventually progressed to the point that he began soloing. His big breakthrough came in 1971 when he made the second solo ascent of the Major Route on the Brenva Face of Mont Blanc. Later that summer, he claimed the first solo ascent of the American Direct Route on the west face of the Petit Dru, causing quite a stir in Alpine circles.

In addition to these audacious solo climbs, Droyer also knocked off a number of important winter ascents, including the first winter ascent of the Contamine-Mazeaud Route on Mont Blanc du Tacul in 1971 and the first winter ascent of the Mollaret-Seigneur Route on Mont Blanc du Tacul in 1974. In 1975 he traveled to the United States to repeat several classic ice routes in New England, including Black Dike on Mount Cannon, and made the first winter ascent of the VMC Direct-Direct Route on Mount Cannon.

Then, in the summer of 1975, Droyer began his free-climbing crusade. In 1973 he had visited Great Britain and come away convinced that a purer definition of free climbing was needed if continental climbers were to equal or surpass the British. He had written articles suggesting this, but people really hadn't taken notice. He had put up new free routes in the Chamonix area and elsewhere using clean, leader-placed protection such as nuts, but few bothered to emulate his example. So in 1975 he decided to put his words into action. First he climbed Le Triomphe d'Eros (5.11a/b) at the Verdon Gorge with the absolute minimum of aid. Then he began removing wooden pegs from other routes so that climbers would have to free-climb them. Droyer's actions so angered some French climbers that Le Triomphe d'Eros was spray-painted and he was vilified. He had gotten their attention, however, and soon climbers began seriously debating the merits of his approach. His subsequent free ascents of routes such as Yellow Ridge (5.10c) in the Saussois in 1976 provided further evidence that his definition of free climbing was the way of the future in France.

After concentrating on short free routes, Droyer turned his attention to reducing aid on classic Alpine routes. In spring of 1977, he took aim at the east face of the Grand Capucin, a route consisting of a series of laybacks, thin cracks, and wall moves on superb rock. Walter Bonatti had used 150 points of aid on the first ascent of the route. Droyer cut the points of aid to eight, calling the ascent the most difficult route he'd ever done in the Alps. Later that summer, he eliminated all but six points of aid on the Comici Route on Cima Grande di Lavaredo in the Dolomites. The following year he raised the stakes further by dispensing with aid completely on the Comici Route. In 1979 he rose to the front rank of climbers with the first free ascent of the Cassin Route on Cima Ovest and the Carlesso Route on the Torre di Val Grande. Both were graded 5.11b/c, making them the hardest routes in the Alps at that time.

Having pushed the grade in the mountains, Droyer returned to the crags to refine his technique further. In 1980 he climbed La Gougousse in Buoux, the first 5.12a in France. Other short extreme routes followed, and eventually most French climbers came to accept Droyer's approach as the way of progress in free climbing. His ideas laid the groundwork for the amazing advances of recent years that have pushed the grade higher than ever thought possible.

But if Droyer initiated the free-climbing movement in France, he by no means condones the direction it has taken. In 1985 he was instrumental in circulating the Manifesto of Nineteen, a statement against competition climbing. In recent years he has criticized the increasing use of bolts where leader-placed protection such as nuts and Friends would serve just as well and have the added advantages of preserving the rock and keeping the elements of risk and commitment in climbing. At present he is working on a route that symbolizes all these qualities—a seventy-foot overhanging crack in the Chamonix region that he believes will go free at 5.13b/c.

Droyer was born on May 8, 1946, in Paris and grew up in and around the city. His father was a professional soccer player, but Droyer shunned sports as a child and preferred to spend his time studying. He might well have gone into academia had not a chance vacation to the Alps in his teens turned his attention to the mountains. Over the years Droyer has made his living as a climbing guide and technical advisor to outdoor companies. Today he lives in Paris and works at Auvieux Campeur, the largest mountaineering shop in France. He has never married, has no children, but spends a lot of time with his German girlfriend, Kathrin Neuhauser.

While attending the Mountain Summit conference in Snowbird, Utah, Droyer took time out to talk about his contribution to free climbing, among other topics. A tall, lanky fellow with thick glasses, an animated manner, and a halo of dark, frizzy hair, Droyer looks much like the Sorbonne professor he might have become had he not caught the climbing bug and become a top alpinist and free climber instead. He spoke at length about the challenges facing free climbing today and emphasized the need for contemporary climbers to understand the sport's past so that they can better decide where to take it in the future.

Why did you introduce free climbing to France?

At the beginning of the seventies I felt that French alpinists were in a cul-de-sac. They were not pushing the standards. They would climb a few meters, rest on a piton, climb a few meters, and rest on the next one. I thought it was possible to push the standards by returning to the purer rules of the beginning of the century where there would be no resting on pitons.

I was not sure about all this at the beginning, but I wrote some articles suggesting that it was at least possible. Then in 1973 the British Mountaineering Council invited me to observe free climbing in Britain. The British didn't rest on pitons at all, and they were pushing the limits. They were better than us. It was really a shock. When I returned to France, it took me a few years to digest all of this. I reflected and came to believe that free climbing was the way to progress in rock climbing and mountaineering.

Was it hard to change people's minds about free climbing?

Yes. When I first tried to get people to free-climb, they told me, "No way. It's useless." I was alone in this for a few years, and even now in the south of France they don't like to recognize that I was the first. They prefer to say that free climbing came to France with the first visit of the British. But when the British came in 1976 to the Verdon Gorge I had been free-climbing and writing articles about it for more than a year, telling people, "Try to free-climb. You'll like it and it's better for the sport."

I was one of the climbers who discovered Verdon Gorge at the beginning of the seventies, and in 1975 I decided to push the standards. I opened a route called Le Triomphe d'Eros with very few points of aid. The route became the center of a big controversy. It was almost destroyed. People even spray-painted it, which showed that they had no respect for the rock. They should have written an article saying, "Droyer is no good. Droyer is wrong," but they should not have done that to the rock.

Then I did a demonstration by pulling the [wooden] pegs on some routes in Buoux and other places. Without the pegs, climbers were obliged to do the route using only the natural holds or to stay on the ground. There were many polemics against me for doing this. Before I removed the pegs, climbers could do the routes, and afterward they couldn't. They didn't like this because they were not real sportsmen; they were not prepared to fail.

So I was hated at the beginning, but the ascent of Le Triomphe d'Eros marked the beginning of free climbing in France. It took a long time to change people's minds. It wasn't until 1979 that I had a group of young climbers saying, "He's right. We can progress and do new things in this way." Soon the trend increased until there were many people free-climbing in France.

How did you get started climbing in the first place?

My family used to go to the seaside on holidays, but at age sixteen I wanted a change. So we went to the mountains for the first time. I did some hiking and so forth, and after this summer I decided to try rock climbing on the boulders of Fontainebleau, close to Paris. I joined the French Alpine Club and spent my first weekend climbing on the boulders. I enjoyed that very much.

What did you enjoy about it?

I liked the feeling. I liked moving on the rocks. I liked to be on a vertical face. It was fun.

Did you have heroes who were climbers?

After my first weekend with the alpine club, I began to read some books, and I discovered Lionel Terray and Walter Bonatti. They were my heroes. At this time the heroes were mountaineers; there were no rock-climbing heroes back then.

What about them appealed to you?

They were adventurers, and they did hard routes in the mountains. In the alpine club, they told me from the beginning, "You climb on the boulders, but it's to prepare for the mountains." And after six months of climbing in places close to Paris, I went in 1973 for my first summer season in Chamonix. I was afraid of the crevasses in the glacier and of the mixed ground, because it was really different from Fontainebleau and the cliffs. My friends and I were very slow. It took us fifteen hours to climb the regular route on Le Grépon. We got back to the hut very late. I had a lot of epics in the early years.

Did you progress rapidly as a climber?

Not really. I was very weak in the arms and legs. For example, it took me two years to climb 5.7. This was not good progress. I wondered if I could ever become a good climber. After my second season in the mountains, though, I began to progress rapidly.

Did you prefer rock climbing to snow climbing?

At first, I was attracted more by rock climbing. And my third season I began to do some hard classic routes, like the west face of the Petites Jorasses. After that I began to do some classic snow-and-ice climbs, including the north face of Les Courtes. Later I progressed in the direction of classic Alpine climbing, doing the west face of the Petit Dru when I was twenty. And then I began to climb solo.

Why did you start climbing solo?

It's difficult to say. I had some problems finding partners, but also I might have been ambitious too. I began to climb solo in the Prealps. I did some hard routes in the Vercors and then some more in the Chamonix needles and places like that. And the trend continued to the point that I was prepared to attack the hardest routes in the Alps solo. And I soloed the Major Route on Mont Blanc, which only Walter Bonatti had done solo. And then I did a much harder climb, the first solo ascent of the American Direct Route on the west face of the Petit Dru. This made me well known in Alpine climbing circles.

Was soloing more difficult than climbing with a partner?

It was scarier, but I enjoyed taking things on by myself, being very calm, very quiet, studying things in advance. This was my approach to soloing serious routes in the Alps.

Had you climbed these routes previously?

Yes, most of the routes I had climbed before, but normally I had climbed them only once.

Did you ever free-solo?

Yes, I free-soloed most of them, but on the American Direct, for example, I belayed two aid pitches in a ninety-meter groove because I didn't want to trust the pitons. When I climbed an aid pitch, I belayed myself because sometimes you have to hang on a piton, and if it comes away....

How do you choose your routes?

I choose the ones that are attractive and hard, but I am not only attracted by the technical grade. Many young people today see a technical grade and they want to do it for that reason. I am a bit different. I am attracted by the quality of the route, not only the technical grade.

What kind of qualities do you look for in a route?

The quality of the rock, the severity of the line, and sometimes the historical aspect. This is why I like to climb in Dresden and other places in eastern Germany. The climbers there spent many years solving certain problems, and this, too, appeals to me.

> *"MANY YOUNG PEOPLE TODAY SEE A TECHNICAL GRADE AND THEY WANT TO DO IT FOR THAT REASON. I AM A BIT DIFFERENT. I AM ATTRACTED BY THE QUALITY OF THE ROUTE. . . ."*

Did you pioneer many new routes?

After this period of solo climbing, I began to climb more difficult routes on ice, and also I free-climbed a few new routes, like Yellow Ridge in Le Saussois in 1976. This training paid off in the mountains. In 1977 I was the first to consider freeing the east face of the Grand Capucin. I tried it a few times, and I did it with only eight points of aid, instead of the 150 Bonatti had used. This climb illustrated the possibilities of free climbing in the Alps.

In 1978 I did the first free ascent of the Comici Route on Cima Grande di Lavaredo. In 1979 I free-climbed the Cassin Route on the west face of Cima Ovest de Lavaredo and the Carlesso Route on Torre di Val Grande, the hardest routes in the Alps at that time.

When did you begin pushing the grade on shorter routes?

In 1975 the hardest grade in France was 5.10b and we were behind the U.S. climbers. But at the beginning of the eighties we started to progress rapidly. I was the first in France to get to 5.12 with La Gougousse in Buoux (1980) and a little later Lauren Jacob climbed the Angel [5.12] in Le Saussois.

Did you train to do these routes?

I didn't train a lot, I only climbed. I didn't like to train at that time. For me it was like another aspect; it was like gymnastics. I liked to practice moves on boulders, but I didn't like to train.

Was Fontainebleau one of your favorite practice areas?

Yes, and I still like it very much. You can climb there year after year and still discover new things. It's so huge. There may be more than 20,000 boulders. Sometimes I go there three times a week.

Is that where a lot of the French climbers go to train?

There are two poles of climbing in France, the north and the south. The north is centered in Paris, and 99 percent of the climbers in the north go to Fontainebleau. And in the south, they have a few limestone boulders close to Nice and some quartzite boulders close to Lyon; but they don't climb regularly on boulders, they go directly to the cliffs. They climb at Buoux or the Verdon Gorge. In the north, bouldering is part of the habit, and in the south, it's more climbing cliffs. That's why the two poles are a bit different.

Is there a philosophical difference between the north and the south?

I can't see really any philosophical difference between the climbers in the north and in the south. And now the two poles are merging because the best rock climbers in the north spend maybe two months in the south in winter, for example. And since the south is not a very good place for rock climbing in the summer, some climbers from the south travel to the north.

Did bouldering prepare you to climb hard routes in the mountains?

Yes. It was good training for the big routes. It was logical for me, after doing some hard bouldering at Fontainebleau, to go to the Dolomites or to try to free-climb a route in Chamonix.

Is this the case with many of the younger climbers today?

No. Most of them don't like mountaineering. Even to get to the Grand Capucin requires mountaineering skills. It only takes an hour, but you have to carry a rucksack, you have to watch your feet, you have to put up with the cold, and these are things that a lot of them don't want to do.

Is free climbing growing away from mountaineering?

I think so. [Wistfully] Even if some people continue to do both, I think it's dividing. There are a few who have done both, such as Wolfgang Güllich, who free-climbed and went to the Himalaya. But what is interesting is that Güllich didn't like climbing competitions. He was a sport climber, but he didn't go to competitions.

Do the leading competition climbers from France still go to the mountains?

Not now. At the beginning, they did. For example, the first free ascent of the east face of the Grand Capucin was done by Jean-Baptiste Tribout in

1982, and not long afterward he went into competition and stopped mountaineering completely. Didier Raboutou doesn't go to the mountains. Neither does Patrick Edlinger. And this could slow the progress of the standards in the mountains.

Is that happening now?

Not yet, because the divide between the two is too recent. But I have this impression. For example, in the Mont Blanc area a few years ago there were some 5.12b routes climbed, and then there were not a lot of new ones until Alain Ghersen and Thierry Renault began climbing some 5.13 routes a year or so ago.

Should bolts be used to put up new routes in the mountains?

Yes, because bolts allow you to climb in some new areas with really quality climbing. There are many good routes that have been pioneered with bolts. For example, the routes on El Capitan. I think Bonatti and Messner were wrong in completely refusing to bolt. They were wrong to make a general rule that applied to everybody. It's good to reflect sometimes and ask ourselves if truth is so absolute. But the problem is where to stop. If you put some bolts next to a crack, that is too much.

In France there is now a reaction against bolting too much. Climbers want to save a bit of wild nature in the mountains. There are so many bolts on some of the smaller cliffs that it's difficult to follow the routes. And some people were doing this in the mountains to make some of the huts more popular places to visit. But now the French Federation [French Alpine Club] is questioning all this. They may clean up a few routes as an example that they will not accept all of this bolting in the mountains. More and more people agree that it's important to keep a bit of unspoiled nature in the mountains.

Should they be placed from the ground up?

That's the best ethic, but on certain rocks it could be unfeasible. It's still the ethic in eastern Germany and Czechoslovakia; but they have sandstone, and sandstone is soft, so you can put bolts in easily when leading. Limestone is very hard, and perhaps it's necessary to rappel down to place them. And when the bolts are placed on rappel, they may be in better position so that the finished product is perfect for the following teams. When you follow a route, you don't want to worry about how the first climbers opened the route.

Is there controversy in France concerning how bolts should be placed?

Yes, in the mountains there is a war between the purists and some climbers with Bosch drills who place bolts on rappel. And some routes very close to

each other have been opened in very different ways. One Sunday in the early eighties, the two opposing groups met near Chamonix, and a strong discussion and near-fight ensued. The names of the routes reflect this. Michel Piola, who used the ground-up ethic, called his route Black Sunday [5.11c], and Jean-François Hagenmuller, who was rap-bolting, called his route Must We Burn the Prophet? [5.11a].

Ethically speaking, I do find the ground-up approach much better. When you open a route from the ground up, you can't place so many bolts and you have to be more careful where you place them. When you rap-bolt, you can put up so many routes that adventure climbing might not be possible in the future because it may be very difficult to find rock without bolts on it, especially on the smaller cliffs.

Should bolting ethics vary from area to area?

The rock is the main factor as to which rules should apply. It would be silly and completely stupid to put bolts close to Butterballs [5.11c] in

Jean-Claude Droyer.
(Photo by Kathrin Neuhauser)

Yosemite because it's a superb crack line. But it's a bit stupid to refuse bolts on some steep wall in Joshua Tree, because with just a few bolts you can put in superb routes.

How about altering the rock through chipping and gluing holds?

In the beginning of the seventies, I chipped a few holds, but after I saw the progress of the standards, I reflected and thought, "It is not good to chip. Someone in the future may be able to climb the route without these holds."

We chipped a lot in France and I think we went too far in this direction. In Buoux, for example, many of the new routes have been doctored. Sometimes a pocket has been enlarged, which could be okay, but then some routes have been completely opened this way, which is ridiculous. I can't understand why Jean-Marc Troussier, who is a good climber, did some routes in the early eighties like Frank Zappa [5.12d], which has fifteen two-finger pockets drilled with a Bosch. This makes no sense.

Should routes be removed?

Why not? In the United States, for example, if someone puts up a route that goes against the rules, other climbers destroy it. But in Europe, the other climbers would never do this. If there is a stupid route with drilled pockets, people will tell you, "It's your bastard," but they won't remove it. Once someone puts up a route, it's there to stay.

In Fontainebleau, there were some people who chipped holds at night. Sometimes I would use glue to hide the pockets where they had chipped, and I was more attacked than the guys who chipped the holds. It was crazy.

Happily, the chipping in Fontainebleau is becoming very rare. One of the guys was caught and beat up by some climbers, and now the chiseling has stopped. Climbers realize that it's fantastic to have futuristic problems that one day could go. So the consensus in Fontainebleau is not to chip holds. But it's not the same in the cliffs.

Does your refusal to chip grow out of a respect for the rock?

Yes, I have tried to respect the rock. This is also why I am careful in using chalk. If it's really hot, I prefer to wait for another day rather than to use too much chalk and leave many, many marks. Because on some cliffs the use of chalk makes some holds very greasy.

But you do use chalk?

I use it, but I use it carefully. And I don't use chalk at all in Fontainebleau. We had some problems with chalk there. We have such good friction on the sandstone of Fontainebleau, and chalk can make it greasy. The tradition in Fontainebleau is to use resin. Then there are no marks and no problems.

Were you opposed to the first rock-climbing competitions?

Yes. And I was not the only one opposed to them. There was the well-known Manifesto of Nineteen [1985] signed by myself, Patrick Berhault, Jean-Pierre Bouvier, Marc and Antoine Lemenestrel, Jean-Baptiste Tribout, Catherine Destivelle, and twelve other climbers. All were opposed to competition. They signed because they thought competition would change the spirit of rock climbing. And even those who changed their minds and went into competition still realized that it was not the essence of climbing. These guys were pushed by outside elements to go into competition. They thought it would be difficult to make a living from climbing if they did not go to the competitions. And now some of them are stuck in the system, and it's difficult to stop the system, to stop the machine. Antoine Lemenestrel competed once or twice but didn't like it, so he stopped. But there are others, like Tribout, who like to compete very much and discovered it can be a thrilling experience.

Are competition climbers paid well?

The best ones are making a living. In recent years Didier Raboutou has won at least $50,000 a year in competition prize money and contracts with manufacturers. He has two cars. He has a good apartment. He has enough to live. But in the last year or two he and the others are making less money. The media is less interested and several competitions have been canceled and there is less sponsorship from companies. So it's more difficult to make a living as a professional climber.

Why have French climbers done so well in competitions?

Because of their dedication and because of the ground on which they climb. Their dedication is intense. Some of them, like Tribout and Raboutou, spend all their time training. They are very serious about training for rock climbing and competitions.

And we have marvelous limestone in France, and limestone has the best possibilities for the hardest routes. There are many areas, such as Cimaï, Buoux, and Verdon Gorge, where it's possible to climb many 8as [5.13a/b] and 8bs [5.13c/d]. This is why the French climbers are the best now in the competitions.

But I think they could be challenged by other climbers. Stefan Glowacz from Germany is one of the best. Some American climbers could challenge the French. And one of the most gifted climbers, Jerry Moffatt, could be the best if he wanted to. He is sometimes beaten by others because he doesn't like to be so serious and train all the time. If he wanted to, he could be the best, because he's so gifted. But to achieve the level of Didier Raboutou and some of the others, you have to have a strong dedication. You can't be disturbed by the problems of daily life. You have to have a stable relationship with your wife or girlfriend and family. You must only climb.

Is competition climbing alive and well in France?

Yes, the French competition climbing circuit is well established now. But it could be better managed with two changes: we should find out how many people are interested in coming to see competitions and how much money this would generate. Because if we have only a small public, we will have difficulty finding money. And the best climbers are really hungry about money. They believe that there is a lot of money in climbing. I think some of them are completely dreaming. They think they are tennis players. They want to stay in the best hotels. They want to win more and more money, but they don't want to respect agreements with the manufacturers. They don't want to wear the manufacturer's T-shirt. They don't want to do the things the other sports stars do, and yet they want to have the money.

This is a big problem, because the French Federation has few sponsors, and it's difficult to find them, and if the climbers don't respect the sponsors, the sponsors will disappear. For example, at Leeds, the first British competition [1989], the climbers didn't want to wear the sponsor's T-shirt. This was ridiculous. They wanted to have a free life, but at the same time they wanted to have money. In Bercy, when the sponsors were announced, many of the young climbers made noise to drown out the announcement. This was not realistic. If you work for a sponsor, it's necessary to accept the conditions.

How long have you been involved in competitions?

I have been involved since the first international competition in Arco, Italy, in 1985. Manueli Casara, the organizer, phoned me many times, and one morning I was in a bad mood and told him, "Yes, I will come." And after that I was obliged to go. That was the first time I was involved in competition. I was a style judge of that competition.

I got involved with competitions because I was afraid that if I didn't, I would get out of touch with what was happening in climbing. So after the Arco competition, I worked at the Grenoble competition, and then I became a course setter for some local competitions. And I also set courses for the Snowbird competitions.

Do you like doing this?

Yes. We had some problems because we did not have much time to build the routes, but I think we were lucky. The main problem was to create a route that would be equal for different-size climbers. If the course setter makes the route difficult by putting in a lunge move, then that could be unfair for shorter people. But it's difficult to be completely fair; I don't think that the routes are equal very often. We need to improve the design of the walls first, and in France we have been making some advances. We have a few factories working only on climbing walls, and the best designs are really nice to climb on and could make things equal between climbers.

Do you help out the younger climbers with training?

A little bit. I am a mountain guide and rock-climbing teacher and I have pushed some of them. Also, I climbed some of the first 8as with Marc Lemenestrel, but I don't think I helped him very much. He was really confident in himself—maybe too confident.

And I advise some of the younger climbers, but I am not an official. I may become one for the French Federation. I was involved for two years in the federation's sport committee, but there were some problems. We had a break three or four years ago between the mountaineers and the rock climbers. The rock climbers went away to organize an independent federation called the French Federation of Rock Climbing. I stayed in the mountaineering federation to organize the rock climbing. That's why some guys in the independent federation didn't like me. And now the two organizations have come together again, which is good, but now I have to wait for a stabilization of things before I become involved in the French Federation again.

Do you still feel the need to speak out about what's happening in the sport?

I'm no longer on the main front because for the last few years I haven't done the hardest routes. I've tried to train more and maybe get to 8b. I've found a seventy-foot crack in Chamonix that overhangs twenty feet. I plan to open it from the bottom and protect it with Friends. It should be 5.13b or c. But I'm getting older and it's not easy to climb at this level. And when you're not at the top, it's difficult to lay down rules and give advice. The younger guys will tell you, "Shut up. You're not good enough."

For many years I wrote articles about what I was thinking. The last few years I've written nothing, and some people come up to me when I'm skiing or doing something else and ask me why I don't speak about this trend or that trend. But I would prefer to do very hard climbing and then to speak.

The problem for me is fatigue. To climb the harder grades you have to be very strong and have very good stamina. Sure, you have to have a very good understanding of the rock so that you can figure out the moves quickly and place your body in the right position in relation to the holds, and you have to have good balance, but you also have to have strong fingers and you have to be able to climb for a very long time with no tiredness in the forearms. And this is my weakness.

Also, you have to climb with some boldness. When I was young I was bold. I was often afraid before soloing a route, but while I was climbing it I lost my fear. I didn't want to call for a helicopter. I was in the climb and I had to finish it. But now I hesitate before doing hard solos. It's very scary to solo at the 5.11d or 5.12a level. I'm more hesitant about doing this now than I was in the past. On limestone, the holds are very small and could break. When you become older, you think more about these things.

And when you get older, you need to be more cautious. Because if you strain a tendon or break something, it will take a long time to get back to your top level. I think that's why it's difficult to continue at the top level. I know many good climbers who have stopped at thirty-five. They were really good until then, but after that, family life, job problems, and the tendons became more important.

Why do you like to climb?

I like the fact of being able to climb an impossible-looking route. It's not only the gesture of the move for me. It's also the aesthetic aspect that's important: the look of the wall and the structure of the rock. There are two aspects: doing a hard move elegantly and doing it on a rock that is impossible looking.

> *"I LIKE . . . TO CLIMB AN IMPOSSIBLE-LOOKING ROUTE. IT'S NOT ONLY THE GESTURE OF THE MOVE FOR ME. IT'S ALSO THE AESTHETIC ASPECT THAT'S IMPORTANT. . . ."*

And maybe dangerous?

I am not attracted by morbidity, but if there is no commitment, I am dissatisfied. For example, the deepest feeling I have had came after climbing in Dresden. I waited a long time to climb Valley Crack [5.10b] because I was afraid of it. The first ring was so far away and the wall was so impressive. But when I succeeded, I remembered it much more than routes that were very well protected by bolts. Afterward, you remember nothing of these routes.

If a route is not adventurous, it's not in the normal spirit of climbing. For example, in 1981, French climbers like Edlinger and the Lemenestrel brothers began top-roping [protecting from the top of the route] the hardest routes and problems. They realized that it was a good way to push the standard and progress to the 8b level. And then other climbers did the same thing. And now in the Verdon Gorge, you can see dozens of people doing only one twenty-five-meter pitch of the 200-meter cliff. I spent two weeks there last May and I saw very few people leading [protecting from the ground up]. I talked to some Germans who thought that because they had done a pitch on top-rope, they didn't have to lead it. That's very strange.

It's better to lead. It's more fun. If nobody wants to lead it, why put in bolts? It would be better not to have bolts in the rock. The leading climbers have to speak out about these things.

What does the future hold for climbing in France?

The future of rock climbing in France will be in competitions, but also doing new routes at the 8c, even 9a [5.14d] level. It's like a hyperbolic line. It's progressed quickly the last ten years, but now progress has flattened out.

As that happens, do you think that people will go back to the mountains?

I'm not sure if they will. For the last ten years, the gymnastic aspect and the competitive aspect have been well established, and I think most of the young guys will go in this direction. I hope they will not forget other kinds of climbing, but I think they will prefer staying on the crags. But who knows? Even the most gymnastic climbers like to travel and do hard routes, to discover other styles and climb other kinds of rocks. I hope this trend will last. It's very important to travel around, to see different rocks, different people, different techniques, different styles.

And it's also important to keep in mind that rock climbing is part of a tradition. It's not a new sport. Many young guys don't know anything about the history of rock climbing. They believe that climbing was born in 1979. And if they don't know the history, they will have the spirit of gymnasts, not the spirit of rock climbers. And then free climbing could become a mere gymnastic routine.

I think we'll lose something if free climbing becomes like that. But many people are thinking the contrary. They think that the gymnastic aspect is a very good thing and the commitment is not important. For example, we have superb sea-cliff climbing in French Brittany and it's perfect rock for putting in nuts. But we've had much difficulty in stopping the bolting on these cliffs because the guys don't like to bother putting in nuts; they want to be concerned only with the move.

And in the French Federation, too often the trend is toward putting bolts everywhere and attracting people to rock climbing. I call that the easy way out. I think it's a mistake. They are wrong and they will later regret it.

Has your definition of free climbing prevailed in France?

Sure. But at the beginning I also emphasized the commitment involved in climbing, and I tried to tell people to respect the natural rock, use nuts instead of pitons, and climb from the ground up. And these principles have been completely ignored. Free climbing is the only part of climbing from which commitment has mainly disappeared. And free climbers don't want to use even one nut. They are only interested in sport climbing and don't want to bother with natural protection and ground-up ascents. The pioneers, such as Patrick Berhault, myself, and Jean-Pierre Bouvier, have become disillusioned about all of this. Sure, the standards have increased fantastically, but a lot of the traditions we worked so hard to establish are already being forgotten.

JEFF LOWE

Ice climbing is a path of approach to a world apart. It is a simpler, more dynamic world than the one we are used to. Death is close. Social concerns drop away as so many inconsistencies in a logical argument. The truth of an individual's nature begins to emerge as instinct shows its old forgotten face.

—Jeff Lowe, *The Ice Experience*

ICE CLIMBING COULD easily qualify as one of the most useless of human activities. Unlike mountaineering, which at least has a summit for a goal, ice climbing sets its sights on such absurd objectives as frozen waterfalls, black ice couloirs, and the phantasmagorical towers of glacial seracs. It makes no pretense of advancing the cause of scientific or geographic knowledge but seeks instead nothing more and nothing less than the psychological and spiritual transformation of the individual climber, serving as a kind of ritual of purification that strips away the worries, anxieties, and petty neuroses of modern urban life, thereby allowing its practitioners to emerge sole and whole again. Ice climbing is a rebellion against a society obsessed with commerce and material comfort, a discipline of risk that attempts to return a sense of balance and proportion to an individual's life.

Though ice climbers share with rock climbers a desire for dangerous and fantastically impractical objectives, they are in fact even more esoteric in their ambitions. Whereas rock climbers can count on a certain degree of stability and constancy from the material on which they climb, ice climbers perform their dance in defiance of death on an exceedingly plastic and mercurial medium—namely, frozen water. An ascent may take place in early morning on a ribbon of ice that will have melted by midafternoon. This gives the sport an ephemeral, otherworldly quality that distinguishes it from rock climbing and ensures that it will attract only the most dedicated and fanatical of followers.

The high priest of this arcane climbing cult is none other than Jeff Lowe, iceman par excellence, and one of the originators of the techniques and equipment that have made modern ice climbing possible. Lowe began ice climbing at age fifteen in the Grand Tetons and the Rocky Mountains. While still in his teens he completed such routes as the north face of Mount Temple in the Rockies in

1970, Black Ice Couloir/west face combination of the Grand Teton in winter in 1971, and the west face of the Grand Teton in winter in 1972. He gained national attention in 1978 with the first solo ascent of Bridalveil Falls near Telluride, Colorado, a feat that earned him a place on the cover of *Sports Illustrated* and interviews on *Merv Griffin* and *Good Morning America*. In 1982, he and David Brashears completed one of the longest and most difficult ice climbs in history, the north face of Kwangde, a 5000-foot ice face in the Himalaya. In recent years, he has continued to ascend difficult lines in the Himalaya, including a solo variation of the south spur on Pumori in 1983, the northwest face of Kantega in 1986 with Marc Twight, Tom Frost, and Alison Hargreaves, as well as outstanding routes in the Rockies and other ranges.

Though he is best known as an ice climber, Lowe's influence on modern mountaineering is not limited to that branch of the sport. He has pioneered hundreds of rock routes, mostly in Colorado, California, Utah, and Idaho, and has brought the full range of his skills to bear on some of the most technically demanding high-altitude mixed routes, including the north ridge of Latok (1978), where he, Mike Kennedy, George Lowe, and Jim Donini got within a few hundred feet of the summit; the southeast pillar of Nuptse, which he has attempted twice, in 1986 and 1987 with Marc Twight; the first ascent of the northeast face of Taweche with John Roskelley in 1989; the second free ascent of the Yugoslav Route on Trango Tower with Catherine Destivelle in 1990; and perhaps the biggest coup of his career, a nine-day effort on the Eiger in the spring of 1991 that resulted in the first ascent of Metanoia (5.10, A5), perhaps the hardest route ever done on the peak.

In addition to this impressive list of ascents, Lowe has played an important role in the development of modern climbing through his sponsorship of sport-climbing competitions. He introduced these competitions to the United States at Snowbird, Utah, in 1988 and organized a number of them before his company, Sport Climbing Championships, went bankrupt in 1990. Despite the failure of his company, Lowe remains optimistic about the future of the sport, maintaining that if properly funded and promoted, climbing competitions could thrive in the United States and elsewhere.

Lowe was born September 13, 1950, in Ogden, Utah. He grew up there, leaving at age seventeen to attend Tahoe-Paradise College in California. Today he lives in Boulder, Colorado, where he works as an equipment designer.

In 1982 Lowe married Janie Hannigan. They have a daughter, Sonja, who is five years old. Recently the couple divorced and Lowe has learned the frustrations of being a part-time parent for his daughter, whom he describes as "an incredible little girl—the reason I was put on this planet." Since the divorce, Lowe

Jeff Lowe. (Courtesy Agence Temp Sport)

has moved to a modern, wood-paneled apartment where the sparsely furnished front room is cluttered on the one end by his daughter's toys and dominated on the other by a color enlargement of the north face of the Eiger. The interview took place there in early fall when the wind was shaking yellowed leaves off the aspen trees outside the windows.

Lowe is tall and lanky with light blond hair, blue eyes, a mild handshake, and a deceptively low-key disposition. When addressing most subjects he is calm, reasonable, rational—the kind of man you want designing the equipment you're going to use to solo a frozen waterfall—but when the talk turns to climbing, an unmistakable intensity takes over his voice and manner, revealing a side of his personality that is as sharp and precise as the blade of a knife. Normally, Lowe keeps this side of himself carefully folded away, preferring to pass himself off as an ordinary person, but occasionally it comes out, making it clear that whatever his many other talents and inclinations, he remains at heart an unrepentant, unredeemed, unreconstructed climber.

What was your first good climb?

When I was seven I climbed the Grand Teton with my dad. I think I have the record for the youngest person to climb the Grand Teton. I still remember that climb. I remember sitting and looking out from the top. You can actually see the gentle curve of Earth if you look off to the west across Idaho. I noticed that and it was impressive to me.

On the way down I tripped on a rock and bumped my head and cried. And I remember crossing Wallstreet, a section of the Exum Route where you crawl along or hand-traverse. It had a lot of exposure below it and I had nightmares about the exposure for a few years after that.

Was your dad a climber?

Yeah, Dad was a climber. He used to climb a lot in the Tetons in the fifties with the Exum guides, so as kids we all had a chance to climb when we were young. Not all the kids liked it equally well, but three of us—Mike, Greg, and myself—were excited by climbing and stuck with it. And our cousins George and Dave also climbed.

Did you climb a lot with your brothers?

We spent a lot of time climbing together, but we always climbed with other people too. We were members of a climbing club in Ogden. We had weekly meetings and climbed with other club members.

Did people from the club teach you to climb?

No, I learned from Dad. And then Mike and Greg and I learned a lot together. And we climbed with my cousin George. He was a few years older and started climbing later than us, but he went to Europe in the early sixties for a season or two and got a lot of experience. I climbed with George a lot when I was fourteen, fifteen, and sixteen. We built our experience together and were probably the best climbers in the area.

Where did you do most of your early climbing?

Right behind my parents' house we had an excellent bouldering area. And then just above that was good rock climbing on quartzite crags up to 250 feet high. We did a lot of routes there.

And our climbing club opened up City of Rocks in the early sixties. We were really against publicizing it or developing a guidebook—that was part of the ethic. We never did record the routes; by word of mouth it got around that some of them had been climbed. We also did routes on the granite in Little Cottonwood Canyon and on some limestone around Ogden. And we'd go up to the Tetons every summer and then in the latter part of the sixties down to Yosemite. When I was eighteen I did the Salathé Wall, which I really liked.

When did you start ice climbing?

At age fifteen in northern Utah and in the Tetons. I'd always been intrigued by ice climbing. I loved to look in the books and see pictures of people on the north faces in the Alps—that looked really exciting to me. And a pivotal point in this direction was when John Harlin and Layton Kor and those guys [Dougal Haston, Chris Bonington, Jorg Lehne, Günther Strobel, Roland Votteler, and Siegi Hupfauer] did the Eiger Direct in 1966. I remember following that in the newspapers. I became very intrigued by that kind of climbing.

When you started ice climbing was it a relatively new thing in this country?

Ice climbing in Europe had been well established for a hundred years, but in this country there weren't many good ice climbers. There wasn't really that much scope for ice climbing in the United States. In the Canadian Rockies there was plenty of scope, but it was hard to become an ice climber in the United States prior to the days of curved picks and waterfall climbing.

How did you learn to climb ice?

My cousin George was my mentor. He had been to the Alps in 1965 and climbed in Chamonix and a little in Switzerland. His stories of the climbing there really sparked my imagination, and we went out and did quite a bit of climbing in the Tetons and around Ogden. He got me moving on snow and mixed terrain. Later on, in the early seventies, my brother Greg introduced me to waterfall ice climbing.

Did you prefer ice climbing to rock climbing?

I've always liked rock as much as ice, or maybe even more. I just like variety. I like to go everywhere in the mountains, and some of the greatest walls are mixed rock and ice. The architecture or look of a line is really important to me, and often ice can add something to the look of a wall. A dry rock wall is often not very dramatic. You add ice and snow and the features stand out in greater relief and it looks much wilder.

What was ice climbing like when you got started?

It was really adventurous because the gear hadn't been perfected yet. I started with an old army ice axe with a straight pick that I cut down to fit me better. The crampons had no bridge between the two front points, so they were really flimsy and flexible. Front-pointing on those, with boots that were not so stiff, and with these straight picks that you use as daggers, was a completely different experience. To climb a fifty-degree pitch of hard ice with those tools was like climbing 5.8 rock slab, and relatively unprotected, because the ice screws weren't that great. Salewa tube screws were available at that time and offered good protection, but you had to wear them inside your jacket to melt out the cores so that you could reuse them. And sometimes you'd have to sit with your stove and melt the cores out of your tubes just to be able to keep going.

So the changes in gear made a big difference to ice climbing.

They made all the difference. They opened up new terrain to ice climbing. As soon as the curved and drooped picks and good tubular ice screws were introduced you could climb vertical waterfalls. And in the early seventies that's what happened. As soon as the tools were available, climbs started happening. My brother Greg was one of the first to use these tools on steep ice.

Did you play a part in the development of ice tools?

Yeah, my brother Greg and I worked together on the Hummingbird tools and Snarg ice pitons. The Snargs were a joint idea of Greg's and mine. The original idea for a drive-in tube was Greg's, and I came up with the idea for the threads that would allow you to drive it in and screw it out, and with the idea for a clearing slot. It was a joint development.

Later on, things like the RATS screw were more my idea, but Greg always had input and so did Mike. We all had input, but on any given design, one or the other of us would come up with the idea and take it to its completion with input from the others. Greg was the most innovative, but Mike and I came up with good ideas once in a while too. And because I did a lot more climbing throughout the sixties and seventies, I could give feedback based on actual experience in the field.

The Footfangs were Mike's idea and then we worked together to perfect them. And Tom Frost was involved in those too. He's a behind-the-scenes guy, but he was involved in the development of Chouinard's curved-pick gear and rigid crampons as well as second-generation development of Big Bird axes and Footfangs with our company. Tom was seminal in a lot of these equipment improvements; he's quite a brilliant guy.

> *"I HATE EXPEDITIONS."*

Did you enjoy designing equipment?

Oh, yeah. I still do. I still work with companies on a consulting basis that way. That's part of how I'm making a living. The tuber belay device was my idea from start to finish. I've designed a lot of clothing. I'm designing a new generation of ice tools for Stubai. I love doing that kind of stuff.

Did all this experience on ice and rock make it easier to move to the Himalaya?

Yeah, winter climbs in the Tetons and summer climbs in the Canadian Rockies gave me the experience to go to the Himalaya and South America and the Alps. The Rockies are a great range for learning self-reliance and all the skills necessary to deal with bad rock, bad weather, ice, and whatever.

Why did you prefer to do high-altitude climbing with small teams?

Because I hate expeditions. In 1974 I went to the Pamirs in Russia with a big group of Americans and climbers from ten other countries. We were climbing alpine style but we were with these huge groups of people. And fifteen people died that summer, which demonstrates that big groups don't guarantee safety and may in fact be more dangerous because the larger the group, the less the individual climber feels responsibility for any single decision and may be lulled into a sense of safety in numbers that is illusory.

That trip made it clear to me that huge groups of people might work in the city or on the trail but they really don't have any place in the mountains. The group mentality that develops in those situations means that everyone is giving up some of their self-responsibility. That experience confirmed that I didn't want to have anything to do with expeditions.

But it did allow you to get your feet wet in high-altitude climbing?

Yeah, and it confirmed my idea that altitude wasn't such a barrier to good climbing as people had been saying. And in fact, after that experience on Peak 19th Party of Congress with John Roskelley—it was about 20,000 feet—I realized that you could do the most technical climbing at that altitude.

So did you then try routes that were even higher?

Not so much higher. I had come up with an approach to alpine style starting with very difficult routes on some of the lower peaks and gradually working up to the most difficult routes on the highest peaks. And I'm still on that path, leading up to things like the Direct West Face of Makalu in alpine style or Southwest Face Direct on Everest. Alpine-style technical climbing on high peaks really attracts me.

But on most of the high peaks there is not the quality of climbing that you can find on some of the slightly lower peaks. It's hard to find climbing of the quality of Latok in Pakistan, for instance, on any of the highest peaks. The southeast pillar of Makalu is pretty good, but it's not in the same class of technical difficulty as some of the 7000-meter peaks.

When did you climb Latok?

In 1978, Mike Kennedy, George Lowe, Jim Donini, and I climbed all but the last few hundred feet of it. We did about 8000 feet of climbing—really highly technical. It's been tried a bunch of times since and nobody's even gotten halfway up. It's really good ice and granite. I think it's one of the ultimate classics of the Himalaya, but it still hasn't had a complete ascent.

What exactly do you look for in a route?

It has to have good rock on it as well as good ice and has to be clean and objectively safe—no hanging glaciers above you. It has to have a nice symmetry, a dramatic aspect, and has to make me feel excited. The quality, beauty, and technical difficulty of the line are more interesting to me than the altitude. I don't like snow slogging at all. I like to climb when I'm on a route, not slog.

Would the route you did with David Brashears on the north face of Kwangde serve as an example of such a route?

Yes. That's a total classic. It's only on a 20,000-foot peak, but the route's 5000 feet long. It's on these thin tongues of ice over compact granite slabs. It's like an El Capitan ice route. Nothing else like it has been done in the Himalaya or anywhere else. It's in a class with few other ice climbs. People have tried to repeat it and they've done some variations off to the sides, but they haven't succeeded yet. Not that it can't be repeated; it just takes a lot of confidence and commitment. For instance, Dave and I were tying two 100-meter ropes together to get to belays and stuff.

So you would run it out that far?

Yeah, and with a heavy pack. On the lower section we did lots of climbing on thin ice over seventy- to eighty-five-degree slabs with essentially no protection. The rock was really compact and you couldn't find much to anchor to and no ledges for a long, long way. In places it was very thin.

It must have been exciting.

It was good. I like that kind of stuff.

Do you like getting scared?

No, I don't like getting scared. I don't like the kind of adrenaline that hits you and makes you get all nervous. I hate that. Things are out of control when you're getting hit by shots of adrenaline like that. I hate to be out of control. I like to be pushing the edge of my control but always staying in control. I like the heightened concentration that comes from that slight tension between fear and control and just feathering that edge and making sure you're on the safe side of it.

> *"I LIKE THE HEIGHTENED CONCENTRATION THAT COMES FROM THAT SLIGHT TENSION BETWEEN FEAR AND CONTROL. . . ."*

Was the southeast pillar of Nuptse the logical next step after Kwangde?

Kwangde was not really on the progression to things like the southeast pillar of Nuptse; it was its own progression as an ice climb. There's one more step with ice climbs, and that would be something like the north face of Latok, which in the winter ices up completely from bottom to top in one system of vertical gullies about 7000 feet high.

So that's one grade beyond Kwangde. I think that's the remaining step to take in that kind of climbing. I don't think anybody's even thinking about that, but it's on my mind. That would be the end progression of alpine-style ice climbing. There's nothing greater than that available; the terrain's not there anymore.

But there are other types of ice climbing that haven't been pushed to their limits—really thin mixed climbs or waterfalls on alpine faces. Especially in Canada, there are things that are harder and bigger than things that have been done. And as far as thin and mixed climbs go, it can be endless; you can do harder and bolder climbs.

So the southeast pillar of Nuptse was more of a mixed route?

Yes. That's more in line with the progression that Latok was part of. That's easier than Latok overall, but it's at a higher elevation. I went there twice with

Marc Twight. Neither time were we a very strong team and we failed both times. We did some good climbing, but the whole upper part of the route remains to be climbed. Some Canadians went there a couple years ago and got a couple thousand feet higher, but there is still an upper 1500-foot or 2000-foot headwall to go to the summit. It's a harder climb technically by far than the south face of Lhotse, but a couple thousand feet shorter.

Why weren't you and Marc Twight a good team?

We were climbing for different reasons. At that time Marc was climbing to get famous and to impress people, and he didn't enjoy being on the climb. The actual climbing is what's important to me. If there's a way to make a living from it, fine, but the climbing is what interests me.

Also, I was asking too much of Marc to put him on that thing at the level of his experience at that time, and he was overwhelmed. Where we should have been soloing ground he was very insecure, so we would move too slowly. We just weren't a strong team. You both have to be really working in tune on those kinds of climbs.

How do you choose your partners?

I just meet somebody and go climbing. There's not a big process I go through.

Who have been some of your best partners?

Mike Weis was my best early partner. He was just a competent human— indoors, outdoors, socially, whatever. And he's a smart guy; he's fun to talk with; he's well read; he has a good sense of humor; and he's strong. So he was a great partner. He hasn't done much climbing in recent years, so we haven't done anything for about ten years; but we used to do a lot in the seventies together.

In 1989 I did Taweche in Nepal with John Roskelley. Roskelley was a great partner. He's always willing to do as much as he can to make things go well. There wasn't a lot of competition between us; we just supported each other. On a hard pitch we would help each other work it out. And when I was feeling a little under the weather one day, he was really solicitous and made extra brews to fix me up.

He's not the world's greatest technical climber, but he's good and he's strong and he's experienced in the mountains. And he's easygoing about it. By the time we got to the top of Taweche, I felt that he was one of the best partners I'd ever had.

Taweche, in Nepal. (Courtesy Jeff Lowe)

And I like him because he's not like me. His politics are a lot more right-of-center than mine are, but we have a real adult relationship where we agree to disagree and want to learn about how the other guy thinks and respect the other person. So he was good from all those standpoints. Another competent human. I guess that's what makes a good partner.

How did you get started organizing climbing competitions?

In the early eighties there was a lot of rumbling that there were soon going to be sport-climbing competitions in the States. I was concerned about bolts going up everywhere on the rock, and I thought I'd like to introduce sport climbing quickly to the States in a way that would influence the future of it and direct some of the energy that was going into bolting the crags toward competition on artificial walls.

I travel a lot to Europe and I saw how it was developing there. I was impressed with the level of climbing taking place but I was anxious about the changes in the environment. The competitions in Europe were held on natural rock, and they were cutting down trees to make it better for the spectators, sandblasting the lichen to clean off the routes, and bolting, gluing, and chipping holds to make the routes the right level of difficulty. That was all happening in 1985 or 1986.

I went over in the fall of 1987 to the Arco [Italy] competition to learn how to organize these things. When I came back to the United States I went to the Mountain Summit at Snowbird, and Dick Bass and I got to talking. I said, "Dick, you've got a nice lodge here that would lend itself to something that's happening in Europe."

We walked out and looked at the end of the hotel [where the climbing wall would be built]. He said, "I can see that happening, but I'm not going to let anything happen to my hotel without the architect's approval."

Then I went to the architect. At first we were going to build a wall with bolted-on holds, but the architect didn't like that. We started designing a wall that would work for the architect and also work for climbing. It was a compromise all the way. It was never meant to be just a climbing wall. It was supposed to add to the look of the hotel.

That first year [1988] I got committed financially because there was never enough money to make it happen. I started investing my own money, and then since I'd invested money, I didn't want to lose it, so I kept putting good money after bad and trying to grow the thing to where I could get enough sponsorship to make it work. In the end I never did make it work. We went bankrupt.

What were the problems?

Lack of sponsorship and public interest.

Did you get a television contract?

That would have helped immensely. We were working on that, but we didn't put it together before the bottom dropped out. In the summer of 1989 I thought I had a bridge financing package put together before I left for Pakistan. I'd been working for a year on a financing package that would have carried us for several more years till the events were self-supporting, but the bank tightened its loan criteria. I was in Pakistan at the time, and when I came back there was no loan package. I couldn't put it back together after that. It was finished.

Was there the same level of support in the United States as in Europe?

There wasn't because it was taking some time to develop it. But even in Europe it isn't working that easily; a lot of competitions lose money. The special-events business is not an easy business. It takes experience, and I was totally inexperienced.

Do you think there's a future for these kinds of competitions?

Yes. There could be a really nice international competition held in this area. Red Rocks would be a fantastic venue for a world-class event. But it would have to be done right and it would have to be financed well.

What effect has sport climbing had on the rest of climbing in this country?

The competitions and artificial walls have taken a lot of pressure off the crags. They're still doing new routes on the crags, but much more slowly than they were.

Do you think that sport climbing will raise overall standards in climbing?

There's zero question. It's a revolution. Naturally athletic people who have never climbed before train on the indoor walls and in two months they're climbing 5.12; in three months they're doing 5.13. I'll bet you could take some people and in six months have them doing the very highest standard climbs that exist now, just by training them on an indoor wall. It's an absolute revolution.

Why does this training allow climbers to progress so quickly?

It's so efficient. In one hour you can get more concentrated climbing than you can on most crags. And you can work on any particular type of strength or skill that you want—apart from cracks; they're still limited on cracks. But cracks sort themselves out because if you develop strength from overhanging face climbs, learning to jam comes pretty easily. So it's revolutionary for climbing in general.

Does it allow climbers to train for difficult routes in the high mountains if they so choose?

If they so choose. Some people are using it that way—Tomo Česen, myself, Catherine Destivelle, Thierry Renault in France, American climbers Charlie Fowler and Alex Lowe [no relation]. But not many people are consciously training that way for use in the mountains.

When did you first meet Catherine Destivelle?

At the first Snowbird competition.

Why did you become partners?

We had similar ideas about climbing and I had some skills that I could impart to her and I liked her. Also, I had this opportunity to do a film project on Trango Tower. I needed a partner for that and I thought she'd be a good partner. In training for the climb and in the climb itself we got along well and liked climbing together. We complement each other really well. I'm better on cracks and she's better on face climbing. I had more experience in the mountains, but she has more technical free-climbing experience. So we're a good partnership.

Are you romantically involved?

Yeah, but who knows what's going to happen. We'll see.

Was the route on Trango the first climb that you did together?

No, we did a month of climbing around here beforehand to make sure that we were compatible for the climb on Trango. And it worked out fine.

How did the climb on Trango go?

The climbing wasn't as hard as we had hoped for. We had gone there hoping to find some pitches we could just barely succeed on. We wanted something like a hard 5.12 at that altitude because it's time to do that stuff in the Himalaya. But it was actually pretty easy relative to what we had gone over to do.

Did the altitude make a big difference?

No. Once you're acclimatized, climbing at 20,000 feet is nothing. Our hands got cold, but I'm used to that and Catherine got used to it. I climb better in the cold anyway. Your fingers don't sweat and you actually have better traction with your shoes at about 50 degrees [Fahrenheit]; friction is at its maximum.

When did you get the wild idea to try a new route on the Eiger?

Right after the first ascent of the Eiger Direct [1966] I was inspired to do that route alpine style. But I never got over to the Alps, and other people did it. Then in the fall of 1990, with the bankruptcy of the sport-climbing company, which put me into personal bankruptcy—my marriage also went down the tubes—my idea about the Eiger came back. I was figuring what I could do cheaply, and I thought I could get some interest to finance the trip. So that's when I thought I'd like to go to the Eiger. And I thought that doing the Eiger alone in winter by a new route, the hardest yet, would be as close as I could get to the level of commitment of the original pioneers.

There was a story in Outside *magazine suggesting that because of the failure of your business and your marriage you were in a perfect frame of mind to do the Eiger.*

> **"***I WASN'T A DESPERATE MAN GOING OUT TO DO A DESPERATE ACT; I WAS A MAN FULFILLING A DREAM. . . .***"**

That really pissed me off. I wasn't a desperate man going off to do a desperate act; I was a man fulfilling a dream—a totally different thing. I was really upset when that came out because it left totally the wrong impression. My mentality during the climb was that the Eiger is a classic and can be one of the best climbing experiences you have. I was totally comfortable on the whole thing.

So it wasn't a suicide mission.

No, no. I couldn't have done it in that frame of mind. You don't get enough energy from that frame of mind. I don't see how I could have done it if I had had any negative baggage to carry with me. I had to put aside my other troubles. I was very up for the climb.

How did you find the line?

I looked for the existing lines and thought there was a line between the Japanese Route and the Czech Route. It's not the first route you would pick, but when you're on it, the climbing is of real quality and you don't feel like you're crowding things. The face is so huge that lines that look close together in photographs are 200 feet away.

Did you have much problem with rockfall?

No problem with rockfall—in the winter it's quiet.

Avalanches?

Yeah. There were huge spindrift avalanches. There was one storm halfway up that dumped eighteen inches overnight. I almost drowned in that one. I had this little hanging tent, but it was like trying to sleep in a cement mixer. I got tired of it.

How long did it take to do the climb?

Nine days.

What kind of gear did you carry?

Winter clothes, food, fuel, stove, hanging tent, ice gear, ice rack, and an El Cap [rock] rack. I carried this humongous pack up the lower 1500 feet. I think it weighed eighty to ninety pounds. I was doing some seventy-five-degree ice with that. After I got through the first band I broke it into two loads. From there I carried about fifty pounds on my back and I had a bag hanging from my harness that I dangled between my feet. I climbed that way up to the top of the second icefield, where it got hard again. From there I would lead the pitch and then drop down and pick up my pack and bring it up. From the top of the second icefield to the summit was all technical. There wasn't any easy climbing.

Was it hard to stay on route?

Yeah, it's really not one line. You're just going up this huge, amorphous mountain wall where there really aren't many cracks, just long areas of face climbing on limestone. I used eight anchors on little tiny things, all equalized, to set up one belay. From there, I looked up and went, "Where do I go from here?" I didn't have a bolt kit because I decided not to carry one. So I just started wandering up on these little limestone edges, mixed free and aid, doing whatever I could to get up it.

I don't think this route's going to be repeated for a while. You've got to be pretty enthused to do it. To do the first ascent of something like that you can be motivated. But to go through all that stuff just to repeat the route is harder in some ways. The motivation might not be there.

And it's pretty intimidating; it was really feathering the edge. It was maybe a grade harder in each type of climbing than, say, Taweche. I was climbing about as hard as I could climb. I took three falls on the climb. One was just a little aid fall; I was trying to save a certain size nut and I put in one that was a little too small. I knew it might pop, and it did, but I fell only five feet. But the other two falls happened because I was climbing at my limits and popped. I've never done that in the mountains before.

So your belays were solid?

Yes. I took care. Even though I didn't have a partner, I was belayed as well as if I had had a partner.

Did it require a lot of different skills to complete that route?

It took a high level of skill at each type of climbing, and not too many people have all those skills. You have to do A5 nailing, which none of the Europeans can do. Yosemite wall climbers can, but they don't have the ice and mixed skills, the rotten rock skills, and the experience. So I'm not sure that anybody will get it all together to do it anytime soon.

What climbs do you have planned for the future?

Catherine will come back with me to Canada and we'll train for several weeks on ice. Then in January we'll go to the Alps to try a new route on the Walker Spur of the Grandes Jorasses. And later on I might try the Southwest Face Direct on Everest.

With Catherine?

No, I don't think so. Catherine will go in support, but I'd like to finish my Himalayan vision, which is to solo that route or the west face of Makalu. In the next couple years I'll try to complete one of those routes. And I'm going to continue to develop my free climbing. While I'm not traveling I can do a lot of free climbing at home.

Why do you continue climbing?

Why? There are a lot of reasons. I like the physical feeling. I like the emotional and mental challenge. But when it gets down to it, to describe the real reason why I climb, it's like explaining why somebody becomes a writer and somebody else becomes a doctor; it's different motivations. My motivation was to become a climber; I got excited by the idea of climbing.

What does climbing do for the rest of your life?

My life and climbing are so intertwined that they're one and the same. Climbing's my life and my life's climbing. A lot of my life revolves around climbing, but it's not all I'm interested in. The problem is that I got so committed to it when I was young that I didn't develop any other skills. Now I'm kind of stuck with that; but it's allowed me to get involved in equipment design and business and other things.

In one way it's been negative, in that I never failed at something that I really wanted to do with climbing, and I think that confidence carried over into what I thought I could do with business. Success in climbing led me to believe that I could do absolutely anything I wanted to. I thought I could bite off anything and make it work somehow. I found that that's not true. Success in climbing doesn't necessarily translate to other things.

But now that I know that, climbing is a positive thing in my life. It's a good vacation from everyday hassles. If you're concentrating on climbing, you can't be concentrating on money and cars and houses and wives and boyfriends. Those things can drop back into their proper slots. And when you come back to deal with them, you have a better view of their relative importance. Climbing puts things in perspective again.

▲ WOLFGANG GÜLLICH

After you have climbed for a long time, you get to the point where you want your ideas about the sport to materialize by establishing new routes. To do a new hard route is such a challenge, because you have to do everything on your own; learn the mental and physical coordination and come up with the motivation to continue a project which may be impossible. You may not see the way for a long time and quit because no one can help you to realize the possibility. And it's only natural that the more effort you put into something, the more you are satisfied when you succeed. Your creation—made up of the line, the difficulty, the protection, and even the name, expressing all the emotions about the route—has a special, unique character. If climbing is an art, then creativity is its main component.

—Wolfgang Güllich, from an interview in *Climbing*

W
HEN IT CAME TO creativity in contemporary free climbing, no one could hold a candle to the late, great Wolfgang Güllich. The leading free climber in the world until his untimely death on August 29, 1992, the droll young German demonstrated his creativity not only by reeling off a dizzying number of extreme rap-bolted routes, but also by boldly going where few or any free climbers had gone before. In an area of the sport where many are content to simply extend the scale while belayed from the bumper of their VW van, Güllich expanded the range of free climbing to include hard solos, nervy runout routes, and high-altitude epics. Through his strength, dedication, and imagination, he helped revolutionize free climbing and establish it more firmly within the great tradition of climbing.

Güllich got his first taste of free climbing at age fourteen in the Sudpfalz area of Germany, one of the crucibles of the sport in Europe. Under the tutelage of

Wolfgang Güllich. (Courtesy Wolfgang Güllich)

215

such famous figures as Reinhard Karl, the first German to climb Everest, Güllich learned the tricks of the trade. Together, he, Karl, and others eliminated artificial aid on many existing routes, relying instead on strength, endurance, and technique to get them up routes without resorting to stepping or pulling on pitons. His 1977 ascent of Valley Crack (5.10b), a Sudpfalz test piece, presaged a brilliant career in free climbing.

Thereafter, he became a kind of free-climbing vagabond, traveling the globe in search of hard routes. He set out for the Saxony region of the former East Germany in 1979 to learn the secrets of Bernd Arnold, the area's leading climber, who helped him succeed on such classics as the Wall of Sunset (5.11d) and Direct Superlative (5.11d).

Soon after, Güllich made his first trip to the United States, where he fired up Supercrack (5.12d) in the Shawangunks of New York. Moving west, he tried Phoenix (5.13a) in Yosemite, but failed on it. After undergoing an intensive training program, he returned in 1982 and finished it off. Then he set his sights on Grand Illusion (5.13c) in Sugarloaf, California, regarded by many as the hardest sport climb in the world at that time. It took him eight consecutive days to claim the coveted second ascent. Afterward he was so exhausted that he couldn't eat or sleep for thirty hours.

Having paid his dues by repeating the world's hardest free climbs, Güllich turned his attention to establishing extreme routes of his own. In 1984 he climbed the world's first 5.13d, Kanal im Rüchen, in the Altmühltal area of Germany. A year later he traveled to Arapiles, Australia, to work his magic on the area's wickedly overhanging rock. His Punks in the Gym route became the first 5.14a ever, while Wisdom of the Body rated a solid 5.13d. In one short trip, Güllich had not only pulled off the first and second hardest sport climbs on the Australian continent but had pushed the world grade yet again.

Not content with these outstanding accomplishments, he returned home to perfect the training techniques that would allow him to fulfill further dreams. He adapted training routines from other sports, such as basketball and gymnastics, to put up Ghetto Blaster [5.14a] in 1986, a testimony to years of motivation and hard work.

Further training permitted him to succeed on other so-called impossible routes. After finding an extremely sketchy line in the Frankenjura, one of the most popular sport-climbing areas in Germany, he undertook a training routine specifically tailored to it. In 1988 he sent shock waves through the free-climbing community by leading Wallstreet, the world's first 5.14b. Since then, the route has been repeated only once, almost unheard of for a high-level sport-climbing route.

In between working on extreme sport routes, Güllich took time off to do hard solo climbs, such as Yosemite's Separate Reality (5.11d) in 1986, and severely runout routes, such as Broken Mirror (5.12a) at Dresden, in the former

East Germany, in 1984. Such climbs required extraordinary mental as well as physical control and helped prepare him for free climbing in the high mountains.

He took his first step in this direction in 1988 when he attempted the Norwegian Route (5.10, A3) on the middle pillar of the Great Trango Tower in Pakistan. Bad weather near the top of the formidable 6000-foot face forced him, Kurt Albert, and several others to retreat, but after resting a few days they tackled the Yugoslav Route on Trango (Nameless) Tower. Not only did they succeed in repeating the route, they free-climbed nearly all twenty-eight pitches, some of them as hard as 5.12, thereby achieving a landmark in free-climbing history.

With these impressive climbs under his belt, Güllich felt ready to attempt even more intimidating routes. He returned to the Karakoram the following year with Kurt Albert to establish a new route on Trango Tower called Eternal Flame. With one pitch of 5.12b, two of 5.12, many of 5.11, and a few of aid, the twenty-eight-pitch route proved the most continuously difficult line ever climbed.

Then in the winter of 1990–91 he journeyed to Patagonia, Chile, to try an even more challenging route. Battling horrendous weather and icy cracks, he, Kurt Albert, Bernd Arnold, Norbert Batz, and Peter Dietrich attacked the 4300-foot east face of the Central Tower of Paine. It took them ten days to complete the thirty-five-pitch route, which included five pitches of 5.12, many pitches of 5.11, and several aid pitches, making it probably the most difficult and adventurous of contemporary rock climbs. Appropriately enough, they dubbed the route Riders on the Storm.

Rejuvenated by his trips to the high mountains, Güllich threw himself back into training for extreme routes. This training culminated in the fall of 1991 with his ascent of Action Directe, a short, steep, dynamic climb in the Frankenjura with holds so small that they accepted little more than fingertips. Tentatively rated 5.14d, Action Directe may well be the hardest extreme sport climb in the world. The amazing Güllich had pushed the grade once again.

Through Action Directe and other ascents, Güllich took free climbing into a new age, not only extending the scale, but also developing a whole new set of games within the free-climbing category. He accomplished this by adapting the old-fashioned values of adventure climbing—conforming to the environment and overcoming risk—to the newfangled field of free climbing. In so doing, he demonstrated that progress in the sport comes about not through the chipping or gluing of holds, but through a creativity developed in close contact with nature. By learning to read the infinity of nature as revealed in the rock, Güllich transformed the field of contemporary free climbing and provided a blueprint for the future of the sport.

Born on October 24, 1960, in the Rhine Valley of Germany, Güllich grew up there until he was drafted into the army at eighteen. After serving in the army for fifteen months, a period he called "the worst time in my life," he moved to Moselstr, a small town near the Frankenjura. He continued to live there with his wife, Annette, whom he married in 1991, until his tragic death in 1992 in an auto accident. Their house served as a kind of informal headquarters for much of the sport-climbing activity in the area, with climbers from around the world stopping by to crash for the night, get the information, or "beta," on a hard new route, or simply engage in long and involved discussions of politics, philosophy, and the like.

After conducting me on a guided tour of the Frankenjura, an idyllic region of pine forests, clear streams, and fantastic limestone formations, Güllich parked his blue Volkswagen Golf and we entered a small cafe. He greeted several climbers who were lounging in the sun and then selected a table near a water fountain. With the fountain bubbling in the background, Güllich ordered coffee and chocolate cake—he doesn't like beer—and began talking about his approach to climbing. A friendly, enthusiastic young man with dark hair, huge biceps, and a mischievous glint in his eye, Güllich took great delight in spoofing the egotistical aspects of the free-climbing scene while remaining modest about his own extraordinary accomplishments.

What are your goals as a free climber?

My goal is to set the standard in every part of the free-climbing game, to do some extreme routes, such as the first 11 in Germany (Action Directe, 5.14d), do some very hard solos, and some free alpine routes. For me there are different games in free climbing and these games are divided between those in which the physical part dominates and those in which the mental aspect dominates.

If you concentrate on the physical aspect, it will be the numbers race, doing the very hard grades. On these routes it's mostly physical; mentally you need a lot of concentration, but you know you can always fall off and the rope will catch you. You try the move a lot until you perfect it and then you put all the little sections together and do the route.

If the mental aspect predominates, it will be solos, which require total mental control, or perhaps some very challenging routes with only the protection of stoppers. Then you would have to think a lot about tactics. You have to climb with a lot more control because these routes could be scary in some sections. And that's a lot different from some kinds of sport climbing. These days there are very good gymnastic climbers who do very hard routes, but they can't do the mental games at all because they don't have much control. They need the security of knowing that they can fall off anyplace.

And then you can go to the mountains and do a very hard route that puts all of the finest games together. You might have to do an unprotected pitch, a very extreme pitch, and then have to deal with the addition of stress from the length of the route. A single pitch may put stress on you, but if you have twenty pitches you have to learn to recover. It's not like you can do just one pitch and then go home and rest for three days and then come back and do something else. You have to recover at your belay and then do the next section.

So these kind of routes require a lot more stamina?

> "... THERE ARE DIFFERENT GAMES IN FREE-CLIMBING ... THOSE IN WHICH THE PHYSICAL PART DOMINATES AND THOSE IN WHICH THE MENTAL ASPECT DOMINATES. "

And on-sight ability. On gymnastic routes you know every detail and have a very fine coordination program and you just have to run the program— "Fingerpocket, undercling, little swing with your left foot, come to balance with the right." But in on-sight climbing you have to be fast in selecting your information from the rock; you can't take forever, because if you do, you'll get pumped. You have to find what you can use, then analyze how you can work your gravity point and balance, and then make the decision. It's more of an intellectual problem.

How did you get started free climbing?

When I was young I read a lot of books about mountaineering. At that time there was no free climbing in Germany; it was all alpine climbing. I read about the Eiger North Face Route and other climbs and became fascinated with the sport.

Were you an athletic kid?

Yes. When I was young I played soccer fanatically. Then I played tennis the same way—three or four hours a day, every day. But as soon as I started climbing I quit both and became totally fanatical about climbing.

Why did you prefer climbing to soccer or tennis?

The people were different. They were much more interesting. The tennis people in our town were big-headed. They thought that tennis required the most coordination of any sport in the world—tennis! These people didn't look too fit to me. I thought, "There can't be much behind that." So I told myself, "I will show them." I trained very hard and was good in tennis, but then I lost interest—not because I had reached what I had wanted to reach, but because I learned about climbing.

Were you good at climbing right from the start?

Good? Maybe not. My father was a gymnast and we had this little game. He would pay me five marks if I could do fifteen pull-ups. I wanted to earn that money, so I did the pull-ups. I thought, "I'm quite fit, I'm quite strong." I thought I could climb immediately. I took a climbing course and thought I would be in the advanced group. They had these little test pieces and I couldn't believe how pumped I got on this Grade III. I learned that there's a lot to develop. But I developed very quickly; after a year I climbed a Grade VI, which at that time was the highest level.

Did your parents approve of your climbing?

Not really. When I started, my parents didn't like to give me money for the forty-kilometer train ride to the Sudpfalz climbing area. They wanted me to stop climbing because they thought it was dangerous, not only because of the injuries you could get, but also from the influence of the other people in our free-climbing group. These people were about twenty-five, all students in college, and I was fourteen, by far the youngest. And my father said they were all a little bit suspect.

Why did your father consider them suspect?

After the war, in West Germany things were very conservative. People got on a track from their youth. They were supposed to work, get property, and things like that. There was not much tolerance or a chance to fulfill a dream. Free climbing was an alternative sport with different ideals and a different lifestyle. Free climbing in West Germany has to do with the ideals of the 1968 generation, which is something like the hippies.

Why did you find the climbers interesting?

I admired their lifestyle. They didn't need much money to do what they wanted to do. They didn't care too much about social acceptance; they went out climbing, had their fun, and played their game. They didn't need a good house; they spent their money traveling.

When did you begin free climbing?

That second year when I climbed Grade VI, I met Reinhard Karl, a German climber. He did the Eiger north face and was the first German to climb Everest. He had gone to America and learned about the idea of free climbing. When he came back to Germany he tried to free some aid climbs.

In the beginning of 1977, we tried Valley Crack in the Sudpfalz. I belayed him as he worked the sections. My goal then was to do the routes no matter how. I just wanted to repeat the routes; I didn't want to push the grade. If you try something that hasn't been done before, you have to work hard and push yourself. I thought, "This is too hard. I'd rather pull on the pins and be on the top of that cliff."

I belayed him for a long time, and finally he said, "You have a try." I tried it and I did the route. "That was a great job," he said.

I thought, "I should do more of that." That was the beginning of my free climbing.

When I started free climbing there were only about ten of us in Germany and the alpine climbers called us "the Outsiders." And, of course, they thought we were crazy. But now it's really become a fashionable sport in Germany.

Was Reinhard Karl one of your early models?

Yes. I thought he was a very interesting person. He had traveled to all these places in a VW bus with his friends. He told us about driving to India and getting into an ambush at Khyber Pass. I was fascinated by his lifestyle.

So first it was him and then Bernd Arnold, who was the leading climber in East Germany. I went there a lot and found it incredible how hard they climbed compared to West German or Alpine standards. There were special routes such as the Wall of Sunset. As soon as I'd done that, I wanted to do Direct Superlative.

When did you decide to go to the United States?

I remember *Mountain* magazine came out with a series of articles called "The State of the Art." It was about Supercrack and Babylon and Phoenix. So in 1979 I went to the States and did Supercrack in the Shawangunks, and as soon as I'd done that, I went to Yosemite and tried Phoenix. I was still too weak and couldn't do it. So I went back to Germany and had this training plan with Phoenix written on top of it. I trained for Phoenix and came back in 1982 and did it. And then I did Grand Illusion [second ascent]. These were some of the landmarks in free-climbing history.

Why do you continue to go back to the United States to climb?

I really, really like the States. In all my vacations combined I have lived in Yosemite for six or seven months. I like the people. They are very friendly and funny. I like the atmosphere, the whole scene. It's easy living—buy a car, drive around.

So it wasn't just the climbing that you liked?

No. If you just want to concentrate on climbing you could stay in France forever. But I'd much rather go to the States than to France. In France the climbing is very competitive and a lot of people are arrogant. They think they are something special because they climb 8b [5.13c].

When you first started going to Yosemite, was it the center for rock climbing in the world?

Yes, it was the most popular climbing area then. From 1975 to 1982, everybody said, "Yosemite is the mecca of climbing." People were very satisfied with the area, and everybody told the local climbers that they were the best and maybe that's why they lost the edge a bit. After 1982 the climbing in Yosemite stagnated. It was a natural progression. You can't keep up the same level of energy very long. You push it really hard and then you lay back for a while.

> "CLIMBING IS CREATIVITY, AND IF YOU WANT TO DO SOMETHING OUTSTANDING, IT HAS TO BE SOMETHING NEW."

Did the traditional methods employed there prevent people from climbing the hardest grades?

I'm not totally sure. I don't want to say what they should do there. It's not my business. I can understand the traditional climbers; they want to keep their climbing area clean because it's very unique. For me it's okay to go there and do the routes their way, but for Ron Kauk, who lives there, there might not be too many projects left in the classic style.

After doing the hardest free-climbing test pieces in Yosemite and elsewhere, why did you start doing first ascents?

At first I just wanted to repeat the hardest routes. As soon as I heard about a very hard route, I wanted to go there and repeat it. But then my attitude changed and I thought, "The most important thing is the creativity, to do your own routes, put up a new standard, push the limits." Climbing is creativity, and if you want to do something outstanding, it has to be something new.

Do you top-rope your first ascents?

Yes. First you anticipate the line, then you rap down and check it in detail, and then you place the bolts. Because the very hardest routes are like gymnastic routines. They're so hard that you'll definitely fall off a lot. You place the bolts to make sure that you won't hurt yourself.

And then you might work on special sections, like a sprint section, which you have to do very efficiently and economically. You won't be able to hang around and rest. You have to be quick. And then you might get to a hold that's a little better. Usually you use that hold to clip into a bolt. And maybe you rest there for a while—just drop your arm and get better blood circulation—because if you sprint something it takes a lot of static strength and it stops the blood in your muscles from circulating. You loosen them up because maybe the next section is another sprint.

So you break it down?

You break it down, yes. And before you start, you concentrate on maybe two or three very complicated moves. You memorize them very well. You program your brain in detail. It might look very natural to do such a move, but in fact there might be a lot of very specific moments.

There might be just one point on the wall that is not even a foothold but where you can put your foot and jump to hit a finger pocket. And if you stood on the ground and tried to hit a finger pocket like that with one finger it would be very hard. And if you've already climbed twenty meters and are tired and under stress you really have to concentrate to hit the target.

For the next hold you might have to kick your right foot back to counterbalance the barn-door effect and then still get enough energy for a swing. And if you hit the next hold with too much energy, you'll shoot too high and miss the target. And if you have too little energy, you won't get far enough. And if you pull your elbow too far out, you won't be able to hang on. Some holds are very small and you have to grab them from the right direction. If you pull down on them they're positive, but if you pull back you lose the most efficient grip and you slip off. It comes down to exact body mechanics for one move.

So it's very sequential and often very complicated. In one very extreme move you could have eight moments to remember. You can't just pull and grab, because at the borderline of possibility everything has to be *exactly* right. There's no margin for error.

How do you train for these kinds of routes?

I think the most important training is to climb. I do a lot of bouldering and that's by far the most important thing. If you're bouldering, it's important to imagine that you can do very extreme moves. And then you transfer this imagination to hard routes, because of course there are holds everywhere, but first you have to learn how to use them and relate them to the ability of your body. If you want to do something new, the most important thing is the idea. Once you have the idea and know that it's possible, you can do the climb; but to get the idea takes imagination, and bouldering helps develop your imagination.

So you transfer what you learn bouldering to harder routes?

Yes, you transfer it. The most extreme routes these days are like extended boulder problems; they're not endurance problems. On a very hard route, there must be a very hard boulder problem. And sometimes you're working a week just to do a single move on a twenty-five-meter pitch.

For example, there's one route in the Frankenjura [Wallstreet, 5.14b] with a very difficult boulder problem. I discovered the problem and I thought it might be possible. Through the winter I went to this training center in Nuremberg, and with the help of a physical education professor I worked specific muscles, training intramuscular coordination combined with reaction time so that I would be able to do the moves for this problem. Nowadays you don't just go someplace and do a route; you need a lot of other training. And if boulder problems like the one on Wallstreet are possible, then you open up the spectrum for other routes. You say, "If I can do this, then this might not be too far away."

If you want to push the level of difficulty, you don't just look for a blanker wall; you have to think about new climbing techniques and styles of training.

Can you borrow techniques from other sports and apply them to climbing?

I think so. If you take a close look at other sports, you can learn something that you can take to climbing and so help develop it.

What sort of things do you take from other sports?

From basketball you can take the moment of deadpoint, the top of the arc when you jump up. It's a real calm moment, and you throw the ball with the most control at that moment—not when you're coming down and not when you're jumping. You can adapt that to climbing. The deadpoint is also the moment with the most control in reaching another hold; you don't even have to hold on very hard. Things like that, and there are lots more.

Do you have a special training diet?

Cheesecake. [Laughs] No, but I like to eat good things. I think the diet of a lot of climbers is very bad these days. A lot of the girls who do competitions are anorexic; they're losing a lot of body functions. I've known them for a long time and they look so ill now. Strength/weight ratio is very important for climbing, so they starve, only drinking mineral water and eating a few things. It's crazy.

What kind of lines attract you?

Routes that are not contrived, routes that are the only possible way through a certain area. I call this the line of least resistance. You look for the hardest possible wall—overhanging, very small holds, compact—and there must be only one possible line to climb. You want to find the easiest possibility through the blankest wall. That's the challenge.

Would your routes be different from someone else's?

Not necessarily. Here [in the Frankenjura] we look for natural lines. In France they often chip holds. They want to do hard routes and they know

Wolfgang Güllich climbing on Lotus Mountain in China.
(Courtesy Wolfgang Güllich)

their climbing ability, so they think about moves and then construct routes. Around here we want to accept the natural structure as a test, as a given. We want to read nature and solve that natural puzzle.

Why do you accept nature rather than constructing routes?

Because otherwise the whole challenge goes away. Otherwise you could just climb in a gym. You don't have to think about coordination anymore. Like I said, you want to select the information from the rock, you want to analyze it, you want to relate it to your ability, and then finally you want to find the program to do it.

And if you don't accept nature but chip, the whole thing falls apart and it's not challenging. It means you're not trying to find the secret of the impossible. If you go to a cliff, you might climb up for twenty meters and then find a blank section for three meters. At first you think, "This is impossible." If you chipped a hold it would be possible, but you want to push the limit of the impossible as far as you can. So you go through your analysis and you put it down to maybe, and then finally you might do it.

Around the Frankenjura there are some routes that I can't do now but I know are possible. They are open challenges. But if I chip a hold, I do them and I lose that challenge.

Why haven't you participated in many climbing competitions?

Climbing competitions have changed the attitude among climbers. That was my feeling from the climbing competition I took part in at Bardoneccia [Italy] in 1985. A lot of climbers at that competition just had the route in mind; there was no fun involved. Everything was so serious. On the first day Russ Clune [American climber] and I were really pissed because of the change of attitude. We thought we might go on to another climbing area and just leave all that behind. But they said, "We'll have a big discussion to sort out the different opinions."

So we stayed for the discussion. We talked about what we liked about climbing, especially the lifestyle, which is very unique. And this journalist got up and said we should shut up because we were really there to win money and nothing else should be important to us. I thought that this was so stupid because I just went there to meet some friends. I didn't even think about the money. The whole thing was totally unsatisfying.

But then Jerry Moffatt made some jokes. The English are much more fun than the French or the Italians. The Italians introduced him, and he went up in front of the audience, but they had no interpreter for him. He didn't know what to do, so he grabbed the microphone and said, "Well, boys, I guess I'll sing a song."

They had no sense of humor. They didn't understand it. They thought he was making fun of the whole thing.

And then later on, Jerry was holding a beer in front of the TV camera. Jerry looks at the TV camera and says, "Do I look good? How do I look?" The sponsors hated it.

And Russ and I made some jokes, too, because everything was so serious. So they called us the anarchists. They said we weren't good for the young people because we weren't serious enough.

Usually I never drink very much, but that night I was really frustrated after the discussion. And these organizers walked up to us and said, "You should go to bed because you have to climb tomorrow." Never before had anyone told me that I had to climb. They turned off the lights on us, but we stayed up, drank red wine, and got very drunk. I don't remember how I got back to my tent.

But I guess competitions have changed a bit. Some people say it's different if you go there with friends; then you have a good time and a lot of laughter. I think there should still be some humor. I don't care who climbs the route. It's not the most important thing. It's much more important how the people act.

It seems that camaraderie is one of the things you enjoy most about climbing.

Yes. There are people who do very hard routes but are no fun, and I really don't care so much for them. And then there are people who are fun and who climb 5.7. I don't care whether someone climbs 5.11 or 5.7 or 5.14, as long as everyone is happy with his result. You climb with a 5.7 climber, he belays you on your hard route, and then you belay him on his hard route. You're satisfied with your result and he's satisfied with his result.

Some people get so arrogant, and I hate that very much. There was this Australian here in the Frankenjura and he was telling Ron Kauk and me how he worked on this very serious 5.14 route at Smith Rocks and there were some 5.11 climbers disturbing him. And he said, "I wanted to do this 5.14 climb and these people were talking to me or singing little songs. And these 5.11 bumblies disturbed my concentration so much that I failed. Can you imagine? People climbing only 5.11?"

And Ron and I had to laugh so hard because he was serious. Here he's concentrating on this very serious 5.14 route and he thinks it'll change the future if he does this route. It's really so unimportant whether someone climbs a 5.14. It's only personal satisfaction.

Why did you attempt to free-climb the Yugoslav Route on Trango Tower?

For me that was the ideal of a long, sustained alpine route. I thought we might have a chance to free-climb it from what I had heard, although some people thought it would be impossible because of the altitude and ice in the cracks. They said, "Forget about it. You'd be lucky if you could put one foot in front of the other at that altitude. There's no way you could free-climb it."

We were on a German expedition that was made up of alpine guides and free climbers. The alpine guides had this arrogant attitude toward the free climbers, who wore these colorful shorts and were used to climbing in the sun. They thought that we wouldn't even make it to base camp and that even if we got there we wouldn't be able to stand the isolation because we were used to going to bars and talking with people. They said, "They look good in the photographs, but they won't even want to touch the rock. Yes, they think they can climb it—Fantasy Island."

So they were surprised when you completed the route.

Yes. They were really surprised.

How long was the route?

It was twenty-eight pitches of very continuous climbing. There were two 5.12 pitches and several 5.11 pitches. There were only five pitches easier than 5.10. We had three bivouacs, one at the base of the cliff and then two on the wall.

Was it difficult to acclimatize?

No. We spent some other time on an aid climb to get acclimatized. But high-altitude free climbing is a different game from other kinds of high-altitude climbing. When you're walking you can pace yourself. If you get tired, you can slow down. But if you have to free-climb a crack fifty meters long, you have to keep going. There's no way you can slow down. Otherwise you get tired and you can't hang on forever. So the mountain tells you how fast you should go.

What was the hardest part?

Having the confidence to go there with a rack of stoppers and Friends and try. You can't bring too much gear, because if you do, it will slow you down. And if you have a 5.11 crack of forty meters, you may have only three pieces of protection that will fit it. So you use maybe a No. 1 Friend, then a No. 1 1/2, and then maybe a No. 2. But you have to reach the belay soon after putting in the last piece because you're running out of gear. And if you want to free-climb the route, there is this strict rule that you can't rest on any artificial aid. So you might have to run it out for ten meters after you've placed your last piece of protection. And it would be tempting to rest before climbing this last section, just to make sure that you have enough strength left, but you keep going because you want to free-climb the route.

Did your route on Trango Tower represent a new direction for free climbing?

Yes, a totally new direction. There was nothing like that done in all the Himalaya. Now some people are going to some 500-meter walls to do a little free climbing, but not in that style. But there's such a great potential there. It was very exciting to introduce technical free climbing to this huge mountain range.

Which aid route did you attempt prior to climbing Trango Tower?

It's called the Norwegian Route [on the middle pillar of Great Trango Tower] because it was done by some Norwegian climbers in 1985. In the judgment of many climbers it's a big landmark in Himalayan climbing.

We spent ten days on that wall. It's on the most impressive rock pillar I've ever seen. It's 1800 meters vertical—1000 meters of steep snow and ice and then another 800 meters of rock. It's twice the size of El Capitan.

We got really high, 600 meters below the top. There were no clouds and the weather looked fine. And we thought, "We'll make it to this next camp and get established on the headwall." So we jumared up with all the stuff— full ice equipment, specialized aid-climbing gear, and other stuff. My pack weighed about twenty kilos. I got hot carrying it, so I didn't bother to bring my gloves or my Gortex jacket. Then a storm came in and within five minutes it started to snow. The ropes got iced up and I couldn't move my jumars. It was crazy. I was stuck and I couldn't get to my warm clothes. Finally I got back down. I was so scared.

We had walkie-talkies so that we could talk to our liaison officer in base camp, and he would give us the weather report from Skardu, which is in the desert. He would tell us that the weather was going to be fine, but you could forget about it because the region there has its own weather.

And the climbing was really hard. On the lower part we did free climbing up to Grade VII and then aid climbing up to A4 for many, many pitches— at altitude and in terrible weather conditions. Finally we didn't have the mental strength to keep going. We said, "Let's finish here. Let's go to Nameless Tower," which was a playground compared to that route.

That trip was so adventurous. Every day something happened. I've never had such an intense two months as that. Never. We were so isolated up there. We realized that if something happened, just one little accident, we would have been fucked.

The four Norwegian climbers who first attempted the route planned to be on the wall for twenty days. But they found that they couldn't make it in twenty days, so two of them rapped down. The two others continued and continued and continued. They made it to the top after twenty-three days.

But then they had to rap down the same route, which would take three days—it has about fifty-six pitches. They never made it all the way back down. They probably pulled an anchor on rappel. There's a place at the base of the cliff where they hit. You can see their ropes and plastic boots and everything. You always have to walk by it on your way to the route.

Do you worry much that something like that could happen to you?

No, I'm very careful. I don't risk much. And if something happens, it happens. You could be riding in a truck along the Karakoram Highway and it could just drop into the Indus River. I'm not worried about death because I think it's destiny.

Anyway, it's mostly the little things that are dangerous. I went to eastern Germany recently and climbed with Bernd Arnold. We wanted to do a new route and he said we should rap down simultaneously to check this one section and give each other information. I thought, "This is very, very dangerous," but he assured me that it was not, as long as we were both hanging on the rope. We rapped down, and I thought the section was possible; so he gave me this wire brush to clean off some lichen. He didn't have anything to do, so he rapped down. There were lots of people with us, and he got into a conversation with them. He got distracted and untied from the rope.

> *"I REALLY CAN'T IMAGINE A BETTER LIFE THAN THE ONE I HAVE. . . . YOU CAN LEAD A REALLY FULFILLED LIFE THROUGH CLIMBING."*

Meanwhile I was still ten meters up. I tried this one move, and when I leaned back there was no tension on the rope, and I fell. I landed on a huge boulder and then rolled off. I was so lucky that I didn't get hurt.

Has anyone close to you died climbing?

My younger brother died climbing. He was thirteen and was hiking with my parents. When you're young you want to show off, and so my brother ran on ahead and tried to climb this little spire. And then it happened. He fell. It could have happened in a tree.

It was really sad. My parents cared so much about us. After that, I went climbing with my father because he wanted to keep an eye on me, and he wouldn't let me do anything on my own until I was fifteen or sixteen. People from the neighborhood said, "How could you continue to climb after such a horrible accident?"

My parents accepted that I wanted to climb and didn't put pressure on me to give it up. But they couldn't explain it to the neighbors who thought, "They never learn. They lost a child, and here their stupid son continues to climb and they think it's good."

Now my parents are very proud of me, but they have to hold it back because other people in the neighborhood are doctors or belong to the tennis club. They're very proud of their children and play these little games, telling each other, "Yes, my son has very good grades" and things like that.

But now when I go home after my vacations even the neighbors are interested in my trips. I go to China and come back and tell them about it, and then they go to China. So I'm exploring countries for them now.

Why is it that you climb?

It feels good to move on the rock. I don't just climb hard routes; I also love to do some easy soloing or moderate climbs with other people.

There are so many aspects to the sport. It never gets boring because you always do something different. Maybe you train really hard on sport climbing and get tunnel vision for a while, but as soon as you burn out a bit you concentrate on another aspect, like traveling. You go to another country and meet people. You see the the world through the vehicle of climbing.

Through climbing I have seen so many things, gone to all these countries and had all these adventures. I really can't imagine a better life than the one I have. I'm totally happy about my life. You can lead a really fulfilled life through climbing. If you don't want to concentrate on the physical, you might study biomechanics, or write a book, or teach other people how to climb, or do something intellectual, like research. So it's not only working your body around on some rock.

What are the future challenges in free climbing? Extending the scale?

Yes, but this is a very narrow path. It's too bad that a big part of the climbing community looks only at grades. If you're around the Frankenjura, they ask, "What grade have you climbed? Have you done 10 [5.13c]?" And it doesn't mean very much. People work on a grade 10 for half a year, do it, and then put it beside their names.

But someone like Peter Croft doing these solos is so impressive. It's a dangerous game, but he seems controlled. And he doesn't seem to do it for the publicity, otherwise he wouldn't do it so often. Some people do a route once to get famous. They think, "I have to do it." And afterward they say, "Wow, never again, but at least I'm famous now." But he solos Astroman [5.11c] regularly. He does it because he enjoys it.

Some climbers reach a point where they can't go any farther and then they stop. I can't see that happening to me or Peter Croft or Ron Kauk.

So you'll probably keep climbing for the rest of your life?

Yes, but not so intensely. I see no need to train forever, but just to go out and do some routes, maybe just on the weekend. I'll always enjoy it.

A lot of climbers are slaves of their hobby. It becomes a dead-serious job for them. When we went to Trango Tower many of the free climbers here in the Frankenjura said, "You'll never free-climb that. And you'll lose a lot of fitness if you go away for two months. You won't be able to touch a grade 10 this year. I'd never risk spending so much time in Pakistan and then maybe come back with nothing in your pocket. There's a good chance of having bad weather and just hanging around in base camp. I wouldn't take the risk."

For them it's a risk, but people like Ron Kauk say, "You'll discover something different. You'll have a different experience." You never come back with nothing in your pocket or on your record. You always get something out of it.

And unfortunately, in the Himalaya as in free climbing, it now seems that the most important word is "success." Everybody asks you about success. The porters ask, "Did you make it? Success?" Which means, "Have you been on top?" And in the tourist office there, they ask you, "Success?" And then when you get back home, they ask you, "Success?"

So the big deal in the Karakoram was free-climbing the route on Nameless Tower, but that was less strenuous than the ten days on the Norwegian Route. I put much more effort into the Norwegian Route and so I got a lot more out of it. It was so much more of an experience.

But people say, "You spent ten days on it? Did you make it to the top?"

"No, we didn't."

"So, how did you waste your time?"

For them it's a waste of time, and that makes me sick. The main thing is to enjoy the sport and not worry about the result. It sounds strange, but the result really doesn't matter. I see a lot of young climbers try something, and if they can't do it, they shout and hit the wall with their feet. They want to be good, and if they don't reach their goal they just quit.

I saw all my steps in climbing as presents. I wasn't sure if I could reach a certain point, but I didn't get angry if I couldn't. When we went to the Karakoram, we tried. When the weather was bad and we couldn't do the Norwegian Route, well, at least we tried it. I didn't get unhappy or frustrated.

Some people just want acceptance from climbing and they treat it as a job. All they're interested in is "success." But I have so much more respect for people who try without caring about the result. They *live* climbing. And it may sound romantic, but they carry climbing in their heart.

CATHERINE DESTIVELLE

*In the end, climbing comes before all else…and I take
renewed pleasure in doing it for myself alone. It's very important
to climb for yourself; if you do, your enthusiasm and motivation
will allow you to progress faster than the rest. It is true that there
are still difficult times which will not be easy to endure. My
position of being a kind of celebrity provokes jealousy and
backbiting but I try not to take notice of this even though it
seems to be getting worse. Because what will it matter if one day
I have enough of it all and decide to take up my career as a
physical therapist again? However, for the moment, things are
going fine, and I live life passionately; there is great pleasure in
this and it takes care of everything else.*

—Catherine Destivelle, *Ballerina of the Rocks*

DESPITE THE STORM of publicity that has swirled around her since she burst onto the scene in 1985, Catherine Destivelle has continued to climb for herself alone, refusing to let celebrity and success sidetrack her and steadfastly following her own evolution in the sport. Whereas most climbers would be content to master just one of the aspects of the climbing game, she has sought to succeed at all of them, taking on new challenges so as to achieve overall expertise. In so doing, she has become one of the finest all-around climbers—male or female—in the world today, thus serving notice that women have finally arrived at the front rank of climbing.

Her love for the sport began at age five when she visited Fontainebleau, a popular bouldering area outside Paris. A climbing prodigy, she progressed quickly, tackling some of the area's toughest boulder problems while barely a teenager and making them appear trivial. Male partners got used to seeing her breeze up routes that baffled them completely. In no time at all, Fontainebleau had lost its challenge for her and she was ready to turn her attention to the Alps.

At age fourteen, she joined the French Alpine Club, where she met a number

233

Catherine Destivelle. (Photo © G. Lowe)

of top-level climbers, including Pierre Richard, with whom she climbed for some five years. Her precocious talent astonished the older men, who set out to teach her alpine climbing techniques. With their instruction and encouragement, she repeated many of the classic routes in Chamonix by age seventeen, including a seven-hour ascent of the American Direct Route on the Petit Dru in 1976.

Shortly thereafter, Destivelle quit climbing to pursue a career in physical therapy. She enjoyed the work initially, learning the intricacies of body mechanics and injury rehabilitation, which proved immensely useful later, but the long hours and repetitive nature of the job convinced her that she needed a change. When a friend recommended her for a part in the French version of the television series "Survival of the Fittest," she jumped at the chance. Not long after the television show aired, the phone rang again. This time it was the filmmaker Robert Nicod. Would she appear in a climbing film about the Verdon Gorge? She agreed immediately, even though Nicod wanted her to climb Pichenibule, which at 7b+ (5.12c) was a grade harder than any route ever done by a woman in France. She pulled off the now famous ascent with only six weeks of training. The resulting film, *It's Dangerous to Lean Out* (1985), helped her get the sponsorship she needed to become a professional climber.

Later that same year, Destivelle entered the sport-climbing competition at Bardoneccia, Italy, and to her surprise took first place. Though she had reservations about the contests, she stuck with them, winning the same contest the following year despite having had to recuperate from a near fatal fall into a crevasse. She took a break from the competitions to do a film on the Dogon people, a cliff-dwelling tribe from Mali, West Africa, for whom climbing is a way of life. When she returned to competitive climbing in 1987, her reservations turned to frustrations at the World Indoor Rock Climbing Premier in Grenoble, where the competition's sponsors first bent the rules to allow her to compete in the finals and then contradicted themselves and disqualified her. Though she went on to win at Snowbird in 1988 and 1989, she had begun to sour on competitive climbing. Jeff Lowe's invitation to take part in a 1990 expedition to Trango (Nameless) Tower in Pakistan came at just the right time.

Though acutely aware of the drawbacks of competitive climbing, she discovered on Trango that it also had its benefits. The competitions had honed her free-climbing skills enormously, allowing her to negotiate extremely difficult passages even at altitude. Trading leads, she and Lowe were able to overcome 5.12a sections and claim the second free ascent of the Yugoslav Route. Rather than satisfying her, though, the Trango climb merely whetted her appetite for further adventures.

She chose the Bonatti Pillar of the Petit Dru as the first of these adventures, free-soloing the route in just four hours in the fall of 1990. The climb caused a sensation in the press, leading some journalists to make what she felt were unfair comparisons between herself and Walter Bonatti, who had spent six days on the first ascent. To get some idea of the difficulty of opening up a new line, she decided to attempt a new one of her own. She turned to Lowe for help in learning the techniques of aid and big-wall climbing, essential skills for the route she had in mind. After a one-month apprenticeship on the walls of Zion National Park in the southwestern United States, she was ready to tackle her objective.

She had noticed a series of cracks running up the west face of the Petit Dru between the Bonatti and Gross-Grenier routes and suspected that she could link them together into a route. The task proved more difficult than she had imagined. It took her eleven days of aid climbing, some of it as hard as A3 and A4, to complete the 2600-foot line. Her hands were bruised and battered when she topped out, but she knew through her exhaustion that she had achieved something significant. Though she downplays the importance of the climb, it nevertheless represents a breakthrough, a major first ascent by a woman on one of the most technically difficult peaks in the Alps.

A pillar of clean, gray granite that dominates the northern end of the Chamonix Valley, the Petit Dru often has served as the place where each succeeding generation of climbers has made its definitive statement: Bonatti's route in 1955 ushered in a new level of individual commitment to alpinism; Royal Robbins's ascent of the American Direct Route in 1962 showed what could be accomplished with Yosemite-style climbing techniques; Destivelle's route in 1991 signaled the arrival of women at the cutting edge of climbing. Whereas in the past most female climbers were content to repeat routes pioneered by men, Destivelle's ascent heralded an era when women began putting put up new routes and coming into their own as climbers. Her gutsy solo winter ascent of the Eiger's north face in March of 1992 confirmed what many people had already suspected: Destivelle is perhaps the finest all-around female climber in history.

Born in Oran, Algeria, on July 24, 1960, Destivelle grew up just outside Paris. Today, she maintains an apartment in Paris, a house in the south of France, and a loft in Chamonix.

Destivelle is a diminutive woman with dark hair, green eyes, and a captivating smile. She seems curiously uncompromised by all the attention lavished on her by the media and legions of fawning male climbers and comes across not as a jaded sophisticate, but as frank, honest, and open, even retaining a surprising girlish streak that manifests itself in sudden outbursts of giggling. Though she describes herself as an ordinary French girl, there is nothing ordinary about her schedule, which makes setting up an interview considerably more difficult than the longest and most complicated aid climb. After schedule conflicts stymied a number of potential face-to-face meetings, a phone interview finally took place, where even via a wire under the Atlantic, it was impossible to mistake her energy, vibrancy, and unabashed enthusiasm for climbing.

Is there a gap between the climbing abilities of men and women?

It has changed a lot. Now we are quite close to the men. There is a bit of difference because we don't have the same kind of body and hormones. It's the same as in other sports; women will never have the same strength.

Should there be separate competitions for men and women?

Yes, I think this is a good idea. Women don't have the same size or strength as men. When you compare Lynn Hill to François Legrand, there is a lot of difference.

What advantages do women have over men as climbers?

Women are lighter and more flexible than men. They save their strength because they climb in balance.

When you started climbing, was it unusual for a girl to be interested in the sport?

No. I started at five at Fontainebleau. All the children liked to climb there. My parents went there every weekend. I climbed there until I was six or seven, and after that we went to another forest without boulders, so I had to stop.

Were you good at climbing right from the start?

Yes, I was good. That's why I liked it. When you are good at something, you tend to like it.

> "WOMEN ARE LIGHTER AND MORE FLEXIBLE THAN MEN. THEY SAVE THEIR STRENGTH BECAUSE THEY CLIMB IN BALANCE."

How did you progress?

I climbed with older friends and I tried to imitate them. I had good teachers.

Was this again at Fontainebleau?

Yes, at fourteen I came back to Fontainebleau to train after I had joined the French Alpine Club, and one climber, Pierre Richard, showed me a lot. He was a very, very good climber. And after a year I met the best climbers in Fontainebleau. So I climbed with them and tried to imitate them.

How old were you when you joined the French Alpine Club?

Fourteen. I stayed with them for one year and then left and climbed with other friends.

Were there any other women in the club?

There were some but they didn't climb a lot.

How did the men treat you?

[Laughs] Very nicely. They were surprised at how well I climbed and they wanted to help me become better. They showed me how to do everything and helped me a lot.

When did you start going to the Alps?

When I was fourteen I went with some other kids to l'Oisans and areas near Chamonix. We had this little bus, so we slept inside it or camped near the Mer de Glace or just above the Plan de l'Aiguille. We climbed for a month there.

Were you scared by the scale of these Alpine climbs?

No, I wasn't scared. I liked climbing them. I was comfortable. It was no problem.

What climbs did you do?

I did the Couzy-Desmaison route on the north face of Olan, the Gervasutti Route on the north face of Ailefroide. And later, when I was sixteen, I led the American Direct Route on the Petit Dru. It took me seven hours to get to the top.

Why did you give up climbing for a while?

I had had enough. The game had become all the same. I knew all the boulders in Fontainebleau. It was quite boring for me. And then I was at Fontainebleau with a group of climbers and it was raining or something and some people asked us to play poker. And at the beginning we played for a little money, but later on it became big money. We would play all night, so during the day we were tired and had no energy to climb.

Why did you get back into climbing?

I had been working for five years as a physical therapist and I was bored with my job. I knew that I didn't want to do this for the rest of my life, but I didn't know how to move away from it and follow an evolution. Then some people asked me to climb for a French TV show, and after that Robert Nicod asked me to do a climbing film, *It's Dangerous to Lean Out.*

Was it hard to get back in shape to do the climbing movie?

It took me a month and a half. They wanted me to climb Pichenibule in the Verdon Gorge. It was quite a hard climb. At this time no girls had made a climb of this difficulty. I was not sure, but I thought I could climb it because

North Face of Eiger, showing the 1938 first ascent route that Destivelle soloed in winter, 1992. (Swiss National Tourist Office; Diadem Archives)

the most difficult passage was quite short. I was a good boulder climber and I thought maybe I could do it. So I trained a lot; I stayed in the Verdon Gorge and climbed every day. I tried the route three times and finally did it. After I did the film I decided to stop physical therapy and try to make a living as a climber.

Did you get a lot of sponsorship as a result of the film?

Yes. Then I went to the first climbing competition at Bardoneccia, and after that a lot of sponsors came and I realized that I could make a living from climbing.

Which companies sponsor you?

Michel Beal has been my sponsor since he gave me some ropes when I was fifteen. And I have Cassin, Boreal, Le Grimpeur Sports Shop, Neutrogena, Poivre Blanc—a clothing company—and some others too.

Do you ever feel pressured by your sponsors?

Never. When I decide to accept a sponsor, I try to do my best, but I feel no pressure.

What kinds of things do you do for them?

I do some conferences and some lectures. I go to sports shops. I try to do some photos for magazines and organize some films. And I try to give them some advice about technical things.

Do you have a career as a model as well as a climber?

People say that I'm a model, but I'm not. But the fact that I'm a woman helps me a lot. I don't know what image I give to people. Do I give the image of being a model?

It isn't strictly the image of a model. Perhaps it's more of a role model for young girls.

Yes, young girls ask me to autograph little pieces of paper. It's funny. People recognize me everywhere in Paris.

When did you start climbing at the Verdon Gorge?

I started at age fifteen. I climbed with boots, a helmet, a rucksack—it was quite an adventure. [Laughs]

Was it a big center of rock climbing back then?

When I first went there it was more for alpinists and mountain climbers. And later on, around 1978, it became the most impressive place for rock climbers; only the best ones climbed there.

Who were the leading French free climbers of this time?

Patrick Edlinger, Patrick Berhault—guys like that, mostly from the south of France.

Was free climbing just getting started in France at this time?

Yes. Jean-Claude Droyer was the ambassador of free climbing. He convinced other climbers to change their game and climb free.

Was it mainly at Verdon that they were trying to do this?

No, they were doing it everywhere, but mostly on the cliffs.

Prior to doing free climbing, had most people been pulling on fixed protection?

Yes, I used to pull on pitons at the time. And we stopped doing this in 1978.

So the rules became much stricter?

You could do what you wanted, but the game was changing. Even now people still pull on pitons. Older people climb with the older game.

Why have French climbers done so well in free climbing?

I think we had the best cliffs in the south of France. And a lot of people came there to climb—American, English, and so on—and there was good competition between them. So the French climbers did so well because they had a good place to train.

Was it mainly in Verdon that people put up the hard routes?

They were put up on cliffs shorter than Verdon. Verdon is nice, but usually people prefer to put up harder routes on shorter cliffs. Verdon is quite old now. Nowadays people put up some beams and boards and climb in their garages. François Legrand and all of these younger climbers train in the garage.

Why did you enter the first sport-climbing competition at Bardoneccia?

Just to see what it was like. I was against competition, but I wanted to see what climbing competitions were like and to be able to judge for myself whether or not they were good.

Did you like it?

No. [Laughs] I don't like competition. It was not the same as climbing. I was nervous. I don't like people watching me while I climb.

Were you surprised when you won?

I was very surprised. And after that the sponsors came, which was good.

But I had an accident just a week after the competition. I fell into a crevasse and broke my back and pelvis. So I had to train very hard to prove what the media said about me. They said that I was the best and so on.

Was it difficult to come back after your injuries?

Yes, it was hard because I was afraid to fall and hurt myself again. I was stuck in my moves because of this fear. It was not physical; it was mental. I started climbing one month later. I knew from being a physical therapist that I could do this.

And so you returned to the Bardoneccia competition the following year?

Yes. In fact, I won because they counted the speed-climbing competition in with the other climbing. I was very fast, faster than Lynn Hill, and I won for this reason.

Did you like this competition any better?

No. I don't like competing, even when I win.

> *"I DON'T LIKE COMPETING, EVEN WHEN I WIN."*

So you took a break from competition to visit the Dogon people?

Yes, on Mali. Some people wanted me to do a film there. And I thought it would be interesting to meet people who really live in the cliffs. I really wanted to meet these people.

Was it good to get away from competitions?

Yes, it was a little adventure compared to climbing competitions. It was more interesting and I had a chance to climb solo. When I was fourteen or fifteen I climbed solo a lot. But when training for sport climbing I was not able to climb solo very much, so I had to work on myself to be able to climb like that again.

Were the Dogon surprised to see you climbing?

Yes, they were very surprised. They compared me to a witch. That's why I was able to climb, they told me.

Why did you return to competition climbing at Grenoble after that?

Because it was my life. I was around people who competed, so I didn't think of quitting. I just had to do it. I thought that it was my life. I didn't think very much.

Were the rules confusing at the Grenoble competition?

I had problems at Grenoble because they considered me the star of the competition and they changed rules during the competition to help me. On the first route I put my foot outside the lines. And normally I would have been disqualified.

I said, "Okay, no problem. I'll withdraw." It didn't bother me because it was my mistake. But they wanted me to stay in the competition, so they changed the rules.

They told me, "This rule isn't good; it's not fair." And they allowed me to go to the finals. And so there were three of us in the finals.

Then they changed their minds and told me, "No you can't compete because you put your foot outside the line."

So I wasn't allowed to compete. I was very disappointed. It was not fair to the spectators and the other climbers [Lynn Hill and Andrea Eisenhut]. I would have preferred to have stopped at the beginning and not to have gone so far to do nothing. It was disgusting for me. So after that I was paranoid about competition. I was thinking that everyone had it in for me. [Laughs]

Did it take some time for the competitions to establish a consistent set of rules?

Yes. At first the rules were poorly established. Now I think it's okay. I haven't been to competitions in two years, but I think it's better.

What were your strengths in competition climbing?

Speed. I was very fast.

What were your weaknesses?

In my head. [Laughs] And I had some asthma. I failed in one competition [Bercy, France, 1987] because I couldn't breathe. I didn't know it was asthma. I went to a doctor and he told me it was asthma. He told me I would have to take some medicine and that I would not be able to run even ten minutes. So I stopped everything when I found that out. But now I'm able to run for one hour.

Why did you go to the Snowbird competition in 1988?

My mind was still in the competition mode. I was training and that was all. I went to the competitions without thinking.

Did they change the rules for you there as well?

I don't think they changed the rules. I had fallen on the first route, and they thought that I had not gotten high enough to qualify. I wasn't disappointed. I was not in good shape anyway. Before that, I had climbed for a month and a half in the United States on cracks, and I was not trained for competition climbing.

But I had a surprise in the morning. I was eating a big breakfast because I was ready to do nothing that day when they told me that a woman ahead of me [Mari Gingery] had put her hand out of bounds. Jeff Lowe and some of the other organizers reviewed it that night, and the next day they said they had made a mistake and that I would be allowed to go on. They told me it was fair and that I could watch the TV and check the mistake they had made.

Was there a rivalry between you and Lynn Hill at this competition?

Yes, a little bit. I didn't know her and she didn't know me, and I was quite a star in France. But now we are good friends. We are working on some projects together.

And the 1989 Snowbird competition was your last one?

Yes, after that I stopped. I realized that I couldn't both climb in the mountains and do competitions—it's not the same training—and I preferred to climb in the mountains.

Are you a person who is easily bored?

No, but I like to see other things and follow an evolution, not always repeat myself. If I do something too much, I lose interest. That's why I stopped climbing in competitions and started climbing in the mountains again.

Where did you meet Jeff Lowe?

I met him at the first Snowbird competition. And at the second Snowbird competition he told me he was organizing an expedition to Trango [Nameless] Tower in the Himalaya and asked me if I wanted to go with him.

Why did you decide to go?

I had never been on an expedition and I wanted to know what expedition climbing was like. And the photographs of Trango Tower are wonderful. I thought it would be quite interesting to climb it.

How did you prepare for the climb?

Before going to Trango we trained for a month in the United States so that we could get to know each other. I wanted to be sure that he was a safe climber and he wanted to be sure that I was a safe climber. We both wanted to be sure that we could climb together without arguments.

Were you a good team on Trango?

Yes. Together we are a complete team. I'm good at free climbing, and he's good at ice climbing and has a lot of experience. So together we could do good routes and climb at a high level.

Did the altitude bother you?

It's not so high [20,510 feet]. I felt fine.

Was it much different from climbing in the Alps?

It was longer and our packs were quite heavy. We climbed with a lot of clothes, sleeping bags, and gear.

How many days did it take you to climb it?

Normally we could have climbed the route in three days, but because of bad weather we spent two weeks on the wall.

Did you enjoy being up there for that long?

Yes, I liked it very much. It confirmed that I liked being in the mountains more than being in competitions. I just like to be in the mountains.

> "... *I LIKE THE ADVENTURE; IT'S A VERY EMOTIONAL GAME.*"

Is that why you climb?

Yes, the scenery is very impressive; it's like being in a movie. And I like the adventure; it's a very emotional game.

So you couldn't give it up?

I could stop climbing, but I would still want to be in the mountains, just to walk.

When did you decide to free-solo the Bonatti Pillar Route on the Petit Dru?

I got the idea when I was sixteen. I trained a lot for the Dru back then, and we did it in seven hours. I was disappointed. I thought it was going to be harder. And I thought, "One day I will climb it solo."

Was it a hard route to solo?

No, it was okay. I was quite sure of myself. I was ready and motivated. I soloed it in four hours.

Why did you decide to do a new route on the Dru?

After my climb people were comparing me with Bonatti, saying he climbed it in six days and it took me four hours. I thought it was unfair because people didn't understand what it meant to repeat a route as opposed to do a new route. I was upset with them. I wanted to show how hard it was to open a new route; this was the first motivation. But after that I just wanted to do a new route, just to see if I could do it. There was no reason not to do it, even if it was very hard and required aid climbing.

Was it hard to find a new line?

I just looked at some guidebooks. I thought that there was some room between two existing routes. I saw some cracks there.

Why did you want to do it solo?

I wanted to see if I could do it like Bonatti.

And it took you eleven days?

Yes.

Was it mostly aid climbing?

There was a lot of aid climbing on the first part, and after that you could free-climb it. But my gear was quite heavy, so I didn't do a lot of free climbing.

Was the aid climbing difficult?

Yes, it was A3 or A4.

Was it an exhausting climb?

No, but it was boring at the end. At the beginning, aid climbing is a new game, but at the end it's always the same move and the same thing and it's quite boring.

Was this one of the best climbs you've ever done?

No. It was okay, but that's all.

What did other climbers think of this route?

There were two reactions. There were a lot of climbers, such as René Desmaison, who congratulated me and were very happy for me. But other people were jealous. They said, "It's nothing. Why is there so much attention?" There was a lot of media coverage because I am a woman. And they didn't understand why I took a Portaledge. They told me, "Why did you take a Portaledge? It would be harder without a Portaledge." And a lot of other stuff; they were very jealous.

But that was an important new route, regardless of whether it was done by a man or a woman.

Yes, I think so. If a man had done it, it would have been as important but with a little less coverage. *Paris Match* and a lot of women's magazines wrote about it, and there was television coverage and a lot of things. I didn't do it for the media attention; I just wanted to do it. But some other climbers try to find things that will attract the media. Only five or six climbers in France try to make a living off climbing, and they were quite disappointed not to have the television coverage. They were upset because they thought they could have done the same thing. But, in fact, they didn't think of it and didn't do it.

Your route seems significant in that it's as hard or harder than anything done on that peak by a man.

Yes, it was good. But for me it's finished now. When you finish something you just think it's okay.

What are you planning to do next?

I want to do something else now—mixed routes, ice routes. I've seen only a part of alpinism and I want to discover the other parts. I have a lot of things to do.

Are you thinking of climbing something like K2?

No, not yet. First I want to do some climbs in the Alps and some technical routes in the Himalaya on 7000-meter peaks, but not on 8000-meter peaks—not yet. I don't think I'm ready to do that. I just want to enjoy my climbs and not suffer too much.

# LYNN HILL

*People who I compete against are an inspiration; they
provide motivation. If there wasn't a Catherine Destivelle or
Luisa Jovane [one of Italy's top women climbers] or whoever,
then it would be anticlimactic. Competition, in itself, is exciting
for me—it demands total concentration. It's your ego that's on
the line.*

—Lynn Hill, from an interview in *Climbing*

WHILE MANY TOP free climbers have criticized competitions as being contrary to the spirit of the sport, Lynn Hill has plunged into the thick of this new form of climbing and not only survived the hype and hoopla surrounding it, but found a way to thrive and prosper within it. Rather than shrinking from competition climbing, she has embraced it and used it to propel herself to new levels of personal achievement. In the process, she has dominated the Women's World Cup division for many years running and has equaled and sometimes surpassed the performances of the best male climbers. Through competitive climbing she has become perhaps the finest female rock climber in history.

Like many top-flight free climbers, Lynn studied gymnastics as a child and learned much from its disciplined approach to body mechanics. She learned to break down complex movements into their constituent parts so as to analyze and reconstruct them. She learned to perform strenuous and complicated routines with control and aplomb. She learned to remain calm under pressure and harness her adrenaline so as to enhance her performance. Gymnastics taught her many of the lessons she later would apply to competitive climbing.

Hill began rock climbing at age fourteen at Joshua Tree. She progressed quickly through the grades and soon was climbing 5.10—at that time the top of the scale. Fired with enthusiasm for the sport, she took the next logical step for an up-and-coming southern Californian climber: at sixteen she made her first pilgrimage to Yosemite. Rather than cowing her, the area's immense granite walls and the local hotshots' high standard of free climbing merely fed her own ambition. Within two years she was leading 5.11 and undertaking a number of

Lynn Hill. (Photo by Philippe Fragnol)

big-wall routes, including the Nose and the Shield on El Capitan. While visiting Yosemite, she met John Long, who soon became her climbing partner and boyfriend. Together they began pushing the standards of free climbing. In 1980 they ascended Ophir Broke, near Telluride, Colorado, which at 5.12d was one of the hardest climbs in the country at that time.

Eventually, Hill tired of the southern California climbing scene, and in 1983 she split up with Long and moved back East to New Paltz, New York, to climb in the Shawangunks. Shortly after arriving, she claimed the second ascent of Vandals (5.13a), the most difficult route at that time on the East Coast. It proved to be one more step in a career that soon catapulted her into the front ranks of American free climbing. As a result of this recognition, opportunities began to come her way.

In 1986 she was invited to France to tour some of the country's most popular climbing areas. Impressed by the difficulty of the routes, she vowed to return. She got her chance later that year when she was invited to compete at the International Sport Climbing Competition in Arco, Italy.

There she met Catherine Destivelle—the previous year's winner—and the two went head to head for the first time. Though Hill managed to flash the final route—something Destivelle couldn't accomplish—a last-minute rule change gave Destivelle the contest. Disappointed but not dismayed, Hill returned to Europe the same year to compete at the top French competition, the Grand Prix d'Escalade at Troubat. Destivelle failed to show and Hill walked away the winner.

The rivalry between the two women didn't diminish, however. They met again in 1987 at the World Indoor Rock Climbing Premier at Grenoble, France. This time Destivelle was disqualified for stepping out of bounds and Hill took top honors. A seesaw battle between the two ensued. Hill finished first at Arco in 1987 and 1988. Destivelle finished first at Snowbird in 1988. Eventually, though, Destivelle bowed out to devote more time to mountaineering, leaving Hill to begin her reign as queen of the competition climbing circuit. She proved unstoppable, taking first place at the International Climbing Championships at Marseille in 1988; first place at the Masters Competition in Paris in 1988 and 1989; first place at the German Free-climbing Championships in 1989; first place at Arco in 1989 and 1990; and first place at the World Cup competition in Lyon in 1989 and 1990.

In addition to having a hammerlock on women's competitive climbing, Hill also set the women's standard for extreme rock routes. She had climbed a number of 5.13s over the years, but in 1990 she set her sights on an even harder route. After nine days of exhausting effort, she ascended Masse Critique at Cimaï, the first and only 5.14 ever climbed by a woman.

But in recent years Hill's hold on the top slot of competition climbing has slipped. In 1990 she tied with Isabelle Patissier of France for first place in the overall World Cup Championship. Then, in 1991, a divorce and the daily grind of the competition circuit took a toll on her. Disappointed in her performance, she dropped out of the World Cup circuit while Patissier grabbed first place in the rankings. Hill took a bit of a breather before going back on the competitive circuit in 1992. In early 1993, Hill retired from full-time competition to pursue other projects, but she continues to train and climb.

Hill was born on January 3, 1961, in Detroit, Michigan. Shortly thereafter, her family moved to Fullerton, California, where she grew up. She attended nearby Santa Monica College for a couple of years before transferring to the State University of New York at New Paltz, where she completed a degree in biology. While in New Paltz, she met Russ Raffa, a leading Gunks local. After living together for several years, the two married in 1988. They were divorced in 1991. At present, Hill lives in Grambois, France, where she recently bought a house with some of the $80,000 a year she made in competition prize money and endorsements.

After giving a talk at the Mountain Summit conference in Snowbird, Utah, Hill took some time out to discuss her career in more detail. Hill is a petite blond with a disarming smile and a pair of remarkable blue eyes. From across the room they flash out at you, fixing you with an intensity of concentration not unlike that which Picasso reserved for regarding a canvas. During the interview, the eyes temporarily relaxed their Zen-like focus, but when she had answered the last question and it came time to put her words into action on the hotel's artificial climbing wall, the focus returned to them.

Although Hill had recently recovered from a serious fall taken at the Styx Wall in Buoux, France, she showed no signs of fear or hesitation. After tying into the rope, she shook out both arms and then squinted up at the fiberglass-paneled wall on the side of the hotel. Her eyes saw more than just random holds—they saw possibilities, ways of linking the holds together into an intricate, delicate dance. She tested the first hold and stepped onto it. She got under way, moving purposefully, economically, gracefully. Occasionally she made a dyno, or short lunge, to grasp a hold that was beyond the easy reach of her five-foot, one-inch frame. Though the holds were small and the line sketchy, she cruised. The route would have proven arduous for many a top rock climber, but Hill made it look easy. In her bare feet, without even taking off her pile jacket, she climbed quickly, calmly, confidently—all the way to the top.

Why are you such a good competition climber?

There are many different elements. For one thing, I've climbed for a long time—for seventeen years now. Through all my experiences, especially those as a traditional climber, I've learned to concentrate on what is important. On a serious climb, you can't be distracted by the fear of falling. You have to concentrate on getting to a safe place. Through traditional climbing I've learned to think on the spot, to go for it, to tune out distractions such as the fear of falling or fear of failure.

But the bottom line in competition is that you have to be motivated. You have to want to go to the top. You have to believe in yourself. You have to be capable of it. I was capable, I believed in my ability, and I really wanted it.

How did you get started in competitions?

In 1986 the French Alpine Club invited me and some other foreigners to climb in the Verdon Gorge, Fontainebleau, and Buoux. I think their motivation for offering a free trip was to show the world that the French were doing some of the hardest routes in the world at the time. And it worked. I was impressed by the difficulty of the climbs. In Buoux there was Choucas [5.13c] and Le Minimum [5.14].

On that trip I met Marko Scolaris, one of the organizers of the 1985 competition at Bardoneccia, Italy. He offered to pay my way back to the 1986 competition, so I decided to see what a climbing competition would be like.

How did you do in your first competition?

My first experience in competition was really crazy. I was the only American there; everyone else was European. Not very many people spoke English, so I felt a bit out of place, and a lot of it went right over my head.

The organizers were really ill-prepared and ended up changing the rules at the end so that Catherine Destivelle could win. If they'd used the rules as they exist now, I would have won. I was the only one to do the final route; she fell twice on it and then ran out of time and wasn't even able to complete it. And the way they weighted the points didn't make sense at all. We were actually tied in points, but they didn't even look at the fact that I'd done the final. They decided to break the tie not by doing a superfinal—which was written in the rules—but by a combination of our total time on the three different routes we'd done except for the final, and on our style, which was a subjective evaluation.

My style points were higher, but Catherine was a lot faster. In the end, they decided to give the victory to Catherine.

I was really angry. It was unfair and unsportsmanlike, and there were political reasons that she was chosen to be the winner: her boyfriend and agent was behind the scenes speaking five different languages to whoever was important while I was sitting there alone, totally helpless and totally lost. In the end, they declared her the winner. What could I do?

Did that experience dissuade you from participating in other competitions?

No. I recognized competitive climbing as being a new sport, and I knew that these things were the nonsense that sports have to go through before they can weed out problems.

And a lot of problems existed. Regarding the environment, the organizers thought nothing of chopping down trees and chipping holds in the rock to have a competition. Even then I realized that competition climbing belonged on an artificial wall—for environmental considerations, for problems with cheating and rules, and for viewing.

So I was thinking ahead of the immediate problems of competition. Even before I'd been to that competition, I imagined that eventually there would be artificial climbing walls and big competitions on network television. I'd been to a bouldering competition in San Diego and I saw the potential.

And I've been a competitive athlete all my life, so the idea of competition in sport wasn't something that intimidated me or something that I thought was distasteful. Competition is interesting and a good learning experience.

Competition climbing is also a way of promoting the sport to the general public in a way that people can understand. The top climbers in the sport can communicate how they feel about rock climbing and have a chance to demonstrate the beauty of a fluid, well-executed climbing style.

How did you get started climbing?

I was extremely active when I was young. I climbed trees. I climbed light poles. I just liked climbing. Even though I didn't recognize it as a sport, it just seemed like a good idea. Then I got more involved in formal sports. I was on a swim team. I got into gymnastics. Later on I got involved in track. I did 1500- and 3000-meter runs.

What did gymnastics teach you?

A lot. I learned the basic physical qualities you have to have, such as flexibility and coordination, and the ways of learning—visualization, modeling after seeing people doing a certain trick, and trying to break that down in your mind using very simple cues. I learned to think of two or three images of body position in sequence.

Through gymnastics I learned how to learn, learned how to go for it, learned that you can't start a trick and freak out in the middle. I learned how to combine the physical aspects of flexibility, strength, and coordination with the psychological aspects of initiating movement, controlling movement, and achieving body awareness. In gymnastics your body's spinning very fast, and you learn to control and accept certain sensations.

Climbing is much slower, but more precise. You have to be really sure about the path of your body's movement. That's what I fine-tuned in climbing, but I was still using basic principles of trajectory and things like that. Gymnastics was really important for my climbing.

When did you start rock climbing?

Chuck Bludworth, my older sister Kathy's boyfriend, taught Kathy and me to climb. He took us out to Joshua Tree. [Bludworth later died on the south face of Aconcagua.]

What about climbing did you like?

I liked the freedom of it. I liked the sensation of climbing. I liked the beauty of being in a natural environment. In gymnastics you practice the same routine over and over in a manmade environment. In climbing the environment's always changing.

Did you learn quickly?

I was a natural. I started when I was fourteen and progressed to 5.10 right away. That was when 5.10 was the top. When I was sixteen, I went to Yosemite and did a few 5.11s. I didn't really try to push the standards at first, but when I met John Long we began trying to push the standards a bit. In 1980 he and I did the first ascent of Ophir Broke, a 5.12d near Telluride, Colorado.

What was the Yosemite scene like when you got there?

Free climbing was in vogue at the time. People were trying to do the most difficult climbs with as few bolts as possible and without using any hangdogging techniques. It was all part of the combination of a big-route mentality of adventure mixed in with free climbing and also the clean-climbing concept of keeping the rock natural and adapting yourself to the rock instead of the other way around.

The big walls appealed to me at that time. I was curious to see what it was like to live on a wall for an extended period of time. So I did the Nose [VI 5.11 A3, El Capitan] with Mari Gingery. We learned how to haul, how to use pulleys, and everything else. When we got on the Shield [VI 5.9 A3+, El Capitan] in 1979, we learned to use Copperheads, hooks, Bashies, knifeblades, RURPs, and all that stuff. We learned a lot about aid climbing on those routes.

Who else did you hang out with?

John Long, John Bachar, Ron Kauk, Jim Bridwell, John Yablonsky—a whole crew of southern California climbers. I was there when people started pushing the standards to 5.11. And then I've been in it for a couple more eras, taking it into bold free climbing and then into competitive climbing and now into an era of artificial walls and training in gyms. The sport has diversified and become really specialized. People who are the best in one form of climbing tend not to be strong in the other forms of it.

Why did you move back East?

I wanted a change. I was bored of going to Joshua Tree every weekend and I didn't like the rat race of living in L.A. I had the opportunity to go to New York for a magazine interview, and I discovered New Paltz [near the Shawangunks]. The Gunks offered a different type of climbing experience and a new group of people who were really friendly and straightforward—there was none of the backbiting and slander that there was on the southern California scene. At the time I was looking for an area where I could finish college and climb at the same time. The Gunks seemed to be an ideal setting, so I moved there.

It was a good experience. The rock is much different from Joshua Tree. It's very compact with many features—grooves, corners, overhangs, and horizontal strata. In the Gunks, I learned different climbing styles and how to protect myself better with natural gear. I learned how to place RPs in really complicated small cracks and how to use double ropes on routes that don't follow direct lines.

Because there wasn't a lot of peer pressure I had an open mind and started to experiment with style. A group of us were working on this route called Vandals and we used a siege approach. I was the first person to go up since I was the lightest and had the best chance of being protected in case of a fall onto the marginal gear that was available at the start. We took turns going up as high as we could, placing gear where possible, until we finally reached some reasonable protection in the roof.

> *"The rock is a limited natural resource. We humans shouldn't be so egotistical as to change it for our own benefit. . . ."*

At a certain point I got sick of going up and down, so I began to hang there. Even though I knew it wasn't necessarily acceptable style, it made a lot of sense to me; it was a more enjoyable way of climbing. That was my first step in hangdogging.

About that time, people such as Wolfgang Güllich, Jerry Moffatt, and Patrick Edlinger were making significant advances in free climbing. There are two reasons why they and other Europeans were doing so well. They had this ideal medium—limestone—which is more conducive to sport climbing. The fitness you need to climb on limestone is ideal for pushing standards of difficulty—no matter what kind of rock you're climbing on. It's very physical, and it involves an awareness of body position because most of the rock is overhanging.

They were able to make progress because they had this ideal medium and because they weren't limited by style. They were able to employ hangdogging techniques to work hard routes. And these techniques paid off. They came to America and flashed some of our most difficult routes.

What are your thoughts on some of the ethical controversies surrounding free climbing?

Well, my basic attitude stems from that period of traditional climbing: the purpose of climbing is to adapt yourself to the rock. You work on yourself to overcome the obstacle of the rock. The rock is a limited natural resource. We humans shouldn't be so egotistical as to change it for our own benefit, specifically creating holds so that a particular move is perfect for our finger size or reach.

I believe climbers should leave the rock as unaltered as possible while keeping one thing in mind—the whole objective of climbing is enjoyment. When you take it upon yourself to open up a new route using bolts, it's no longer for yourself; it's also for the enjoyment of others. So you have a responsibility not only to put in safe bolts but to put them in logical places—to do the least possible alteration of the rock to establish the best possible experience for others.

The whole sport is contrived, if you think about it—the shoes, the chalk, the protection, the rope—all these products are artificially created. You can argue ground-up versus rap-bolting, but it's all artificial; it's all a game. And the objective of the game is enjoyment for everybody—and safety. Who wants to die from a bolt that pulled out because it was hastily placed while climbing from the ground up?

To me it's not a problem if somebody places a bolt on rappel. In fact, I welcome that because if it's placed on rappel it's often carefully placed, maybe even reinforced with some cement to keep it from weathering. And usually the bolts are reasonably spaced so that it's easy to clip into them.

I don't condone chipping and gluing. That's changing the rock for your own specific needs. That's not acceptable. And if a route doesn't go, so what? Not every square inch of rock needs to be climbed. It's possible to find a new route where you don't have to chip. And if at some point all the easy, convenient routes have been climbed, then create routes on an artificial wall. You can get tons of enjoyment out of that. You can change the holds and do whatever you want. This creative outlet offers plenty of challenge and infinite possibilities.

Did you formulate these ideas during your early years at Yosemite and Joshua Tree?

Yes. In climbing at those particular areas, I grew up with the ethic of clean climbing that some of the younger climbers don't understand or appreciate.

They think the rock is just a tool to make them a better climber. They want to climb 5.13s and they want to compete. They're so eager to jump into the limelight that they have a tendency to compromise the rock for their own purposes. I don't think you need to do that. A truly great climber can adapt to any environment, whether it's an artificial wall, limestone, or a crack climb.

Is your adaptability one of the reasons for your success?

Yes. My ability to adapt to the rock has helped me a lot. I don't get fixated on one style or one approach to climbing. I enjoy climbing in a variety of places and on many different types of rock.

So you're not a specialist in any one kind of climbing?

No, I've done many different types of routes. I prefer overhanging, gymnastic climbing, but I've done a variety of routes in traditional style. If I find myself in a situation where I have do a little technical frictioning, or get a finger jam, it's no problem since I learned these techniques early on.

How do you train for climbing?

My primary aerobic activity is running. It's not directly related to climbing, but it's good for overall fitness and it keeps my weight down. I have done a bit of weight training for general strength and fitness and to make sure that my shoulders are strong enough so that they don't dislocate. And I do a lot of stretching. I used to be a gymnast, and I still do some gymnastic exercises—handstands or exercises on a bar. They help coordinate you and give you the body sense you need in climbing. Gymnastics is a good sport for keeping your whole body in shape for climbing.

Do you practice on a climbing wall?

Yes. Climbing walls are excellent for developing power and learning to coordinate complex movements. They enable you to focus on learning correct body positions and visualizing complex movements in advance. You can teach your body to do really complex movements on a wall. A lot of people might be able to see the hold, but they don't know how to get in the right position if they don't know how to visualize the right position. That's what my training in climbing is all about.

Take a lunge, for example. A lot of times I break down the movement into different parts, as in gymnastics. I imagine three distinct steps when lunging—the initiation, the apex or deadpoint, and then the final body position after reaching the target hold. I try to find the most natural position from which to initiate a powerful launch, and then as my body is moving upward, I make subtle adjustments of my body position so that I will arrive in the right receiving position to catch the target hold.

It's not just a random process. I find that if I consciously think through this process, I am better able to direct and control these types of movements. Anyone can use trial and error, and in several tries succeed on a particular move, but if you're on a really difficult climb—on sight—it helps to have an understanding of the mechanics of movement and well-developed movement patterns. If you've learned how to do them correctly, you're more likely to fall into those patterns of movement on the first try.

So you think about this process as you're climbing?

Yes, but the ultimate is to be present in that moment, totally focused on what you're doing. It's not necessary to tell your body how to move. This process should occur naturally and spontaneously if directed using some of the visualization techniques I explained before. You focus in on the hold. You see the details of the hold. You imagine the correct body positions and forces required to reach the hold. You see your hand on it before you actually do it.

So there's a previsualization?

Yes, very momentary, and you may not even be conscious of it. That happens in a lot of sports. Most people don't do it consciously. Without thinking about it, they just visualize how to start, how to move through, and how to finish.

This approach must help immensely in competitions.

Yes. At the top end of climbing competitions everyone has the physical ability to win, but it's what goes on in the mind that makes the difference. That's what's so interesting to me.

What's your frame of mind during a competition?

I try to relax. I try to concentrate. I try to be free of thought or any kind of negative self-talk such as, "This looks too hard," or "I'm getting a little tired." It should be pure experience, like a meditation. You should be right there.

Is that the way you feel when you're in a competition?

Not always, but I try to. That's the ideal.

But isn't it easy to get rattled when you're climbing in front of several thousand people?

If you allow that to distract you, then you're not going to do as well. You've got to be there. You've got to be in that experience. It has to register on a level that's not going to interrupt your concentration. Sometimes the energy and encouragements from the crowd can be helpful, but most of the time I am too concentrated on the climbing to pay much attention.

Can you use the crowd to improve your performance?

Yes. Because there are all these people, and it's such an event, your excitement level rises. If you can direct the adrenaline, it can help you. But if you're overstimulated—it's like when you drink too much coffee—you'll become nervous and start shaking. You'll perform poorly. So you have to be able to take that excitement and direct it in a positive way without getting overstimulated.

Can you sometimes climb better during a competition than you might climb out in the mountains?

Sometimes. The motivation is there. There are all these people sharing in your experience. And everyone wants you to make it—well, maybe a few competitors don't want you to make it—but almost everybody wants you to make it.

So the competitions can push you to achieve things you might not have done otherwise?

Oh, yes.

Do competitions discriminate against shorter climbers like yourself?

Very often this can be a problem. Right now competition walls are so randomly designed that you never know whether you're going to come into a short bouldering move that favors a tall person. Route design is really the main problem.

Is it getting better?

It's not an exact science. There's no real standard for it. The people who design these routes are chosen because they have some interest or experience or because they know the organizer of the competition. I don't think it's easy to design a route that's ideal for everyone, but it can be done by using more realistic walls and holds and making sure the designer has plenty of experience and understanding of route design.

Is this one of the reasons it would be difficult to have men and women compete on the same routes?

Yes. I don't think that the technology for artificial walls nor the current route designers are quite at the level to design a route that would be fair for both men and women in terms of height. Competitions should be exciting to watch, and if people fall off at the same point because the move is too reachy, it ruins the show. It's certainly more interesting to watch people battle it out to the end rather than falling off on a move that favors a particular body type. If a woman gets fifteen feet up and falls off at the first reachy move, then the show is not very interesting for the spectators.

Do you think at some point women will be competing with men?

It could happen, but I think there are a lot of things that we're struggling against. My stance used to be, "I want to compete on the same climbs as men," because I felt that for me it would be interesting. But spectators want to see people get to the top. And since most women aren't climbing at the same level as the top men, it's necessary to design a route that's a little easier for women. It's best to create routes that suit the level of people in the sport at the current time. I wouldn't mind competing on the men's routes even if I wasn't able to make it to the top. I like that kind of challenge. But that's me—I'm not thinking about the rest of the women.

And at this point in the evolution of climbing, most women have not accepted the idea that they could be as strong or stronger than men. There are only a few women climbing at a high-enough standard to compete successfully on the men's routes. So why make a rule that's going to be bad for the majority of the women who are in the sport?

Do you think that women will ever equal or surpass men in climbing?

I don't know. I wouldn't say yes or no. I think that climbing, like gymnastics, favors people with high strength-to-weight ratio. In general, women have more body fat, and that's not the best thing to have; having low body fat and a lot of strength is important.

And women are generally smaller. I think ultimately I'm too small to be the best climber. On an artificial wall you can equalize things by adding holds for smaller people, but I think ultimately there comes a point where it's simply too difficult to compensate. There's going to be too big of a gap or too long a lunge.

". . . MOST WOMEN HAVE NOT ACCEPTED THE IDEA THAT THEY COULD BE AS STRONG OR STRONGER THAN MEN."

But theoretically somebody as short as me could be the best in the world because it doesn't depend so much on height now. At this point, the top level of climbing is nowhere near what it could be; 5.13 and 5.14 are nowhere near the ultimate level. And it's a psychological thing more than a physical thing. Of course, you would have to go through an evolution of perception to be able to do harder grades. It would take a really exceptional woman to make such a psychological leap. She'd almost have to be on her own track, pursuing things in a different way than the rest of the climbers.

Are the top female climbers getting closer to the top male climbers?

Closer, yes. Women have the advantage of being relatively light, with the capacity for tremendous endurance. Women might be better adapted for longer endurance routes that involve high-intensity moves and then short recovery sections.

But is there still a psychological barrier that prevents them from surpassing the men?

No, I think that psychologically women are on an equal par with men; there's nothing physiological about the way a woman has to think, but on a physical level, the body fat and the lower center of gravity, especially on really steep climbs, is probably not an advantage.

Are men intimidated by your climbing ability?

It depends on the person. If the person is someone who sees me as a threat to his self-image, then he might feel intimidated by me. But if it's someone who is really content in what he's able to do, and just likes to climb, then he'd probably be positive and encouraging of me, because he sees something in me that he admires. It just depends on each person's sense of security.

What's life like on the competition circuit?

Right now it's kind of chaotic. There are many different competitions going on—the World Cup, the World Master Tour, Masters events, inaugurations of climbing walls, and other competitions. There's too much to try to do everything. Last year I traveled too much and did too many competitions, and over a period of time it wore me down. In the end, my performance took a nose-dive and I lost motivation.

The year before wasn't quite as hectic, but it was the second year running of traveling and competing with not enough of an off-season or a rest period. I was hardly ever in one place for long enough to feel good.

In 1990 I decided I wanted to do a 5.14, so I stopped traveling around so much and climbed in one area for a couple of weeks. I spent nine days on a 5.14 [Masse Critique at Cimaï] and did it. Up to that point I didn't have the opportunity to work on a hard route because I'd been traveling around doing on-sight climbs in preparation for one competition or another.

Do you make a living from all of this?

Yes, and that's another element. There are a lot of responsibilities and commitments that go along with being a public figure. I travel a lot, doing promotions, slide shows, interviews, meetings, ads, photos, and films, and respond to numerous requests for writing projects or appearances.

Last year I got pulled in too many different directions. I realized that to do something well, you have to exclude a lot of other things. And since I've done so many competitions and focused so intensely on climbing for so long, I'm interested in opening myself up to other aspects of life. I want to diversify and experience new things. And that may exclude being a competitive climber at some point because competition climbing doesn't allow much of an opportunity to do this.

So you're thinking of getting away from it?

I'd like to compete one more year on the competition circuit while continuing to pursue some of my other projects and objectives. I want to cap off my competitive career in a way that is fitting for who I am and for what I believe in.

What was your most satisfying win in a climbing competition?

That was in 1990 at the World Cup competition in Lyon. In the competition before that in Nuremberg, Germany, I made a costly mistake. As soon as I stepped off the ground, I slipped and touched the ground. According to the rules I had to stop. I was eliminated after the quarterfinals and didn't earn a single point.

So in order to win the World Cup, I needed to win in Lyon and Barcelona. And at Lyon it came down to Isabelle Patissier and me in the superfinal round. And our superfinal was on the men's final route.

When I walked into the isolation room, François Legrand was explaining the moves on the route to Isabelle. He and Didier Raboutou were the only two guys who had done the final. All the other fifteen men had fallen on it. I listened to this and I couldn't believe it. Then the organizers finally realized that they should separate François and Didier from Isabelle and me.

But the damage had already been done, and that made me all the more motivated to go to the top. I was thinking, "Fine. She thinks it's going to help her; I'm going to be that much stronger." So not only was I coming off a zero, but I saw them telling her about the moves. I became determined to do the route. Period.

It took all of my effort and concentration to pull through the route. The moves I had to make were really spectacular, but I managed to do them. I was so excited to get to the top. So I won that competition [Patissier fell partway up] and I proved a point about women and what we're capable of— a lot of the best men had fallen off that route.

PETER CROFT

To reach beyond what you are, you must ignore the rules
and fashions of the day. Or perhaps better yet, cast them way out
in your peripheral vision where you can still see them but only as
a vague reference point. This doesn't mean that all the rules are
gone. It might mean that you adopt a far tighter code of conduct
to ensure the necessary level of intensity and adventure.

—Peter Croft, "Bat Wings and Puppet Strings" in *Climbing*

FAR FROM THE MADDING crowd of sport and competition climbers, Canadian Peter Croft has followed his own path, extending the boundaries of risk, boldness, and technical difficulty while remaining true to the traditions of adventure climbing. When the tide turned in the mid-1980s and many top rock climbers jumped on the sport-climbing bandwagon, Croft chose instead to push the grade with ground-up methods, refusing to resort to tactics such as hangdogging or rap-bolting. His flash ascents of extreme routes, bold solos, marathon link-ups, and speed ascents of long routes demonstrated what could be accomplished within the conventions of adventure climbing. In greatly expanding the range and difficulty of routes within this category, Peter Croft has become one of the world's premier adventure rock climbers.

Born on May 18, 1958, in Ottawa, Canada, he moved with his family shortly thereafter to Nanaimo, British Columbia, on the east side of Vancouver Island. The beaches and forests surrounding the town afforded endless opportunities for outdoor adventure, and he spent much of his childhood hiking, fishing, swimming, and exploring. At age seventeen he began climbing, first on boulders near his parents' house and then on the mainland at Squamish, one of the premier rock-climbing crags in Canada.

After learning the ropes with partners such as Richard Suddaby, Croft quickly advanced through the grades to become one of the area's best climbers. He then turned his attention to new areas, in 1979 visiting Yosemite Valley, where he climbed Royal Arches, among other routes, and came away impressed by the size of the walls and the high standard of free climbing practiced there. Subsequent visits to the Valley inspired him to push the standards at Squamish,

Peter Croft. (Photo © Greg Epperson)

which he proceeded to do in 1982, when he, Greg Foweraker, and Hamish Fraser free-climbed University Wall, which at Grade V, 5.12b, was one of the hardest long free climbs in the world at that time.

Although he had soloed occasionally at Squamish, he began doing it systematically in 1983 on a visit to England, where he climbed many of the country's classic rock routes in this manner. When he returned home, he immediately put his well-honed soloing skills to use in the Bugaboo Range of interior British Columbia, where he ascended the Chouinard-Beckey Route on Howser Tower, the McCarthy Route on Snowpatch Spire, the northeast ridge of Bugaboo Spire, and the McTech Arête on Crescent Spire—all in fourteen hours. In the fall, he returned to Yosemite to free solo the Steck-Salathé Route on Sentinel Rock and the northeast buttress on Higher Cathedral in a day.

Over the next few years, Croft continued his soloing progression, completing longer and harder routes before soloing Astroman, a landmark free climb with five pitches of 5.11 and five of 5.10. By the summer of 1987, he was ready, and after psyching himself up, climbed the route in an hour and a half, causing a sensation in Valley climbing circles. Since then, he has repeated the feat several times. He remains the only climber ever to have soloed the route.

More recently, Croft has concentrated on link-ups of classic Yosemite free climbs. On one particularly motivated day in 1990, he soloed the Steck-Salathé Route on Sentinel Rock, the north buttress on Middle Cathedral, the northeast buttress on Higher Cathedral, Royal Arches to the south face of North Dome, and the Arrowhead Arête on Yosemite Point. His only disappointment was that darkness prevented him from squeezing in another route that day.

In addition to his remarkable soloing achievements, Croft is one of the few contemporary climbers who employs ground-up tactics to push the grade on short extreme routes. In 1987 he made the first ascents of University Wall (5.13) and To the Hilt (5.13) at Squamish in this fashion. In 1989 he added Excellent Adventure (5.13) and Whippersnapper (5.13) in Yosemite. He accomplished all of these climbs without hangdogging, previewing, or rap-bolting, techniques that many contemporary climbers consider mandatory on routes of such difficulty.

In recent years, Croft has added speed ascents to his repertoire. In 1990 he and Dave Schultz climbed the Nose and the Salathé Wall on El Capitan in a day. The next year they did the Nose in four hours and forty-eight minutes. In 1992 Croft teamed up with Hans Florine to climb the Nose in four hours and twenty-two minutes. In the coming years, Croft plans to continue doing such speed ascents, as well as hard solos, solo link-ups, long free routes, and all the various other games within the adventure climbing category.

Today, Croft lives in Yosemite Valley, where he works as a guide at the Yosemite Mountaineering School. In 1987 he married Jo Whitford, a talented local climber who often worked as a waitress at Yosemite's Mountain Room Bar. They divorced in 1992.

The interview took place one summer afternoon at an outdoor table behind the Yosemite Lodge cafeteria. Croft talked modestly and circumspectly about his own extraordinary climbing achievements, while heaping praise on predecessors such as Walter Bonatti, Warren Harding, Royal Robbins, and John Bachar, among others. A quiet, self-possessed man with large, sturdy legs and muscular arms covered with cuts and scrapes, Croft has a round face that breaks out in a wide, Huckleberry Finn–like grin when he talks about climbing, revealing the intense, boyish enthusiasm for the sport that has never left him as he has progressed through the grades.

What's the appeal of soloing?

There are no interruptions. There's no one saying, "On belay. Off belay. You've got ten feet of rope left." There's no stopping to place gear. It's just you and the environment deciding where and how far you go.

And on longer routes, you get a certain rhythm going. You're just reacting to things and the decisions you make are almost subconscious. You're not thinking, "If I grab the flake like this and push my foot like that, it should work." It's all instantaneous. It all just flows.

Do you worry much about the dangers of soloing?

Oh, sure. If I just went for it all the time, it would be crazy. A lot of people think that I never back down. I back off loads of things. I may plan to go soloing one day and then think, "I don't really feel like it." I'm not superstitious, but unless it's really fun, there's no point, because there is some risk, and if you're going to accept a certain amount of risk, there should be some reward.

It's not as if soloing changes your life every time, but it reinforces certain things in your head. It requires that you concentrate pretty hard, and depending on the type of concentration, it can bring different things to you. Sometimes when I'm soloing I find the beauty of the climb just staggering. I'm living life intensely and the rewards are intense. If they weren't intense, I wouldn't bother.

> *"FOR ME AN ADVENTURE IS SOMETHING THAT I CAN TAKE AN ACTIVE PART IN BUT THAT I DON'T HAVE TOTAL CONTROL OVER."*

Is it psychologically draining?

If I solo on a day when I'm not fully into it, it might be draining. But on the days when I'm really psyched to be there, it's the opposite. It's psychological food. It just gives me energy. On a lot of the biggest soloing days, I've felt totally charged up at the end and disappointed that the sun was going down.

Is soloing the ultimate climbing adventure?

It's not that I want to solo all the time, but in terms of adventure, the more equipment that I can get rid of, the better. For me an adventure is something that I can take an active part in but that I don't have total control over. And the more active a part, and the more intimate the relationship with the surroundings, the better. So it's possible to have an adventure in a car, but it would be better on a bike. And better than a bike would be hiking, and since hiking is generally the same sort of movement over and over, better than that would be roped climbing. And better than roped climbing would be to eliminate all the equipment and climb solo without ropes.

But I don't see soloing or even climbing as the only way to have an adventure; it's just the way I've gone after it. In fact I think children have the purest vision of adventure. The closer I can get to the childlike ideal of adventure, the better.

Did you have a lot of adventures as a boy?

Yes. I grew up on the east coast of Vancouver Island in Canada, and as a kid I just loved the adventure of being out in nature. We lived near the ocean and in the summertime the water warms up enough that you can swim. We would do the Tarzan thing of swimming out to these little islands offshore, exploring them, and then swimming home.

How did you get started climbing?

I hiked a lot and that brought me into contact with people who went climbing. At first I wasn't interested in it at all. I thought it was for tough guys trying to prove something. Then a friend recommended that I read *I Chose to Climb,* by Chris Bonington. After I read that book I decided to try climbing. I'd tried so many sports up until that time—karate, hockey, soccer, tennis, track and field—but the rules and organized nature of those sports didn't appeal to me. But once I tried climbing, I realized that was it.

Were there other climbers besides Bonington whom you looked up to?

Yes. Joe Brown, Don Whillans, Hermann Buhl, but Walter Bonatti more than anyone else. Bonatti's spirit came through very strongly in his books. It impressed me that he was using climbing as a vehicle rather than as an end in itself. Obviously he was totally into the climbing and loved the beauty of the mountains and everything, but he was also using climbing to find things out about himself and the world. That really influenced me.

Where did you start climbing?

I started climbing on some boulders about a mile away from my parents' house. After that I went to Squamish, which is like a smaller, wetter version of Yosemite. The weather is worse, but the climbing is quite similiar.

In 1979 I came down here for a month, mostly to do short routes. It didn't even occur to me to do any big walls; I didn't do them up in Canada and I certainly wasn't going to do them in Yosemite, where the walls are so big. But the longer I climbed here, the more I realized Yosemite's potential. What other area in the world allows you to climb such big routes with such reliable weather? I can't think of anyplace. It seemed like the place to be.

When I started coming down here, it was *the* place to go. It was the rock-climbing mecca. The climbing scene was really energetic, and climbers were doing a lot of the world's hardest free and wall routes. You'd see a lot of the hotshots from Europe and everywhere else.

And then there was a backlash. People began to say, "Oh, Yosemite's not that great. This is wrong with Yosemite and that's wrong." The tide turned, people started sport climbing, and then different places were heralded as the hot new cragging spots. People started saying, "You've got to go to American Fork in Utah," or "You've got to go to France."

There are fewer climbers in Yosemite now than ten years ago because people are out doing sport climbs. But for some types of climbing, Yosemite is still a really important place. To me personally, it's the most important place.

When did you start soloing?

I'd done some easy soloing before, but in 1982 I soloed this overhanging finger crack called ROTC Crack [5.11c] on Midnight Rock in Washington State. It was just two pitches of climbing, but you start 700 feet off the ground, so it was really exposed. That was the first time I really felt out there. I didn't feel like it was do or die, but I knew I had to concentrate pretty hard. All I had to do was look down to see that there was an awful lot of air below me.

And then in 1983 I did some soloing in England. I'd read *Hard Rock,* which describes a lot of classic routes, and I really wanted to do a lot of those. I didn't have a partner, so I just went up and soloed them. That was the first time I'd done much on-sight soloing, which is much different from soloing a route you've done a whole bunch of times before.

One day I was sitting in a bar there watching it rain and I started thinking, "It would be great to go back to the Bugaboos and link up a lot of routes." And so I did that. But I never thought, "Oh, this is how I'm going to make my mark." It just happened. Soloing was just so much fun.

And then in Yosemite Valley there was a logical progression in terms of modern hard-soloing. The first route was New Dimensions, which John Bachar soloed in the early 1980s. And then several years later he soloed the Nabisco Wall. And to me the next step in the order of the classics was the Rostrum, so I did that a little later. And then the next obvious one after that was Astroman.

A lot of people started asking me, "When are you going to solo Astroman?" I kept saying, "I'm not going to solo it. I'm not interested at all." I didn't want any feedback about it, negative or positive. It's really important for me not to listen to other people about something like that. I just wanted to look at myself honestly and decide for myself, "Is this smart or stupid? What are the reasons for doing this?" And since the reasons were good ones, I went for it.

I first thought I should go up a few days beforehand and do it with a rope and check it out. I'd climbed the route two or three times before but I hadn't done it for maybe four years. But then I figured that to get the best adventure, I didn't want to do it just beforehand.

I really wanted to follow the soloing progression that day. So I did New

Dimensions and Nabisco Wall and I wanted to do the Rostrum, but it was really hot and I didn't want to do it in the heat of the day; so in the end I did those two shorter routes and I waited until the afternoon to try Astroman. I remember walking out into the forest past Curry Village and looking up at it, waiting for it to go in the shade. The route is mostly overhanging and it's on this beautiful orange granite. It's one of the most beautiful faces in the Valley.

As I looked at it from the forest there, I started psyching myself up, getting it engrained in my head that this wasn't a dangerous thing, that I was totally ready for it, and that it would be a totally successful climb. I saw myself hiking up there and saw myself climbing the whole thing.

And then I started getting an overpowering urge to do it. It was hard to stop myself from going up there immediately. Finally I saw it go into the shade. I forced myself to wait a little longer for it to cool down and then I hiked up there. It was about five o'clock or so.

"AFTER THE FIRST PITCH, I REALIZED THAT I WAS GOING FOR IT NOW AND I STARTED GETTING REALLY JACKED UP. I HAD TONS OF ADRENALINE."

When I got up to the base of the climb, there was no one else around. I dithered around the first 5.11 pitch, because it's the technical crux [5.11c]. I had a little toothbrush and I scraped some of the chalk off it. Then I went for it. It was thin, fingertip laybacking, but it felt really solid.

After the first pitch, I realized that I was going for it now and I started getting really jacked up. I had tons of adrenaline. I was climbing fast and hardly ever stopping to chalk up. I knew that I wasn't going to enjoy it if I kept climbing that quickly, so I got to a ledge a little more than halfway up and stopped, took off my shoes, wiggled my toes, and looked over at Half Dome. I sat there for a while enjoying the view, and then put the shoes back on and started climbing, but more slowly.

I got to the top as the sun was setting. I'd been concentrating so hard and all my senses were incredibly sharp and my perception was super vivid. I looked over at Half Dome and down a couple thousand feet to the Valley floor. I could see everything in perfect definition and I was just amazed at how intensely beautiful everything looked. It was so much fun and totally worth the effort and risk. It was an adventure, a true adventure.

And I've soloed it a few times now. There are harder, long free climbs around, but there are none that have the classic status of Astroman. I can't see any other ones becoming more classic, because Astroman was so instrumental in the history of climbing. Warren Harding, Glen Denny, and Chuck Pratt did the first aid ascent in 1959. Then in 1975, John Bachar, John Long, and Ron Kauk did the first free ascent. There are pitches on Astroman that are just about as hard as the hardest single free pitches in the Valley. They did all the pitches free, but the second two guys just jugged [jumared] pitches after the leader climbed them. And then Ron Kauk went back and led every pitch free with no falls, so he got the first complete free ascent.

The Valley is one of the most impressive rock-climbing areas in the world, and Astroman is one of the classic climbs here. I can't think of anything that would have the same effect on me as soloing that route—not even free-climbing the Nose.

What were people's reactions to that climb?

There was a big reaction, which is still going on. I was just down in southern California and these guys came up to me and shook my hand for having soloed Astroman six years ago. But also I run into lots of climbers who say, "Yeah, I was going to solo it but I heard you did it, so I'm not going to do it now."

John Bachar, who was probably more qualified than anyone else to solo it, came up to me afterward and said, "Way to go. I'm glad you did it so that now I don't have to." He knew it was an obvious challenge but he was glad that he didn't have to do it. I appreciated his honesty.

Did John Bachar influence your climbing?

Yes. He was an inspiration to me and a lot of other people because he pushed both the difficulty and boldness of climbing. When I first came to the Valley, he was doing the hardest climbs and the boldest solos. If it had been just technical difficulty it would have been impressive, and if it had been just boldness it would have been impressive, but you put the two together and he was way beyond anyone else. There were good climbers and there was Bachar.

I didn't really get to know John until we did the Nose and Half Dome in 1986. I had been doing several big solos in a day, and I guess he decided if I could do those, I could obviously handle a fair bit of climbing. When he asked me to go with him, I felt like God had touched me on the shoulder. He had done so much for climbing.

I got a lot of inspiration from him, but I didn't want to copy him. He specializes in shorter routes and I specialize in longer routes. I'm not

Peter Croft. (Photo © Greg Epperson)

naturally super strong, but the stuff that I've excelled at is endurance stuff, stuff that goes on for more than a couple of hours.

Why do the longer routes appeal to you?

The long solos give me a lot of time by myself. I start off at midnight, trying to psych up, trying to convince myself that it's not stupid, going through all the doubts, thinking about my weaknesses, and saying, "Just keep going. You can always turn back." And it's real easy to say, "Maybe I should just take the easy way out." And then it gets light, and as I'm dealing with the difficulties of the climb, I have a lot of time to think about what I'm doing. I've learned a lot about myself through doing those kinds of things.

Doing a bunch of long routes in a day is a much bigger deal than some of the other things I've done. It's one of the things I've been most pleased with, but most people just don't understand it. It's not like I'm trying to get praise, because in the long run that doesn't really stay with you; but the fact that they don't understand this kind of climbing just reinforces my feeling that if I want to get something lasting out of climbing I have to do it for myself. To orient my climbing toward what other people think is the latest rage would be a big mistake.

A lot of times when people say, "It's so amazing you did such and such a climb," I know it wasn't amazing. A week ago I did the Nose a bit faster than I'd done it before, and people were saying, "That's so amazing!" But it wasn't that big a deal. It was just a lot of fun.

What was your time?

Four hours and twenty-two minutes.

Is there a competition between you and other climbers for speed ascents of routes such as the Nose?

No. This last time I did the Nose with Hans Florine, the guy who everybody said I was so competitive with.

How do you climb the route so quickly?

There's one section where we climb about a thousand feet without switching the lead so that we're not changing over gear. We have to make sure that the rack that I have lasts for that amount of rope. A lot of the time we're moving together, simo-climbing.

You must know that route well?

Yeah, I've climbed it seven or eight times. It's probably my favorite route in the world. The last time I did it was the fastest time ever, but it didn't seem like we were climbing fast; it was just so much fun. I couldn't believe how much fun it was. I felt stronger on top than at the beginning of the climb.

Is Dave Schultz normally your partner on those kinds of projects?

Yes. Dave is a great partner. It would be hard to find a partner who's half as good as Dave for the big El Cap routes. He's got so much energy that it's hard for him to sit still. And he's one of the funniest guys I've ever met. He'll be reracking the gear and making all these weird animal and machinery noises. Or he'll make up a song about something—with sound effects.

When I first met him, I didn't like him at all. I thought he was a cocky little jerk. He comes across that way to a lot of people. But if you get to know him, you can see it's a joke; he just pretends to be cocky.

Late at night, I'll say, "Dave, we should do such and such a climb tomorrow." And we'll get up at midnight, drink some strong coffee, and drive down toward El Cap in his beater Volkswagen van with some heavy metal music playing loud to wake us up.

Dave is definitely my best climbing partner. It isn't just my show and it isn't just his show and it's better because of that.

Does living in Yosemite Valley make you more aware of the area's climbing history?

Sure. I can feel the history here. And it's not a burden; I get inspiration from it. I probably respect it more than some people, but I've gotten so much from the past that to spit in its face just makes no sense. You get a lot from it and so you take that into account. You don't just take the good parts of it and forget about the parts that might hold you back. And I don't think of the history as holding me back in any way. I think of it as loose guidelines.

Is it hard to strike a balance between a respect for the past and a desire to innovate? Is there always a tension between those two things?

A lot of it comes down to your reasons for doing something. You have to put aside feelings of competition, look honestly at yourself, and ask, "What are the reasons for doing this?" And if the reasons are good ones, there won't be much of a conflict with the past.

I didn't get the idea to solo a lot of big routes in a day from the past, or at least the past in Yosemite. People really didn't do that here. But I think that sort of thing is in the same spirit as a lot of the other climbs done here. The past is more than just rules or guidelines; it's also the spirit of adventure you can get from those guys.

Do you see climbs like your solo of Astroman as a progression in the climbing history of the Valley?

I guess it's a progression, but I have a bit of a problem with the word progression. It was pretty amazing that Harding and those guys were able to do the first aid ascent back then. So yes, technically speaking, soloing is a progression, but I don't necessarily see that as being better than what people did before. If they hadn't done the first aid ascent, then maybe there wouldn't have been a first free ascent, and if there hadn't been a first free ascent, then maybe I wouldn't have done the first solo ascent. Time moves on and things change, but I would hesitate to say that because I soloed Astroman I'm better than the climbers who did the first aid ascent.

Do you see yourself as building on what they did?

Yeah, I guess so. Using what they did and going on. But, for example, there's no way I would ever presume to say that I'm a better climber than Walter Bonatti. I've climbed far harder free pitches than he has, but to say that I'm a better climber would be ridiculous. And I'm not just trying to be modest or polite. Given what he accomplished in his era, he was amazing.

Nowadays, people think they've got to climb 5.14. I'm not trying to say that doing 5.14 isn't a big deal, but people tend to think that doing 5.14 has advanced climbing so much further than ever before and so new rules are needed for the sport. But 5.14 is just like 5.7: the holds are smaller and the route's maybe a bit steeper, but you're doing the same kind of thing.

And if you want to use new rules, fair enough. I don't have any problem with hangdogging. Go for it. But don't try to make it sound like what you're doing is so special, because it isn't. And don't try to say climbing is so space age now that you can't judge it in terms of older climbing. I don't buy that at all.

Young climbers see the "now" as all important—the ultimate statement. But how can you look at anything in isolation? No matter what you're looking at—climbing, nature, politics, relationships—nothing can be looked at in isolation. It doesn't mean anything in isolation. And so for someone to say that so-and-so doing this one route is the most rad thing in the history of climbing is just ridiculous.

Have you rap-bolted any of your routes?

Years ago I rapped lots of routes to clear them and sometimes fix pins or nuts. I don't feel bad about it because I don't see rap-bolting as this horrible thing. I don't rap-bolt now because it allows me to find out too much about the route and makes the climbing less interesting. But I don't hate rap-bolters. Dave's my best friend and he rap-bolts; fair enough. He likes it; I don't.

Do you think that there's any consensus on the issue in Yosemite?

Most people think rap-bolting is fine. If I had my way, there wouldn't be any rap-bolting here because when I first started climbing in new areas, I enjoyed the fact that in each area there would be different rock, different people, and different climbing styles. When sport climbing became prevalent in all the areas it took away the variety in styles, and that's a shame.

Why do you think that rap-bolting took over?

Why do you think that climbing's a lot more popular now? All you have to do is take away the boldness, take away the risk, and it's another sport.

Is ground-up climbing more adventurous than rap-bolting?

Yes. Because you don't know what's coming up. The bottom line is the adventure, not the grade.

"*WHY DO YOU THINK THAT CLIMBING'S A LOT MORE POPULAR NOW? ALL YOU HAVE TO DO IS TAKE AWAY THE BOLDNESS, TAKE AWAY THE RISK, AND IT'S ANOTHER SPORT.*"

How does this philosophy apply to your climb Excellent Adventure?

Well, it's not the most excellent adventure that I've had, but for a hard free pitch it has incredible air on it. To me it was something good because it was steep, direct, and followed Warren Harding's first aid ascent route. It's an endurance pitch; it's not technically that hard. There's a 5.12 thin bridging crux for the first half, a 5.11 roof, and then a 5.12 finger crack going directly up the headwall. It's almost a straight line.

Do you think that there are plenty of routes like that left to do?

There's a ton of stuff to do here, particularly up on the big cliffs. People could spend centuries doing those kind of routes here. And there are some smaller cliffs that are almost untouched.

Could you do them in ground-up fashion?

Yeah. But again, it's whatever people want to do as long as they don't put bolts all over the place, chop away at the rock, or leave a mess. More areas are closing and more regulations are coming down, and one of the main reasons is that a lot of climbers have been pretty irresponsible. The bottom line is that you don't trash the place that you're in.

Will you keep doing short, extreme, ground-up routes?

Yes, if I see a really good-looking route like Excellent Adventure, but I don't go around searching desperately for other new routes to do. If I see one that looks good, I'll do it. But I'm not interested in doing something just for the sake of doing a new route. Not every bit of climbable rock has to be climbed.

Do you have any interest in entering a climbing competition?

No. I got into climbing because it was so different from a normal sport. There wasn't someone saying, "You have to start climbing at quarter past ten, finish by eleven, and then start again at eight o'clock tonight." Climbing competitions have had the same effect as sport climbing; they've turned climbing into more of a sport.

I've seen some climbing competitions on television—edited—and I don't mean it as a joke, but I would have preferred to watch a good tennis match. Climbing competitions are so far removed from what I do.

What effect has sponsorship had on climbing?

It's changed climbing in good ways and bad. It's allowed some people to concentrate heavily on climbing, and that's good. But one of the bad things is that people are now sometimes more willing to stretch the truth or lie through omission. That part of it is really sad. They might say, "If I had another few days, or if I wasn't quite so tired, or if it hadn't started raining, then I could have done it—I'd worked out all the moves anyway." There are so many rationalizations. There are so many ways you can cheat about things. There are so many excuses for being less than honest. One of the good things about competitions is that they're totally honest.

How do you make a living?

Most of my money comes from guiding, but I get quite a bit from slide shows and some from sponsorship. There's nothing wrong with having sponsors, if you're honest about it—to the climbing world, yourself, and the sponsors. You can be honest and still make a living through climbing.

Is climbing becoming too specialized today?

Yes, but I think it's wrong to get cynical about the future of climbing. If you look at any fad, what happens? All kinds of people go into it at first, and then after a while they start going back to the other things they were doing before. A lot of people are into sport climbing now, but I was climbing at American Fork not too long ago, and I was amazed at how many of the sport climbers there were planning to go wall or crack climbing in Yosemite. Sport climbing is here to stay, and there's nothing wrong with that, but over the last year it seems like a lot more people are going back to crack climbing or alpine climbing or wall climbing. They're getting back into those things because they're realizing that sport climbing doesn't have all those facets those other kinds of climbing do.

Do you think that at some point Yosemite will reemerge as the climbing mecca?

Not to the extent it was before. But there could be an upsurge of free climbing on the big walls or linking up routes. There are more long, hard free climbs to do here than just about any other place in North America.

What projects do you have planned for the near future?

There are some solo link-ups I'd like to do. And then Dave and I would like to link up the Nose and Half Dome and Mount Watkins in a day. And then he and I would like to free-climb a route called Southern Belle in a day. It has fourteen pitches, five of 5.12, and it's no specialist's route. If you're just a sport climber, there's no way that you're going to be able to deal with the 5.12c overhanging endurance crack and long runouts. If you're just a crack climber, you won't be able to do the 5.12 low-angle and overhanging face pitches. And if you're not in really good hiking shape, you'll have trouble because it's a solid three hours uphill to get to it. You have to be good at pretty much every aspect of rock climbing to do that route.

But there's so much to do. There's an incredible amount to do. The more imagination that you have, the more you can find to do in Yosemite. And it's not so important that what you do is the latest and greatest. It's just as important that you have fun and really enjoy what you're doing. The best way to push yourself the hardest and do the most amazing things is by having fun—not going up on something because someone said it would be impressive, but because you can't imagine any other place on the planet you'd rather be.

It's not like I see what I'm doing as the most important thing that anybody could be doing, but for me, climbing these big routes in Yosemite is such a combination of fun and rightness and taking complete advantage of what climbing has to offer. To me it's unreal that this kind of stuff is free. How can this much fun not cost anything and not be illegal?

TOMO ČESEN

I am convinced in any case that Lhotse took part of my
soul, the part that wants to know true adventure linked with a
sense of uncertainty. This is a perilous path, where one must
constantly make decisions and act on them: a path like life, with
a small difference, that everything happens at the extreme limit,
where it is sometimes difficult to know which way to turn.
Fortunately, more distant summits are always being discovered;
the true limit is bounded only by the infinite. Through the fog,
man throws a stone—his desire—into the unknown, then throws
himself in pursuit.

—Tomo Česen, *Solo*

TOMO ČESEN'S ASCENT of the south face of Lhotse represents one of the most spectacular achievements in the history of climbing. With one bold, breathtaking stroke, the brilliant Yugoslav changed not only the face of Himalayan mountaineering, but the whole field of climbing in general. His on-sight, free-solo first ascent of a wall often referred to as the last great problem of the Himalaya represents not just a quantum leap forward in terms of high-altitude climbing, but a new synthesis of all the various specialties within the sport. His route demonstrates that it is not only possible to excel at all aspects of the climbing game, whether on rock, snow, or ice, but that such comprehensive mastery is the best way to ensure that adventure and commitment remain at the core of climbing in the future. His ascent of Lhotse brought the sport's divergent branches back together and secured his reputation as the finest all-around climber in the world today.

Though Česen seems to have leaped into the spotlight from out of nowhere, his ascent of Lhotse was in fact the culmination of years of training and dedication. He describes his development as a series of steps, though some of the steps seem more like broad jumps when measured by ordinary standards. He began climbing in 1975 at age sixteen on the crags outside his native town of Kranj, Slovenia, formerly the northern republic of Yugoslavia. After learning rock-climbing basics,

Tomo Česen with his son, Nejc. (Photo © Janez Skok)

he ventured onto snow and ice, ascending Mont Blanc the following year.

Although he liked climbing, he didn't get serious about it until 1979, when he had to choose between going on an expedition to South America or continuing in the normal academic track in school. He decided in favor of the expedition and ended up making a first ascent of the south face of Alpamayo in the Andes as a member of a Yugoslav team. He returned home excited by the possibilities of the sport, but not completely committed to it.

In 1980, Česen teamed up with Nejc Zaplotnik, one of Slovenia's best climbers, to climb the Bonatti Pillar of the Petit Dru, the Gabbarou Couloir on Mont Blanc du Tacul, the north face of Les Droites, and other classic routes in the Alps. These routes confirmed his enthusiasm for climbing and convinced him that he should pursue the sport more seriously.

In 1983, Česen ascended the north face of Peak Communism (24,580 feet) in the Pamirs, giving him the high-altitude experience he needed to take part in the 1985 Yugoslav expedition to Yalung-Kang (27,896 feet), the west summit of Kangchenjunga. The Yalung-Kang expedition proved a pivotal one for Česen. After making a first ascent of the peak's 11,000-foot north face, he and his partner, Borut Bergant, ran into trouble as they descended in the dark. While rigging a rappel, Česen looked up to see Bergant slump over from sheer exhaustion and fall to his death. Deeply shaken, he decided to bivouac in the open at 27,600 feet rather than to risk proceeding further. He had gone four days without food and two days without water, but somehow he summoned the strength to survive the night without frostbite. At first light he continued down and eventually arrived safely at base camp.

Česen's bivouac on Yalung-Kang served as the crucible for making a good climber into a great one. By revealing the incredible reserves on which he could draw, it gave him the confidence to attempt even more ambitious climbs. Shortly after Yalung-Kang, Česen enchained the three great north faces of the Alps—the Eiger, Grandes Jorasses, and Matterhorn—by soloing them in four consecutive days during the winter of 1986. His star was on the rise.

Later that same year, Česen soloed Broad Peak (26,414 feet) and then took aim at completing a new route on the south face of K2. Without bivy gear or food, he quickly soloed up the southeast spur, passing the high point reached by Doug Scott in 1983. He reached the shoulder of the Abruzzi Spur (26,500 feet) in time to see the weather deteriorating. Though he quickly retreated, other climbers above him on the Abruzzi Route weren't so lucky. Not long afterward a terrible storm moved in and claimed many of their lives.

In 1987, Česen took part in his last traditional expedition, an unsuccessful attempt on Lhotse Shar. He discovered on that trip that he could acclimatize best by climbing continuously, going high quickly and then immediately descending. Such an approach did not fit within the confines of traditional expeditions, so he decided to forgo them in favor of solo climbing at altitude.

In addition to these high-altitude routes, Česen continued to push the grade on Alpine climbs. In September of 1987 he soloed No Siesta (5.11a) on the Grandes Jorasses while wearing plastic boots and alpine gear. In 1988 he did a number of difficult solo winter ascents in the Julian Alps, helping prepare him for the bold leap forward he was about to make.

After gleaning important information from every climb he had undertaken, he began thinking about ways to put his high-altitude experience together with his Alpine-climbing experience so as to do something new and innovative. The result was a climb so visionary that even he hesitated to think about it: a solo of the immense north face of Jannu (25,294 feet), a 9000-foot wall he had seen while on the Yalung-Kang expedition. But after doing winter solos of Modern Times (5.11a) on the south face of the Marmolata and the Gabbarou-Long Route on the Pilier Rouge of Mont Blanc (5.11d) in 1989, he felt psychologically ready for Jannu. On April 27, 1989, he started up the enormous face. He encountered long pitches of thin ice over granite slabs, some A2 sections and a free-climbing crux of 5.10, which at that altitude proved incredibly strenuous. After twenty-three hours of continuous climbing, he finally reached the summit. It was the most difficult solo ascent ever achieved in the Himalaya.

When Česen described Jannu as the shape of things to come, he was not indulging in hyperbole. After Jannu he realized that light, fast solo ascents were not only possible at altitude, but that they provided some distinct advantages over big expeditions. Such ascents could be completed within a narrow window of good weather and sometimes could be safer than expeditions because they allowed a climber to spend less time in dangerous places. After mulling these things over, Česen decided that the next step would be to employ these tactics on an 8000-meter peak, specifically the much sought-after south face of Lhotse, where such an approach might give him some advantages over the big teams that had failed in the past.

Česen is a master at analyzing a climbing problem and coming up with a solution. He studied the south face in great detail. He talked to other climbers who had attempted it. He considered all this information for a long time and then developed a plan, a kind of "beta" for an 11,000-foot free solo. He decided to climb much of the face in the morning or at night so as to avoid avalanches and rockfall, which had wiped out many other parties. It was a brilliant scheme, a masterpiece of tactics, but it still needed to be carried out.

After months of preparation, Česen finally put his plan into action. He climbed the lower portion of the face at night and then holed up during the day as avalanches and rocks roared by. Once the face quieted down, he continued climbing till evening, reaching the base of the rock band, where he bivouacked again. At first light, he tackled the upper portion of the face, moving quickly through the rotten rock and mixed terrain. At 2:20 P.M. on April 24, 1990, he topped out. The "last great problem" of the Himalaya had been solved.

Word of his ascent spread like wildfire through the climbing community. Most climbers reacted with unabashed admiration for the amazing climb. Others, however, let jealousy interfere with their better judgment. They questioned whether he had climbed the face at all, claiming that his photos of the climb were doctored. Eventually cooler heads prevailed and Česen could bask in the glory of his magnificent achievement. His ascent of Lhotse is now the standard by which future high-altitude climbs will be judged.

Česen was born on November 5, 1959, in Kranj, Slovenia, a small city in the foothills of the Julian Alps. He has lived there ever since, never moving from the house in which he grew up. He and his wife, Nada, and their sons, Nejc and Ales, now share the upstairs, while his parents occupy the ground floor. Česen receives a salary from the Slovenian Sport Association that allows him to train and climb year-round. In addition, he writes a climbing column for the local newspaper and narrates a television program, which makes him a celebrity in Slovenia. As he walks around Kranj or any of the neighboring cities, people stop to ask him for his autograph, a request with which he most graciously complies.

In some ways, Česen seems almost too good to be true. This hardest of the hardmen is a devoted family man as well. He somehow manages to reconcile the risk and uncertainty of the adventurous life with the stability and tranquility of domesticity. Moreover, he accomplishes this remarkable balancing act without making it seem like an effort at all. He spends the mornings helping out around the house and the afternoons climbing at the local crags. No problem!

Česen is tall, lean, and muscular, with large, thickly calloused hands from which he is constantly peeling layers of skin. He is obsessive about his hands— the most valuable tool of the solo-climbing trade—to the point that he prefers not to swim so as to avoid softening them up.

The interview took place on a hot summer day in the sitting room of Česen's house in Kranj. He spent the morning and the better part of the afternoon fielding questions—his attention never flagging, his concentration never faltering, his whole personality radiating calm and confidence, as if he had not only climbed all of these immense mountains but had found a way to internalize them as well.

Why do you prefer to do most of your climbing solo?

I like to solo because it requires that I do everything exactly right. I have always been interested in things that require precision, where I have to concentrate and do exactly one and one thing only. This kind of thing is attractive for me, and I have found it in solo climbing. Because if I keep my concentration at the proper level, I am always inside this situation. I am not affected by anything outside it. I don't hear anybody. I don't see anybody. I am like somebody else. I am not on this planet.

And yet aren't you extraordinarily aware of what's going on around you?

Yes, of course. When I solo I feel the place where I am more intensely. I am always on the move, always doing something, but I can concentrate on things better. If I am with a partner, I climb, I belay, I sit, I rest, I wait around, and so on. And when I am not doing something, I have time to think about other things. But if I am always on the move, if I am climbing continuously, then I can really feel the whole—myself, the mountain, and everything else.

Why is solo climbing more difficult than climbing with a partner?

The difficulty is that you have to do everything by yourself and can't expect help from anybody else. And you have to be able to deal with the feeling that you are alone. If you aren't comfortable with this, it could present some problems. But I've discovered that if I'm aware that everything depends on me and only on me, I can concentrate 100 percent. And if I have 100 percent concentration, I can pull out of myself all of the power and strength that I have.

So it might be safer for you to solo than to go with a partner?

Sometimes, yes, because it's not necessary to pay attention to a partner when you solo. You can concentrate only on your own climbing. And it can be safer because you spend less time on a route when you're soloing. This is especially true in the Himalaya on ice walls and so on.

Do you ever get scared when you're soloing?

Yes, sometimes. I get scared when the situation is not in my hands, when I cannot control whether or not the seracs will fall down. I'm most frightened of objective dangers—avalanches and such things.

How do you overcome these dangers?

It's a matter of choosing the way. You see the face and then you decide where to go and in which period of day it will be safest. There are ways of getting around objective dangers with as little risk as possible. You need a lot of information, together with a lot of experience, to decide these things. You need to think logically and prepare very carefully.

Have you always liked to do things by yourself?

Yes. When I was a boy I was quiet and shy. It was not easy for me to talk with other people. But I always had a serious approach to the things I did.

I was interested in a lot of things, especially sports. I started skiing when I was seven years old. I trained and competed quite a lot, but when I was fourteen I quit. The system of training was not very serious or very professional. I got the feeling that I was wasting my time. I wanted to be serious in what I did.

Did you prefer sports in which you could train on your own?

Yes, I think I'm more of an individualist. I don't have anything against team sports, but I prefer sports where I can do everything by myself. I don't like to depend on other people—not only in sports, but also in life. Most of the things I want to do, I want to do by myself. And I don't like to trust others too much. Most things I prefer to do myself rather than giving them to somebody else.

> *"I DON'T LIKE TO DEPEND ON OTHER PEOPLE— NOT ONLY IN SPORTS, BUT ALSO IN LIFE."*

This is not only a matter of character; it's also a matter of experience. I've had some bad experiences with work and other things. For example, when we organized a climbing competition, I asked a guy to help me out with some things. He said, "Yes, okay." And two weeks later nothing was done. In the end, I had to do it myself.

When did you start climbing?

At sixteen. I started with the climbing school in Kranj. First we studied the theoretical part, and then for the practical part we climbed in the afternoon at some local crags. Later I climbed with some friends from the climbing school in the Julian and Carnic Alps around Kranj.

Did you start climbing on rock?

Yes. And then we climbed some easy routes here during the winter, mostly couloirs. And the next year we went to Chamonix and climbed Mont Blanc. After Mont Blanc, I began doing more difficult routes on ice and then started climbing ice waterfalls. My career was step by step; it was not a quick progression. I think it is important to go slowly so that you can think about whether something is good or not so good.

Why did you like climbing?

This could be a very easy or a very difficult question. Maybe I should just say that I liked it. I am a person who likes to be out in nature. I am a person who wants adventure. It's difficult to give a logical explanation of why I liked to do this.

Did you want to get away from town?

Not really. I like to be around people very much. I'm not a person who wants to run away from society. I simply like the feeling of being in the mountains. I like the feeling of being around a steep wall. I was born between the mountains and I can't imagine living somewhere where it's flat.

Were you a good climber when you started?

Yes, but even after I completed this school and had climbed for a few years, I was still not very serious about climbing. I was still trying to find out if it was the right thing for me.

Then in 1979 my climbing club organized an expedition to South America and I had to decide whether or not to go. At the same time I had exams at the university, and one professor wouldn't allow me to take his exam at another time. So when I decided to go on the expedition it meant I couldn't take his exam, and because of that, I couldn't go into the second year of studies. And if you're not a student you have to serve in the army; so before I went into the army I got married, and when I came back from the expedition, I had to put all these things together—school, work, climbing, family. This was not so easy.

This expedition was the beginning of many struggles and conflicts for me, but it was the turning point in my life. A year or two after South America I became sure that this was the sport that I wanted to do. It was not that I wanted to be the best at it or get outstanding results; it was just a question of doing this because I liked it. Maybe somebody likes to play tennis in the afternoon. My activity was climbing.

Were there other climbers whom you modeled yourself after?

I read stories about climbers and I was sometimes quite impressed. Bonatti, Buhl, and Cassin were some people who impressed me by what they did, their approach to the sport, and by the way they thought about life in general. Because for me it's very important what kind of a person someone is. You can be a perfect climber, but if you're not a good person, this is not impressive to me. It's not possible for somebody to impress me only because he is a climber. It is more important that he be a nice man, or, as we say, that he be a man with a capital *M*.

Who taught you to climb?

Nejc Zaplotnik taught me a lot. He was very well known in Slovenia. He had climbed three 8000ers. He also soloed a lot. We did not have the same personality—he was very extroverted and liked to go to parties, and I don't like to do this kind of thing—but we were in the same position. He was sometimes without a job, like me. We climbed and wasted a lot of time together. We just sat and talked and said crazy things, not useful things. Sometimes we were lazy maybe, but this is relative. Maybe to average people we were not very efficient, but average people think you have to work eight hours a day in a factory; otherwise they think you don't want to work.

When he was killed on Manaslu [spring of 1983] it was really a shock for me. This was the first and the last time that I was really shocked that someone was killed. Even in 1985 on Yalung-Kang, when my friend Borut Bergant fell and was killed, I didn't suffer so much. But I was shocked when Nejc died. And the whole of Kranj just couldn't believe it. We didn't think that it was possible that something could happen to him.

Was he a safe climber?

In general, yes, he was very sure about what he was doing. But sometimes he wasn't careful enough. He did some things that I wouldn't do, mostly when it came to objective dangers. If we were going to pass under some seracs, he would say, "No problem," whereas I would go around.

How was he killed?

A stupid way. He and another climber were a little way from base camp. They were crossing a snowfield. It was easy, nothing, but then a serac broke off above them and avalanched. The avalanche hit them and they were finished.

Did that make you question your climbing?

No. I never doubted I should continue climbing. I never thought of quitting. I was climbing in the south of Yugoslavia when I heard that he had died. Someone told me in the evening and then I got all my things together and went back home. I just couldn't climb the next day when I knew that my friend had been killed. But I never doubted what I was doing. It was never this kind of question.

When did you start doing hard routes in the Alps?

In 1980. Nejc and I did the Bonatti Pillar on the Dru, the west face. And then we climbed the Gabbarou Couloir on Mont Blanc du Tacul and the north face of Les Droites.

Were these routes harder than the ones you'd climbed in Yugoslavia?

No, we have a lot of routes that are much harder. The most difficult Alpine routes I've done have been here in the Julian Alps. We also have routes 1000 meters long but they are not well-known. But I like to climb in the Alps because I like to climb in new places. And you can climb much better if you have different experiences. You can compare the situation here with the situation other places.

When did you get the idea to enchain the big three north faces of the Alps?

I was sitting around with some friends talking, and somebody said it would be interesting to link these three faces together by solo-climbing them in the winter. I started to think about it, and I said, "Yes, this would be a fun thing to do. You start with one face, descend, and then go to another."

Did Christophe Profit plan to do this too?

Yes, but my idea was born independently of his. All these magazines and newspapers wrote that there was competition between us, but we didn't know of each other's plan at first. I started with the Eiger, then came to Chamonix and stayed with a friend, and he told me that Christophe Profit also had this plan. That was the first I'd heard of it. I said, "No problem." When I got on the Shroud of the north face of the Grandes Jorasses, he was already on the Croz Pillar, which is a longer and more difficult route on this face. I didn't know that he was on the route, but I saw helicopters; so I realized that somebody important must be there.

And this was his first face. Then he went to the Matterhorn by helicopter. I got to the Matterhorn a day or two later. I went from the Italian side because it was closer. And a man there told me that Profit had come one day before and didn't climb because he saw that he couldn't finish all of the faces in twenty-four hours, and so he quit. But I went on and climbed the Matterhorn. So he was the first to enchain them in the summer [in twenty-four hours], and I was the first to enchain them in the winter.

I met him the following summer in Chamonix; we just spoke a few words. This is the whole story. It's quite simple, but some magazines made a big thing out of the competition between us. That was really stupid.

And once you'd enchained those faces, was it easier to get money to go climbing?

No, it was the same. I don't know how it will be in the future, but in the past in Yugoslavia we had this system for all sports where you were rated at the republic level, state level, or international level of athletics, and depending on your rating, you could get some money for training or travel. And the sport association in Kranj and our climbing club also gave some money. If you climbed some good things, these places would give you money for travel and so on. Not for living, but to help pay the expenses.

For example, when I linked these faces, I made a report of how much it cost, and they reimbursed me. There was a lot of publicity in newspapers and on television, and I gave a talk here in Kranj; but otherwise everything was the same after the three faces.

Did you try to climb fast on these faces?

No. I never climbed fast just to climb fast. I was always within the limits of control. It was not like running. It would be better to call it climbing continuously. But speed is important. If you are fast, then the possibilities of weather change and also objective dangers, such as falling rocks, are lessened. So speed also means safety.

Maybe my style of climbing is a little faster than some climbers, but a lot of people climb even faster. And if you solo without putting in protection, it's natural that you climb faster than when you have a partner on the rope. So it's misleading to compare the time of a solo climb with one done by two climbers. If you climb by yourself, you spend about a third of the time on a route that a rope team would spend.

Do you belay yourself when you solo?

Sometimes yes, sometimes no. It depends on the situation. If there is aid climbing, yes, because I don't want to depend on one piton. With ice climbing, usually you can't take all the ice screws you need to protect yourself very well, and on big faces in the Himalaya, you can't protect the whole face, otherwise you would never finish the climb; so you have to go without protection. In difficult free climbing, it's a matter of ability. A few years ago I might have soloed a route using belays, and if I soloed the same route now, I probably wouldn't need protection. When I solo now, I usually climb without protection.

There are a lot of systems to protect yourself in solo climbing. You can protect yourself nearly the same as if you had a partner belaying you. When you finish the pitch you have to go down and jumar back up. This takes a lot of time and it's not such a big challenge. For me it's much more interesting to climb the routes free, and without any protection, so that everything depends on me.

And you now solo routes that you haven't climbed before?

Yes. But the first step was to solo routes that I knew and that were not difficult. I started solo climbing the same way I did my other climbing, step by step. I soloed my first route at the end of my first year of climbing. It was an easy route. And then I did maybe 150 or 200 solo climbs on easy or middle-grade routes before I made the next step, which was a difficult route that I had climbed. And then I started to solo easier routes that I didn't know. So it was like that.

When did you first go to the Himalaya?

In 1985 to climb Yalung-Kang.

How was it different from other climbs that you had done?

It was different to be in the Himalaya at that altitude and to be on a big, classical expedition with camps and fixed ropes and so on. But I was lucky because I teamed up with a man [Borut Bergant] who was very experienced. He had been to the Himalaya many times and helped me a lot.

His job on the expedition was food and my job was equipment. We stayed together in base camp to get things organized while the other climbers went on ahead to find the route through the glacier. The following day we climbed together. And so we became partners.

Borut taught me a lot of things by his example. I learned small things that are not important at low altitude, but that are very important at high altitude—how to acclimatize, how to put on your crampons so that they don't slip off, how to use gloves for getting snow rather than your bare hands. Somebody who is there for the first time wouldn't know how to do these things.

How did you feel on the expedition?

Okay. But the night before we started from Camp IV to go to the top, we melted some water and Borut put something in the water that I didn't like. I drank it and during the night I vomited. In the morning I told him I would make the water and drink half, and then he could put whatever he wanted in the rest. But he put something in the water again, and I drank the water and vomited immediately. And because of this I felt very weak.

If I had been alone, I would have gone back. I came out of the tent and I was dizzy. The slope was very steep, and I said, "I have to go down." But he encouraged me. He said it would be okay. So I took some oxygen and then we started, and after an hour or two I felt okay. And then the closer we got to the top, the better I felt. It took us fourteen hours to get to the top. We reached the summit at 5:00 P.M. and then descended in the dark. Going down, I felt better and better, but he got worse and worse. He became exhausted. He had a problem with his concentration. His psychological preparation was not good; mentally he was not good.

What do you mean by that?

He was concentrating only on getting to the top, and when he got to the top, he relaxed. I found out later that he had had similar problems in the Alps. After he had climbed the route and reached the top, he always was exhausted on the descent. But when you get to the top in the Himalaya, it's not finished at all.

When did the accident occur?

It was at 8400 meters on the most difficult part, a pitch of twenty meters with some ice between seventy and eighty degrees and some 5.8 rock climbing. At that altitude it would have been quite difficult to climb down; so I had left a piton there because I knew that we would have to rappel off it on the way down. And by the time we reached it he was not aware of what he was doing. He had already started to say that he couldn't manage, that he was too tired, and that he would die.

So I rigged the rope to do the rappel. He rappelled down to a small ledge and said that he was already down, but I knew that he was about ten meters before the end. And I rappelled down and of course saw that we had to descend ten meters more. I hung on the rope and tried to put in a piton so I could put in another rappel. And when I was putting it in, he fell. I don't think he was even aware that he fell. I think he had gone to sleep because he didn't scream or say anything. He just fell.

But I'm sure that he couldn't have survived the night anyway. He was so tired. I can't imagine how I could have kept him from sleeping, and if he had gone to sleep, he would have died.

After he fell, I bivouacked on the ledge. During the bivouac I knew very well what I must do and what I must not do. I moved my fingers, I tried not to sleep, and so on. It was a matter of concentration and a matter of will. And in the morning everything was fine for me. I survived and I didn't have any frostbite or anything.

How were you able to survive?

I don't know if I have more stamina than other people, but I do have an ability to concentrate. And I was there and I had to survive. It's that simple or that complicated.

Did you have trouble descending?

No. As I got lower, I felt better and better, but I was still concentrating very hard. When I reached Camp II, some of the climbers met me and we talked a little and then went down to Camp I. We spent the night there, and the next day we walked over the glacier and at the end of the glacier I felt my concentration going. It became harder and harder just to walk. There were these small rocks and I couldn't manage to see how far I was from them, so I fell sometimes because of this.

And at the end of the glacier I had to climb 100 meters to the top of this moraine. I rested every ten meters and sat down. I had a very heavy rucksack because I had carried all my equipment by myself. I don't know why, but I didn't want to give it to my friends to carry. I wanted to carry all my things myself. And I was thinking whether to leave the rucksack there and to go on without it. But I decided that I wanted to reach base camp with the rucksack, with all the equipment, with everything, and that I wanted to do it myself. I wanted to finish everything myself. I wanted to finish clear.

And then base camp was the end of the story for me. I was so tired that I couldn't sleep. The doctor offered me an intravenous injection, but I said

I would try to manage without it because it's not good to get an injection unless you really need it. And the next day it was difficult to do anything. I tried to pack up my equipment but after ten minutes I had to stop and rest. It was hard just to walk to the toilet, which was 200 meters from base camp. And so I asked him for the injection. He gave it to me and also something to help me sleep. And after that, I slept twenty hours continuously. Sometimes the other guys came into the tent to see if I was still alive. I woke up for lunch or dinner—I don't remember which—and then I slept again for about fifteen hours. And after that I felt okay.

> *". . . THE MOST IMPORTANT*
> *THING I LEARNED*
> *WAS MY LIMITS.*
> *I FOUND OUT HOW MUCH*
> *I COULD STAND*
> *AND STILL SURVIVE."*

What was the most important thing you learned from the Yalung-Kang expedition?

I learned many things on Yalung-Kang but the most important thing I learned was my limits. I found out how much I could stand and still survive. You can't find this out in some other way. This kind of thing you have to experience. And because of this, Yalung-Kang was for me the most important point in my high-altitude climbing career. After Yalung-Kang I knew how far I could go. I knew what I could manage. But of course I still try to avoid such situations.

Like on K2?

Yes. I was there in 1986 and I had climbed Broad Peak before, so I was well acclimatized and conditions were very good. But I had a bad feeling about the weather when I was on the shoulder. So I descended, and then the weather got worse and worse. And this sudden change of weather cut off the descent route for climbers higher up on the mountain.

I spoke with Kurt Diemberger later. He said that they couldn't see five meters in front of them. There was fog, clouds, and snow. And of course they knew that they could get lost on the slope from Camp IV down, so they decided to wait a day, which was logical. And then they waited another day. And then another day. And then after four or five days they saw that they would have to do something even if the weather was bad, otherwise they would die. And the rest of the story you know.

Was Lhotse Shar in 1987 also an important expedition for you?

Yes. Lhotse Shar was an important expedition, although it was not successful. It was important because I found out on that expedition that for me it's much better to climb continuously than to go slowly and to sleep. I feel much better if I climb continuously, without rest. Then I don't have much problem with altitude.

The first day we arrived at base camp, and the next day we put in the fixed rope up to 6500 meters and went back to base camp. We rested two days and then climbed up to 7200 meters. And I had no problem. I would have had big problems if I had stayed there, but I didn't. I went back to base camp. If you go up and down the same day, it's not dangerous.

And so I started thinking about this, started analyzing acclimatization, and I realized that if could do this, I could also climb a 7300-meter peak in one push and then go back down. Himalayan climbers used to think that you should spend at least three weeks acclimatizing, but I found out on Lhotse Shar that this is not necessarily true. And so I decided that this was the last traditional expedition for me. In the future I would go with one partner or alone. I promised that to myself.

Did you get invited on other traditional expeditions?

Yes, in 1988 I was invited on an expedition to K2. And because I didn't reach the summit in 1986, I thought it would be important for me to go back again. But then I decided that it was not so important. I thought it would be pointless to go there just to reach the summit. Because it meant going with a big team.

And there was another reason. At that time I worked as a steeplejack. Summer is the best season for that work, and the expedition was during the summer. And in 1986 when I came home from K2 we were without money. We were in a really critical situation. It was not a good feeling. I had to sell some of my climbing equipment so that we could get money for living. And I felt guilty that my family had to suffer because I was off climbing. Of course, nobody saw our situation. Nobody knew. But I promised to myself that I would never let that happen again. I would first take care of the family so that we would have enough money and then afterward I would go climbing.

And this was also a good excuse for not going. I didn't want to go with a big team on a classical expedition anyway, but this gave me a real excuse and a true excuse. I said, "If you will give me a job and allow me to take care of my family obligations, I will go, but otherwise we can't make a deal." I explained this to the expedition organizers and told them that for this reason I had to turn down the invitation. Some people were not happy about this and criticized me, but they later apologized.

So in 1988 I stayed home. I worked and concentrated more on rock climbing. I thought that I should improve my abilities in rock and ice climbing if I wanted to do something innovative in the Himalaya. And one year later it was obvious that I had made a good decision. I did some difficult solo climbs—a few winter climbs in the Julian Alps, Modern Times on the

Marmolata, the Gabbarou-Long Route on the Pilier Rouge of Mont Blanc, and some other good routes on the crags. So I think I did the right thing.

When did you first get the idea to climb the north face of Jannu?

I saw this face for the first time in 1985 on the way to Yalung-Kang. I looked at it and said, "Wow," and started thinking about climbing it. And then later I got more serious about it. And then I decided to try. It was just a logical progression. But with Jannu, the decision to go was not so easy. I thought about it for a long time. It took me much longer to decide to go to Jannu than to go to Lhotse because Jannu was a new step.

How did you prepare for that climb?

Mostly by climbing difficult routes and then by thinking about this face so that I could imagine what kind of situation would be there. You have to live a certain time with something like this. You have to make a plan in your mind, calculate everything correctly, and then you go and finish it—just like that. The time that you spend doing the route is just a small percentage of the whole work.

Did you have a photograph of the route?

Yes, but the line I imagined from the photograph was different from the line that was on the face. I had one good picture but it was taken in the afternoon, when the sun was from the west. There are some overhanging roofs on the face, and I thought that there would be an ice gully in the shadow behind these roofs. In the photograph it looks like there should be a ramp or gully there, but this is an illusion. It is just a vertical granite face, with no gullies, with nothing to climb.

When I got there, I saw that it would not be possible to climb that route, so I had to change my plans. Sometimes it was very difficult to decide where to go because the face is very steep and there are a lot of small ice gullies, and I couldn't decide which ice gully to take. And once I took the wrong one. The ice ended in the middle of the rock and I had to make a pendulum to reach the next ice gully.

What kind of equipment did you take with you?

A six-millimeter rope of sixty meters—more for rappelling than anything else—ice pitons, rock pitons, crampons, ice axes, three liters of water, a little food, a sleeping bag but no tent—just like in the Alps. Sometimes it was very steep and I had to rest on an ice axe—not such a pleasant situation—and I thought, "Maybe I should throw away some of this equipment that I don't need now." But I didn't do it. And this was good, because on the descent, I needed my sleeping bag and other equipment.

Tomo Česen. (Photo © Janez Skok)

What was the crux of the climb?

The crux was a crack of about fifty meters, about 5.10. If you climbed it here, using chalk and rock shoes, it would be easy, but with plastic boots and gloves at that altitude it was really bad. Luckily, from time to time it was wide, so I could put my whole leg inside and rest. And the edge of the crack was very sharp, so it was the kind of thing I could climb with gloves, which was good because I didn't want to take my gloves off in the cold.

It must have been very difficult to do that kind of rock climbing at altitude.

Yes, of course. If a route is rated 5.9, it's always 5.9, whether it's here or at 7000 meters. But at 7000 meters it feels like it's 5.11 or 5.12. You can't climb the same grade at 7000 meters that you can at sea level. If you can climb 5.9 here, you won't be able to climb 5.9 there. This is the reason you have to push your limits here so that you climb difficult things at altitude.

How did you feel after getting up the face?

It was a really fantastic feeling when I reached the ridge and was on snow. I looked back, saw how steep it was, and had an immense sense of relief that I was out. You just can't climb this kind of route more than once or twice a year. It's psychologically too demanding. You really need a lot of preparation to convince yourself to do such things.

Was climbing Jannu a significant step for you?

Yes. I was very satisfied with my climb of Jannu. It was steeper and technically more difficult than anything I'd ever done. It allowed me to put together my Himalayan experience with my soloing experience in the Alps. Jannu is not so high—7800 meters as compared with 8500 meters on Lhotse—but for me it was much more worthwhile than Lhotse. Because on Jannu I could concentrate only on climbing. There was a certain percentage of objective risk, yes, but in comparison with Lhotse, the face was very quiet. On Lhotse I had to think about objective dangers such as avalanches and rockfall.

Why did you choose the south face of Lhotse as your next objective?

Because it was a challenging and very famous face. A lot of expeditions had tried to climb the face, and unfortunately some people died, and in the last years a lot of people spoke about this face.

It was supposed to be the "last great problem" of the Himalaya.

Yes. Now there will have to be a new one.

Was your preparation for Lhotse similar to that for Jannu?

Yes. I got a lot of information from Ales Künaver, the leader of the 1981 Yugoslav expedition. He had studied this face really carefully for ten years. He had a lot of pictures and a lot of notes. And the year before I climbed it, he sent two climbers to the base camp to watch the face for two months and mark every single avalanche on one big picture. I looked at this and got a lot of information.

And I spoke with the climbers from the 1981 expedition. I compared different stories, different information. And in 1987, on Lhotse Shar, I had had a good chance to see the face from the side. I could see which time of day was the most dangerous for avalanches. So I had a lot of information and experience to draw from. I wrote everything down and I thought about it a lot so that I could find the safest route.

And I respected certain things that you have to respect. For example, every afternoon there is bad weather, so you have to be in a safe place then. I think the most important thing on this climb was tactics—how to climb, when to climb, where to stay, where to rest, and so on. And I was prepared 100 percent. I don't think anyone had ever been as well prepared theoretically for this face as I was.

Was the route on Lhotse more difficult than the one on Jannu?

It was more dangerous. We can't compare these two mountains directly because there is a big difference in altitude. There is a big practical difference between 7800 meters and 8500 meters. And on Lhotse the main difficulties are at about 8000 meters. If you have the crux at 8000 meters as opposed to 7000 meters it's a big difference.

Plus south faces are complex problems. They have bad rock, bad weather, avalanches, rockfall. Put all these things together with high altitude and it's not so simple. If there had always been good conditions and good weather on this face, it would have been climbed many years before.

Did you get a period of good weather?

It was relatively good weather, but it was never completely good. In the morning it was usually sunny, but in the afternoon some clouds would form, the wind would start, and some snow would fall—sometimes just ten centimeters, but quite enough for an avalanche. And then in the afternoon there was usually bad weather. This is the usual pattern on Lhotse.

So during the night it's okay to climb and the next morning it's okay, but at 8:00 A.M. the sun hits the face and the avalanches and rockfall start, mainly from 9:00 A.M. to noon. And at this time you have to be in a safe place.

And you climbed part of the route at night?

Yes, the first part, which is the most dangerous.

Was it hard to climb it at night?

No. It was just like climbing in the Alps during the night. It was difficult only because I was tired. I climbed at night the first day, and then the second day it was almost dark by the time I got to this upper snowfield. And above that it was rock, and it was not possible to climb during the night; so I bivouacked. You can climb during the night on ice, but not on rock, because you can't see.

How many times did you bivouac on that route?

Three. Two on the way up and one on the way back.

And you learned about the descent route from the leader of the 1981 Yugoslav expedition?

Yes. Because they left all these pins on the south side. I also had the possibility of going down the normal route on the western cwm, which leads to Everest base camp. This normal route is technically not so difficult, but it's much longer, and if there's bad weather you can get lost. And I don't like the feeling of not knowing where I am. I prefer to go on a more difficult route if I know where I'm going. It's a matter of feeling that you control where you are and you know what direction you're going in.

Did it take part of your soul to climb Lhotse?

Yes. I had to put so much of my energy into concentrating on these dangers, because the south face of Lhotse is one of the most dangerous faces in the world. I just kept thinking that some avalanche could come at any time, that I was in a dangerous area and had to go quickly. I just hoped that everything would go okay.

After Lhotse I needed to take some time off. Once per year for Himalayan climbing is quite enough for me. I have to rest from this kind of work. I have to rebuild this kind of energy again. I felt as if I had spent all my energy for this and was empty. I felt completely empty after Lhotse.

Did you take photographs on the way up?

Yes. And all these photographs were published. I took more pictures on this expedition than on any other. I took a photograph of Makalu that makes it clear where the photo was taken from. And I took a photograph from the top where you can see Everest and down the western cwm. How can anybody say I wasn't up there? How can this [French climber Ivan] Ghirardini say that these are not real pictures? He should not make these accusations without proof, which of course he does not have. He has never been there. He has no high-altitude experience at all.

How did you respond to these accusations?

At first I said, "I don't care," but then I became so angry. And my friends told me, "If they attack you without a reason, then you should do something." So I have had interviews, press conferences, and have published the photos.

Was it your ability to climb very hard grades of rock that allowed you to succeed on Lhotse and these other hard routes in the Himalaya?

Yes, I'm sure. If I can climb at a high level here, then I can do the same in the big mountains. I can easily do a grade that is difficult for other alpinists.

What grade of rock can you climb?

Last year I climbed Brave Men at Verdon, which is 5.13d. This year I plan to climb 5.14.

It's rare for someone to be able to climb hard grades of rock and also do difficult routes in the Himalaya.

Yes, but I don't see the reason for not doing all of these things. I have also competed in climbing competitions on artificial walls and I also liked that. I don't see the reason why climbers are arguing among themselves about these things. Free climbers think that free climbing is the best thing. Alpinists say that big mountains are the best thing. All this arguing about what is the real thing, what is the best thing, what is the hardest thing, is stupid.

At the moment there is nobody who has done both difficult new routes on 8000ers and 5.14 routes on the crags. And this is my dream for this year. Not to be the first, but to show the people that it's possible to do something like this and that it's important to practice all types of climbing.

Why is it that you climb?

Because I like it. I really like to do this—not only climbing itself, but writing about climbing, doing lectures, books, working in a climbing school or a climbing club—all kinds of things having to do with climbing.

And in other sports you are old when you are twenty-five or thirty. In climbing you are not old at all. If you train a lot, you can do extreme things when you are forty or fifty.

Do you have much margin for error on your climbs?

No. If something happens, I don't have a chance. It's logical.

So you're willing to accept the risks of climbing?

Well, yes. But I don't think that I take much of a risk at all. Sometimes I know that I am taking a certain risk, but these times are very rare. I hardly ever feel that I'm taking a risk. I try to avoid risks. I think it's possible to avoid risk with everyday training, technical training, psychological training. When experienced climbers get killed it's usually because of some stupid mistake or on some easy route. I think you always, always have to be a little scared. And you have to take every climb seriously. And I do take every climb seriously, even if it's a normal walking route on Mont Blanc.

Does your wife worry about you?

Yes. It's logical that she's worried when I'm on an expedition, but for the rest of the climbing—sport climbing, for example—she knows that this is safe and not a problem.

And you wouldn't be happy if you couldn't go climbing.

Sure. For me, climbing and having a family are necessary parts of being alive. If I didn't have either, I wouldn't feel alive.

Have your routes on Jannu and Lhotse changed the climbing game?

No, my climbs are just one example; people can do what they want. I don't have anything against routes like the one done by Russians on the south face of Lhotse [fall of 1991], but they're twenty years behind in their style of climbing. If you get twenty or thirty very good climbers, with a lot of equipment, with oxygen, they can do anything. They can drill a hole through Lhotse. But this is not interesting. Today, to fly in a jet plane from Europe to the United States is not interesting. But 100 years ago it was quite a different thing. The time for big teams has already passed; these big expeditions should have been finished ten years ago.

> *"I TRY TO AVOID RISKS. I THINK IT'S POSSIBLE TO AVOID RISK WITH EVERYDAY TRAINING, TECHNICAL TRAINING, PSYCHOLOGICAL TRAINING."*

So you seek out routes on which the outcome is uncertain?

Yes, but the most important thing is the way you climb. More things in climbing should depend directly on you and your ability. I don't think a lot of technical equipment should be used. If it's not possible to climb a face without a lot of this equipment, then the face should be left for somebody else to do in good style. It's the same with chopping holds on the crags. If you can't climb it without chopping holds, leave it for somebody else. If you can do it in good style, okay. If you can't, then leave it. Not for any price should you do a climb.

What are some of the routes you have in mind for the future?

I think about the west and south faces of Makalu; the West Direct Route is still unclimbed. It's the same altitude as Lhotse, but it's technically more difficult, although not so dangerous. The south face has the Yugoslav Route and the [Pierre] Beghin Route, but it's possible to climb some other routes. I think the Himalaya will go in the same direction as the Alps: first the easiest route, then more difficult routes, and so on.

And it's quite clear that the future of high-altitude climbing will be with small teams, alpine style, no oxygen—the necessary equipment, but nothing else. This is the future.